Conspiracy Journal Publications

GIANTS
And The Lost Lands Of The Gods
By
Peter Kolosimo & Nick Redfern
With A Prologue By Timothy Green Beckley

GIANTS
And The Lost Lands Of The Gods
By
Peter Kolosimo and Nick Redfern
With A Prologue By Timothy Green Beckley

Copyright 2017 by Timothy Green Beckley
dba Global Communications/Conspiracy Journal

All rights reserved. No part of these manuscripts may be copied or reproduced by any mechanical or digital methods and no exerpts or quotes may be used in any other book or manuscript without permission in writing by the Publisher, Global Communications/Conspiracy Journal, except by a reviewer who may quote brief passages in a review.

Published in the United States of America By
Global Communications/Conspiracy Journal
Box 753 · New Brunswick, NJ 08903

Staff Members
Timothy G. Beckley, Publisher
Carol Ann Rodriguez, Assistant to the Publisher
Sean Casteel, General Associate Editor
Tim R. Swartz, Graphics and Editorial Consultant
William Kern, Layout, Format and Art Consultant

Sign Up On The Web For Our Free Weekly Newsletter
and Mail Order Version of Conspiracy Journal
and Bizarre Bazaar
www.ConspiracyJournal.com

Order Hot Line: 1-732-602-3407
PayPal: MrUFO8@hotmail.com

CONTENTS

Prologue by Timothy Green Beckley v
Giants In History by Nick Redfern ix
The Origins Of Mankind 1
Cosmic Catastrophes 9
The Age Of Giants 17
The Mark Of The Titans 23
Nightmares In Stone 31
The Lost World Of Mu 39
Legends Of The Stars 49
The Colonies Of Mu 57
Secrets Of The Pyramids 65
An Empire In The Sahara 77
Pangs Of Rebirth 85
The Wandering Masters 91
The Mystery Of Atlantis 99
The Realm Of Forgotten Knowledge 111
The White Gods 119
Greeks In America 127
Constellations In The Jungle 135
The Lords Of Fire 143
The Spaceships Of Tiahuanaco 153
Children Of The Sun 161
The Heirs Of Atlantis 169
Myths Of Vanished Lands 177
Unthinkable Journeys 183

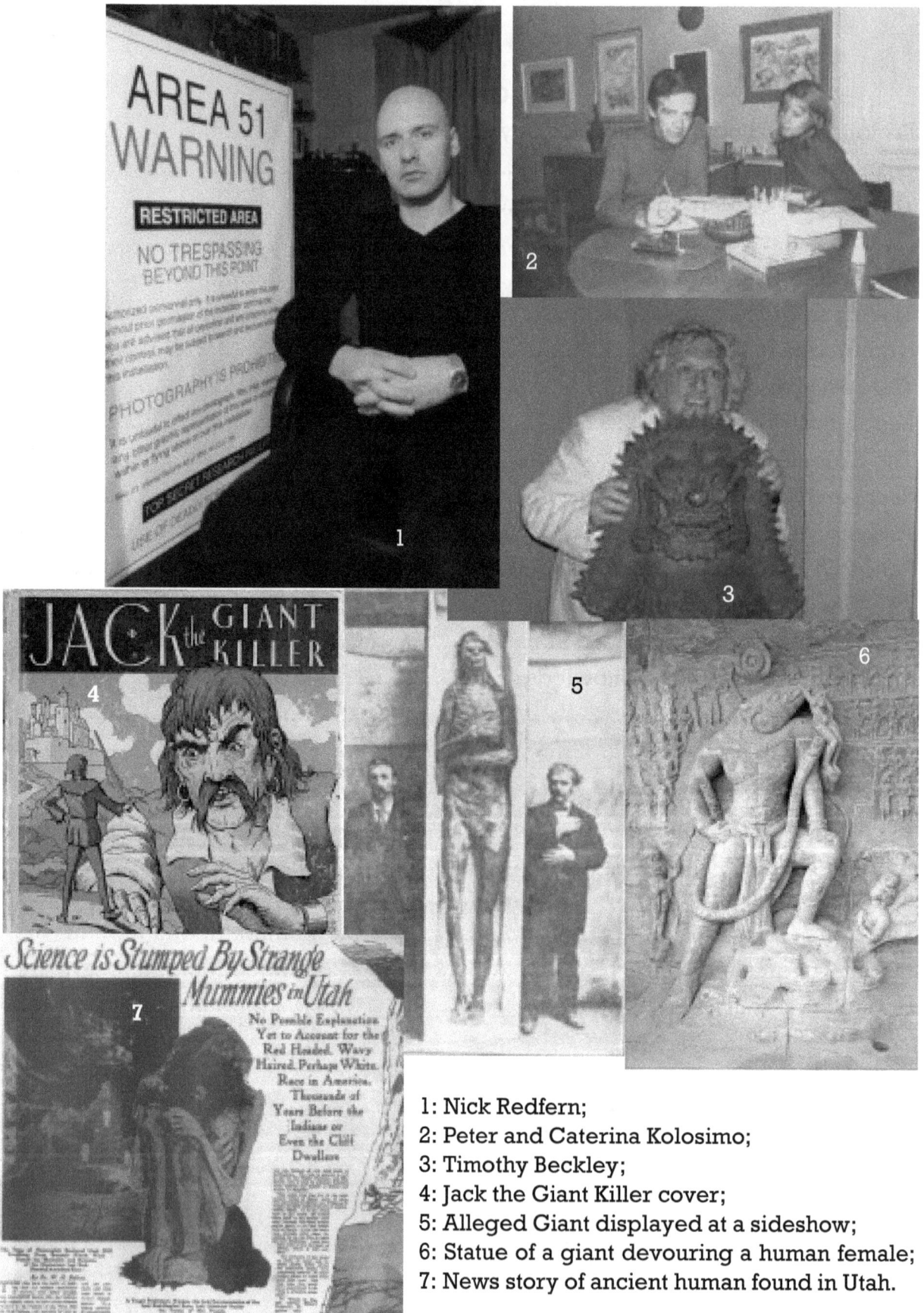

1: Nick Redfern;
2: Peter and Caterina Kolosimo;
3: Timothy Beckley;
4: Jack the Giant Killer cover;
5: Alleged Giant displayed at a sideshow;
6: Statue of a giant devouring a human female;
7: News story of ancient human found in Utah.

TRAVEL INTO THE REMOTE PAST
WITH PETER KOLOSIMO AND NICK REDFERN

By Timothy Green Beckley

I think we can all agree that Peter Kolosimo was what you would call a "bold individual" – that he lived his life to the beat of a different drummer.

He was a true innovator known for his rogue concepts and ideologies.

Peter Kolosimo was not his given name, and no one that I know has been able to surmise why he selected the nom de plume that he did. His birth name was Pier Domenico Colosimo and he was born on December 15, 1922, in Modena, Italy. His father was a police officer and his mother came from suburban New York. They lived a rather modest, but more or less middle class, lifestyle. He went to university and began writing at an early age. He was interested in the remote past, but no one suspected to what degree. He spent many hours in seclusion studying rare scholarly texts, which put him at odds with academia's "agreed upon" chronology of our distant past and made him especially irksome to his professors at the University of Leipzig,

Kolosimo was one of the earliest – if not the earliest – researchers to tackle the ancient astronauts concept which maintains that beings from outer space arrived here in a virtual caravan of UFOs and ended up becoming involved in the evolution of our earthly species and advancing our moral and technical fiber.

Some may think that Kolosimo latched onto a sure thing by hitching himself to the coattails of ancient astronaut pioneer Erich von Daniken, whose "Chariots of the Gods?" raised the hackles of many skeptics who poo pooed the entire AA concept. But the fact of the matter is that the astute investigator of antediluvian matters had never heard of von Daniken or embraced him as a contemporary. Peter's initial offerings in the field came prior to the eventually famous Swiss pop culture figure in the world of what the skeptics called Fanta-archeology or pseudo-archeologia.

As early as the 1950s Peter was writing a column on time travel which developed into "Timeless Earth," a book that was translated into an unheard of 60 languages, including Russian and Chinese, while they were still solid members of the "red bloc of nations."

Apparently those that followed Felix Ziegel's writing in Russian literature might have gotten wind of Kolosimo's similar beliefs because Peter was a devoted Communist who had become radicalized while in University. As a journalist of some renown in Europe, Kolosimo had caused quite a stir with his leftwing outspokenness in the press and at public street rallies.

But the subject of this work is not politics. Heaven knows we get enough of that on a daily basis at home. What we are interested in is Kolosimo's overview of the origins of humankind and its relationship to extraterrestrial life forms. Kolosimo took the subject matter, some say, to extremes, with these revelations concerning the secret history of our planet. He wrote of cosmic catastrophes and how extraterrestrial disasters affected our ancient planet. And how giants might have once roamed the earth, and how cosmic rays from outer space may have created these 10 feet tall "hybrids" and the modern anthropological evidence that bears this out. He also wrote about the Mark of the Titans and how some of these hybrid-mutant-giants might have been cannibals. Nor were lost worlds and unknown civilizations beyond the realm of possibility when Peter pondered what our ancient globe might have consisted of. To him, Atlantis and Mu might have been very real, as was the notion that the Children of the Sun had come down from the sky to mingle with Homo sapiens.

What you are holding is a new, updated version of Kolosimo's "Timeless Earth." It is exactly as written with minor "corrections" for clarity, thus preserving what is considered to be one of the most remarkable books you will ever read on the development of civilization with the help of "outside, off-world influences."

Though the author repeatedly came under fire from skeptics, this work was essentially critically acclaimed by European audiences, thus enabling Kolosimo to found and coordinate the Italian Association for Prehistoric Studies, as well as to produce several more books on the same broad theme.

ENTER NICK REDFERN

Of the various topics discussed herein, the most popular would have to be a belief in giants. Now we know about David and Goliath in the Bible, and unless you think he also had the facial features of a cyclops and the powers of a superhero's villain, chances are this Old Testament figure was just a muscle-bound geek who towered over his adversaries, scaring the shit out of those who were confronted by his superior brawn and warrior's brazenness.

But now, with the advent of ancient languages scholar Zachariah Sitchen and his pronouncement about the Anunnaki, gigantic figures who came to earth during a prehistoric planetary cycle to plunder our resources, there is an even more widespread interest and belief in giants who many rebellious students of archaeological chronicles say were not as rare upon the earth as one might have been led to believe. Nevertheless, the acceptance of the ancient giants remains almost nonexistent among those with "proper training" and credentials showing a "higher education" on their resume.

Wishing very much to expand upon the ancient alien findings of Peter Kolosimo, I knew I had to call upon a young, more active member of the AA community to tout the current beliefs of an expanding audience, people who have become mesmerized by numerous books on the subject as well as a highly popular History Channel adaptation of the theme. The network's "Ancient Aliens" is watched by tens of thousands on a regular basis and these highly provocative, sensationally edited and illustrated broadcast epics have become hugely accepted by an increasingly sophisticated audience.

Nick Redfern describes himself as a fan of punk rock music, dark chocolate, a horror film aficionado, as well as a person who loves to wear black clothes. To relax he enjoys downing a couple of Tennents Super and a Carlsberg Special Brew or two.

A personable Briton who has since adopted the fringes of Dallas, Texas, as his home, Redfern is one of the top writers in a field we can generally term "paranormal" in nature, though he can write on almost anything, staying up late at night and pounding the computer keyboard like the drummer from his favorite "Smashing Pumpkins-style" band.

According to his online posted bio, Nick is the author of many books, including:

"A Covert Agenda;" "The FBI Files;" "Cosmic Crashes;" "Strange Secrets (with Andy Roberts);" "Three Men Seeking Monsters;" "Body Snatchers in the Desert;" "On the Trail of the Saucer Spies;" "Celebrity Secrets;" "Man-Monkey;" "Memoirs of a Monster Hunter;" "There's Something in the Woods;" "Science Fiction Secrets;" "Contactees;" "Monsters of Texas" (with Ken Gerhard); "Final Events;" "The NASA Conspiracies;" "Space Girl Dead on Spaghetti Junction;" "The Real Men in Black;" "Keep Out;" "The Pyramids and the Pentagon;" "The World's Weirdest Places;" "Wildman!;" "Monster Diary;" "Sinister Tales of the MIB;" "Monster Files;" "Close Encounters of the Fatal Kind;" "The Zombie Book" (with Brad Steiger); "For Nobody's Eyes Only;" "Secret History;" "The Bigfoot Book;" "Bloodline of the Gods;" "Chupacabra Road Trip;" "Weapons of the Gods;" "Men In Black;" "Nessie;" "The Monster Book;" "Immortality of the Gods;" "365 Days of UFOs;" "Secret Societies;" and "Women in Black." Forthcoming books include: "Shapeshifters;" "The New World Order Book;" "Control;" and "The Black Diary."

Nick has also appeared on more than 70 TV shows, including: Fox News; the BBC's *Out of This World*; the SyFy Channel's *Proof Positive*; the Space Channel's *Fields of Fear*; the History Channel's *Monster Quest, America's Book of Secrets, Ancient Aliens* and *UFO Hunters*; Science's *The Unexplained Files*; the National Geographic Channel's *Paranatural*; and MSNBC's *Countdown with Keith Olbermann*.

Redfern believes that the Bigfoot and Yeti might have to be "lumped together" when considering the various types of giants discovered – and possibly still inhabiting – the world. Giants have been with us for eons and, like Kolosimo and Redfern, we may very well have to consider the fact that they inhabit the "land of the Gods" that exists around us, unseen and unacknowledged by the rest of the world.

http://nickredfernfortean.blogspot.com/

GIANTS IN HISTORY: ALIENS, MEN & MONSTERS

By Nick Redfern

As you press forward through the pages of this atlas of ancient arcane knowledge, you will have the unique privilege of being presented with much in the way of "forbidden historical facts" that have been kept from an unenlightened public in order to maintain the status quo among the academic communities, in particular archaeologists who seem smug in their attitude in regard to who has lived on earth, when and under what set of circumstances. Their belief system seems rigid and unmovable, and they detest anyone coming along who they see as trying to buck the establishment. Giants, aliens and what we would identify as "monsters" have played an important part in our planet's history, regardless of the attitude of academia toward the content of this noteworthy book – TGB

Extraterrestrial Giants

It has been suggested that the legendary "giants" of the *Old Testament* were, in reality, either the extraterrestrial Anunnaki or, at the very least, their half-human and half-E.T. offspring. On this particular issue, researcher Angela Sangster says: "Were the giants spoken of in Genesis actually aliens from another planet? The *Enuma Elish* (the creation story according to the ancient Babylonians) has many parallels with the Christian Bible. The *Book of Genesis* speaks of these giants (also called Nefilim) who were said by the Church to have been angels who came to Earth and cohabitated with the daughters of Man (*Genesis* Chapter Six). *The Book of Enoch*, which was removed from the Christian Bible, speaks of the resulting hybrids of humans and these giants, or 'watchers.'"

Zecharia Sitchin, not surprisingly, had things to say on this matter, too: "Who were the Nefilim, that are mentioned in Genesis, Chapter Six, as the sons of the gods who married the daughters of Man in the days before the great flood, the Deluge? The word Nefilim is commonly, or used to be, translated 'giants.'"

He continued: "I questioned this interpretation as a child at school, and I was reprimanded for it because the teacher said 'you don't question the Bible.' But I did not question the Bible. I questioned an interpretation that seemed inaccurate, because the word, Nefilim, the name by which those extraordinary beings, 'the sons of the gods' were known, means literally, 'Those who have come down to earth from the heavens.'"

Further evidence of ancient giants absolutely abounds in the pages of the Bible, as the website, *Beginning and End*, clearly shows: "When Moses sent his spies to scout the Promised Land so the children of Israel could enter it, the spies reported seeing beings there who were giants. The Bible makes it abundantly clear that there were races of people at that time who were so large that regular sized men appeared as 'grasshoppers' before them…And we see that when the great servant of the Lord, Joshua, was sent to conquer the Promised Land, that God commands him to kill all of the men, women and children of these giant races. They were to be wiped out as if any remnant of their kind would pose a great danger."

The words of *Numbers 13:31* confirm this particular story: "But the men that went up with him said, 'We be not able to go up against the people; for they are stronger than we.' And they brought up an evil report of the land which they had searched unto the children of Israel, saying, 'The land, through which we have gone to search it, is a land that eateth up the inhabitants thereof; and all the people that we saw in it are men of a great stature. And there we saw the giants, the sons of Anak, which come of the giants: and we were in our own sight as grasshoppers, and so we were in their sight.'"

Moving on, there is *Genesis*, Chapter Six, the words of which point in the direction of cross-breeding between the giant alien men and human women: "That the sons of God saw the daughters of men that they were fair; and they took them wives of all which they chose. There were giants in the earth in those days; and also after that, when the sons of God came in unto the daughters of men, and they bore children to them, the same became mighty men which were of old, men of renown."

Goliath, the Ultimate Giant

All of this raises an important question: is it possible that the legendary giant, Goliath – perhaps *the* definitive giant, of all time – was an extraterrestrial, one of the Anunnaki? Certainly, the question is a controversial one. That does not mean, however, that we should outright dismiss it.

The Old Testament story of Goliath's death, at the hands of David (who ultimately went on to become the second king of the United Kingdom of Israel and Judah), is a well-known and thought-provoking one. It can be found in *Samuel 1*,

Chapter Seventeen. It tells of a violent confrontation between Philistine forces and those of the Israelites – at the Valley of Elah, which is located on Palestine's West Bank, near the city of Hebron.

So the story goes, for no less than forty days, the most feared soldier of the Philistines, Goliath, taunts, goads and dares the Israelites to send a soldier to try and defeat him. Goliath asserts that whoever wins – he or the chosen Israelite – will also decide the outcome of the entire battle. The stakes, then, are high in the extreme. David is the only one who dares to take on the mighty giant. And he does so in a decidedly alternative fashion: whereas Goliath is heavily armored and equipped with a large shield and a powerful, razor-sharp sword, David elects to arm himself with nothing more than a sling and a handful of stones.

Select parts of the story, as told in the Old Testament, follow: "…the Philistines gathered their forces for war and assembled at Sokoh in Judah. They pitched camp at Ephes Dammim, between Sokoh and Azekah. Saul and the Israelites assembled and camped in the Valley of Elah and drew up their battle line to meet the Philistines. The Philistines occupied one hill and the Israelites another, with the valley between them.

"A champion named Goliath, who was from Gath, came out of the Philistine camp. His height was six cubits and a span. He had a bronze helmet on his head and wore a coat of scale armor of bronze weighing five thousand shekels; on his legs he wore bronze greaves; and a bronze javelin was slung on his back. His spear shaft was like a weaver's rod, and its iron point weighed six hundred shekels. His shield bearer went ahead of him.

"Goliath stood and shouted to the ranks of Israel, 'Why do you come out and line up for battle? Am I not a Philistine, and are you not the servants of Saul? Choose a man and have him come down to me. If he is able to fight and kill me, we will become your subjects; but if I overcome him and kill him, you will become our subjects and serve us.' Then the Philistine said, 'This day I defy the armies of Israel! Give me a man and let us fight each other.' On hearing the Philistine's words, Saul and all the Israelites were dismayed and terrified.

"Now David was the son of an Ephrathite named Jesse, who was from Bethlehem in Judah. Jesse had eight sons, and in Saul's time he was very old. Jesse's three oldest sons had followed Saul to the war: The firstborn was Eliab; the second, Abinadab; and the third, Shammah. David was the youngest. The three oldest followed Saul, but David went back and forth from Saul to tend his father's sheep at Bethlehem.

"For forty days the Philistine came forward every morning and evening and took his stand.

"David said to the Philistine, 'You come against me with sword and spear and javelin, but I come against you in the name of the Lord Almighty, the God of the armies of Israel, whom you have defied. This day the Lord will deliver you into my hands, and I'll strike you down and cut off your head...'

"As the Philistine moved closer to attack him, David ran quickly toward the battle line to meet him. Reaching into his bag and taking out a stone, he slung it and struck the Philistine on the forehead. The stone sank into his forehead, and he fell, face down on the ground. So David triumphed over the Philistine with a sling and a stone; without a sword in his hand he struck down the Philistine and killed him. David ran and stood over him. He took hold of the Philistine's sword and drew it from the sheath. After he killed him, he cut off his head with the sword."

Those who accept the Bible precisely and unswervingly might be inclined to suggest that Goliath was simply a tall man; a giant possessed of such incredible fighting skills and appearance that they made him feared throughout the land. Perhaps, however, Goliath was far more. Maybe something part-human and part-extraterrestrial.

A King Who Towered Above All of the Rest

In early 2003, an intriguing discovery was made in the heart of conflict-ravaged Iraq. It was, many suspected, the final resting place of a legendary, long-dead king; one who ruled over the city of Uruk, from which the country of Iraq takes its name. He was Gilgamesh. Just about everything we know about this ancient ruler comes from the *Epic of Gilgamesh*. It's often, but quite incorrectly, described as being a book. In reality, however, the story of Gilgamesh was actually recorded on a series of clay tablets, more than 4,000 years ago.

The Epic of Gilgamesh tells of the mighty king, after death, having been buried in a tomb below the Euphrates River when it diverged, leaving the previously water-filled area dry. Today, there is still a high degree of controversy regarding whether or not the tomb in question really is that of Gilgamesh. The fact is, however, that the location is broadly correct, as is the timeframe in which the tomb was constructed. And, of course, the discovered remains of a long-gone city point strongly in the direction of Uruk, itself.

The story of Gilgamesh, of his life, his adventures, of his quest for immortality, and, ultimately, of his death, are detailed in the form of an extensive poem, one which surfaced out of Mesopotamia millennia ago. By all accounts, Gilgamesh was feared just about as much as he was revered. There was a very good reason for this: like Goliath, Gilgamesh may have been something more than human. He is said to have reigned for an astonishing 130 years and, as an adult, stood at a height of sixteen-feet. Part-human and part-Anunnaki? Perhaps, yes.

Massive Apes or Primitive, Human Giants?

Bernard Heuvelmans, one of the most important figures within the field of cryptozoology, said that during the course of his research into the Yeti of the Himalayas, he had learned of no less than three distinct kinds of creature that roamed the vast mountains.

"This opinion," said Heuvelmans, "was confirmed in 1957 by a Tibetan lama called Punyabayra, high priest of the monastery at Budnath, who spent four months in the high mountains and brought back the surprising but valuable information that the Tibetan mountain people knew three kinds of snowmen."

There was the *rimi*, a man-beast of close to three meters in height that dwelled in the Barun Khola valley, in eastern Nepal, and which was specifically omnivorous. Then there was the rackshi bompo, a beast of roughly human proportions, and which Heuvelmans said "must be the Sherpas' reddish *yeh-teh* or *mi-teh* which leaves the footprints 20 to 23 cm long that the *Daily Mail* expedition...found in such quantity." Finally, there was the imposing and terrifying Nyalmo.

Heuvelmans came straight to the point: "The *nyalmo* are real giants, between 4 and 5 m high, with enormous conical heads." He continued: "They wander in parties among the eternal snows above 4000m. In such empty country it is hardly surprising that they should be carnivorous and even man-eating."

Heuvelmans asked of the Nyalmo: "Do they really exist, or are they just a myth?" He admitted to having heard of accounts of Yetis with feet around 45 to 60 cm in length, but was careful to qualify this by stating that: "...the evidence is far too slender for us to draw any satisfactory conclusions. Possibly the *nyalmo* are an invented addition based on the belief that *yetis* increase in size the higher you go."

Loren Coleman says: "When [Sir Edmund] Hillary went to the Himalayas to look for the Yeti, he and his collaborator, journalist Desmond Doig, noted that there were several unknown primates said to be there still undiscovered in any formal way. Among the varieties was one called the 'Nyalmo.' Hillary and Doig learned of the Nyalmo in north-central Nepal. It was said to be 'giant-sized (up to twenty feet tall), manlike, hairy, and given to shaking giant pine trees in trials of strength while other Nyalmos sit around and clap their hands.'"

The matter of the curious behavior of the Nyalmos – to which Coleman refers – was most graphically told by one Jean Marques-Riviere. It was in 1937 that the details of Marques-Riviere's account first surfaced, one that was eagerly picked up on by Bernard Heuvelmans. According to Marques-Riviere, he had occasion to speak with an Indian pilgrim who personally encountered a group of Nyalmo in the wilds of Nepal. *Crypto Journal* describes the extraordinary encounter in a fashion that suggests the beasts have a high degree of intelligence and may even have some form of spiritual belief-system:

"The creatures were standing as they formed a circle and were chanting, as if they were doing a religious ritual or something of that sort. One of the Yeti-like creatures was enthusiastically beating a hollow trunk of a tree, like a man hitting his drums to create some music. The others continued their 'chants,' but their faces seemed to be filled with a sad expression. With this sight, the adventurers thought that the creatures acted like typical persons and that they should not be feared. But eventually, fears set in due to the creatures' massive build, and they decided to walk away stealthily to avoid conflict."

What may very well have been a description of the huge, and reportedly extremely dangerous and violent, Nyalmo came from Charles Stonor, a former assistant curator of the London Zoo, England, who embarked on a quest for the truth of the Yeti in December 1953, an expedition that was organized and funded by the British *Daily Mail* newspaper. While in Darjeeling, Stonor was told of a creature known as the Thloh-Mung that, with hindsight, may very well have been the Nyalmo.

The story told to Stonor went like this:

"Long ago there was a beast in our mountains, known to our forefathers as the Thloh-Mung, meaning in our language Mountain Savage. Its cunning and ferocity were so great as to be a match for anyone who encountered it. It could always outwit our Lepcha hunters with their bows and arrows. The Thloh-Mung was said to live alone, or with a very few of its kind; and it went sometimes on the ground and sometimes in the trees."

The account continued: "It was found only in the higher mountains of our country. Although it was made very like a man, it was covered with long, dark hair, and was more intelligent than a monkey, as well as being larger."

It seems that, to a significant degree, the beasts were fighting for their very survival: "The people became more in number, the forest and wild country less; and the Thloh-Mung disappeared. But many people say they are still to be found in the mountains of Nepal, away to the west, where the Sherpa people call them the Yeti."

Eskimo Legends of Mighty Giant Men

Within the culture, legend, and lore of the Eskimos – people of Greenland, Canada, Alaska, and Siberia – there are stories of giant, marauding creatures with whom they had a highly fraught relationship. They were the Tunnit, a race of creatures that were human-like, but clearly not human in the way we understand the term today.

Certainly, no one did more to uncover the truth of the Tunnit than one Ernest William Hawkes, whose book, *The Labrador Eskimo*, which was published in 1916, demonstrates. Hawkes was a noted anthropologist who spent a great deal of time in Canada and Alaska, and along the Bering Strait, speaking with the indigenous people, gaining their trust and friendship, and securing a wealth of material on their lives, cultures, and beliefs.

It was during the course of his summer 1914 expedition to Hudson Bay, in northeastern Canada, that Hawkes learned of the terrifying Tunnit. He recorded the following, which demonstrates just how deeply, carefully, and extensively he listened to what his Eskimo informants had to tell him:

"Tunnit ('Tornit,' in Baffin Island), according to tradition, were a gigantic race formerly inhabiting the northeastern coast of Labrador, Hudson Strait, and southern Baffin Island. Ruins of old stone houses and graves, which are ascribed to them by the present Eskimo, are found throughout this entire section, penetrating only slightly, however, into Ungava Bay. Briefly we may say that there is evidence, archaeological as well as traditional, that the Tunnit formerly inhabited both sides of Hudson Strait. The oldest Eskimo of northern Labrador still point out these ruins and relate traditions of their having lived together until the Tunnit were finally exterminated or driven out by the present Eskimo.

"According to the account given by an old Nachvak Eskimo, the Tunnit in ancient times had two villages in Nachvak bay. Their houses were built on an exposed shore (the present Eskimo always seek a sheltered beach for their villages, where they can land in their kayaks), showing that they had little knowledge of the use of boats. When they wanted boats, they stole them from the Eskimo. From this thieving of kayaks the original quarrel is said to have begun.

"For all their bigness and strength, the Tunnit were a stupid slow-going race (according to the Eskimo version), and fell an easy prey to the Eskimo, who used to stalk them and hunt them down like game. They did not dare to attack them openly, so they cut them off, one by one, by following them and attacking and killing them when asleep. Their favorite method was to bore holes in the foreheads of the Tunnit with an awl (a drill in the Greenland story in Rink).

"Two brothers especially distinguished themselves in this warfare and did not desist until the last of the Tunnit was exterminated. The Tunnit built their houses of heavy rocks, which no Eskimo could lift. They used the rocks for walls, and whale ribs and shoulder blades for the roof. At the entrance of the house two whale jawbones were placed. Ruins of these houses can still be seen, overgrown with grass and with the roof fallen in. They may be distinguished from old Eskimo igloos by the small, square space they occupy.

"The Tunnit did not use the bow and arrow, but flint-headed lances and harpoons with bone or ivory heads. They were so strong that one of them could hold a walrus as easily as an Eskimo a seal.

"They did not understand the dressing of sealskins, but left them in the sea, where the little sea-worms cleaned off the fat in a short time. The Tunnit dressed in winter in untanned deerskins. They were accustomed to carry pieces of meat around with them, between their clothing and body, until it was putrid when they ate it. The Tunnit were very skillful with the lance, which they threw, sitting down and aiming at the object by resting the shaft on the boot. For throwing at a distance they used the throw-stick.

"They did not hunt deer like the Eskimo, but erected long lines of stone 'men' in a valley through which the deer passed. The deer would pass between the lines of stones, and the hunters hidden behind them would lance them. Remains of these lines of rocks may still be seen.

"Their weapons were much larger, but not as well made as those of the Eskimo, as can be seen from the remains on their graves. The men used flint for the harpoon heads, and crystal for their drills. The women used a rounded piece of slate without a handle for a knife. They used a very small lamp for heating purposes, which they carried about them. For cooking, they had a much larger lamp than the Eskimo. Until trouble arose between them, the Tunnit and the Eskimo used to intermarry, but after it was found that an alien wife would betray her husband to her people, no more were taken. A Tuneq woman, who betrayed the Eskimo of the village she lived in to the Tunnit, had her arms cut off. After that no women were taken on either side.

"The Tunnit were gradually exterminated by the Eskimo, until only a scattered one remained here and there in their villages. How these were overcome by stratagems is handed down in the tales of the giant at Hebron, said to be the last of the Tunnit, and Adlasuq and the Giant. The giant allows himself to be bound in a snow-house and is slain by the Eskimo hunters. This story has attained a mythological character in Baffin Island, but is ascribed by the Labrador Eskimo directly to the Tunnit. A story about the Tunnit, giving considerable circumstantial detail, was obtained from a Nachvak woman:

"'At Nachvak the Tunnit were chasing a big whale (this was before the time of the present Eskimo). They were in two skin boats, about twenty men and women in each boat. They had the whale harpooned and were being towed round and round the bay by him. Somehow the line got tangled in one of the boats and capsized. The other boat with the line still made fast to the whale, went to pick up the people in the water, and was capsized too. Another boat came off from the shore, and picked up some of the people in the water. Most of them were drowned.

"They were buried under a hill on a big bank near Nachvak. There are some thirty graves on this bank, with pots, harpoons, and knives buried by the graves. Even the remains of the boats are there. The knives and pots are of stone. The harpoon blades are of flint. The umiaks were much larger than the present boats."

On the specific matter of what, precisely, the Tunnit were, Jonathan Downes and Richard Freeman, of the Center for Fortean Zoology, have made some noteworthy observations:

"Although the Tunnit seem to have achieved a far different culture than the Eskimo people, they do not seem to be Neanderthals. They are too tall, for one thing, and also the level of cultural sophistication that they have reached seems to be beyond that ever achieved by Neanderthals. Our best guess is that they were a very primitive race of people, probably kin to the Mesolithic hunter-gatherers whom we suspect still live in the Transcausacus, who keep their hairy skin and evolved a large size in order to cope with the climate of the frozen north."

In that sense, Downes and Freeman are of the opinion that the Tunnit may also be the Almasty of Russian lore – creatures that have been reported on a regular basis from the Caucasus Mountains.

Beware of the Big Gray Man

A large and mystery-filled mountain in a Scottish range called the Cairngorms, Ben Macdui is said to be the lair of a sinister entity known as the Big Gray Man (BGM). Legends of its existence date back centuries and they show no signs of stopping. The Big Gray Man reputedly possesses paranormal powers that allow it to plunge the unwary traveler into states of terror and panic. A form of monster-based mind-control, one might be justified in suggesting. Without doubt, the foremost expert on the BGM is anomalies expert, Andy Roberts.

Andy has noted that witnesses to the creepy phenomenon describe how they have heard heavy footsteps on the often fog-shrouded mountain, felt a distinct sensation of a threatening presence, and experienced an overwhelming feeling of unbridled terror. The experience is graphic enough to compel witnesses to flee – in fear of their lives – and, in some cases, to run wildly and in crazed, fear-filled fashion for miles. Taking into consideration the fact that encounters almost exclusively take place on rocky, dangerous ground, and often in weather conditions involving mist and snow, Andy stresses that "we should not underestimate the power of the experience."

As far as can be determined, the first encounter of any real note with the BGM occurred in 1791. The witness was a poet and shepherd named James Hogg. He reported seeing a massive figure on Ben Macdui, which appeared to manifest out of a strange halo. Says Andy: "As he watched the halo which had formed around him due to the combination of sunshine and mist, he suddenly noticed a huge, looming figure. It was vaguely human in shape and he imagined it to be the devil. Hogg fled in terror, not stopping until he reached fellow shepherds."

Moving onto the 20th century, in 1921, the Cairngorm Club Journal reported that a recent letter-writer "…called attention to a myth prevalent in Upper

Deeside to the effect that a big spectral figure has been seen at various times during the last five years walking about on the tops of the Cairngorms. When approached, so the story goes, the figure disappears."

In 1925, Professor Norman Collie revealed the facts concerning his very own encounter with the Big Gray Man, decades earlier. Collie recalled, in Volume 15 of the Cairngorm Club Journal: "I was returning from the cairn on the summit in a mist when I began to think I heard something else than merely the noise of my own footsteps. For every few steps I took, I heard a crunch and then another crunch, as if someone was walking after me but taking steps three or four times the length of my own. I said to myself: 'This is all nonsense.' I listened and heard it again but could see nothing in the mist. As I walked on and the eerie crunch, crunch, sounded behind me, I was seized with terror and took to my heels, staggering blindly among the boulders for four or five miles nearly down to Rothiemurchus Forest. Whatever you make of it I do not know, but there is something very queer about the top of Ben Macdui and I will not go back there by myself, I know."

A man named Alexander Tewnion told of his very own encounter with the terrifying thing of Ben Macdui in the 1940s: "In October 1943, I spent a ten-day leave climbing alone in the Cairngorms. One afternoon, just as I reached the summit cairn of Ben MacDui, mist swirled across the Lairig Ghru and enveloped the mountain. The atmosphere became dark and oppressive, a fierce, bitter wind whisked among the boulders, and an odd sound echoed through the mist – a loud footstep, it seemed. Then another, and another. A strange shape loomed up, receded, and then came charging at me! Without hesitation I whipped out the revolver and fired three times at the figure. When it still came on, I turned and hurried down the path, reaching Glen Derry in a time that I have never bettered. You may ask was it really the Fear Laith Mhor? Frankly, I think it was." Tewnion's account appeared in The Scots Magazine in 1958.

Cryptozoologist Dr. Karl Shuker says: "Even more incredible, however, was the entity reportedly spied one night on Ben MacDui by a friend of climber-writer Richard Frere. Having pitched a tent beside the Cairn, Frere's friend awoke to see a brown shape standing between his tent and the moon. So as soon as the shape moved away, his friend peered outside his tent, only to discover (according to Frere's subsequent description, which follows) that just 20 yards away…"

"…a great brown creature was swaggering down the hill. He uses the word 'swaggering' because the creature had an air of insolent strength about it: and because it rolled slightly from side to side, taking huge measured steps. It looked as though it was covered with shortish, brown hair…its head was disproportionately large, its neck very thick and powerful. By the extreme width of its shoulders compared to the relative slimness of its hips, he concluded its sex to be male. No, it did not resemble an ape: its hairy arms, though long, were not unduly so, its carriage was extremely erect."

From September 2006, we have the following from someone using the pseudonym of Big Max. "I was climbing back down Ben MacDui in May 1988 when I experienced the footsteps phenomenon mentioned by others. It was pretty misty and I was alone. But it was like 'something' was behind me, only 10 meters or so, keeping track of me. I backtracked to see if anyone was there. I didn't see anything, but it was weird enough to scare me, particularly as the sounds occurred both when I was moving or was stationary. It was only after I told this story to a Glasgow cousin years later that I first heard about the Gray Man."

As for what the Big Gray Man may be, Dr. Karl Shuker says: "During the 1970s, inorganic chemistry specialist Dr. Don Robins proposed that some minerals may be capable of encoding a type of electrical energy, in turn yielding a moving image that could be projected under certain specific conditions, i.e. a veritable geological hologram. Could it be that the BGM is one such hologram, stimulated by certain specific, mountain-related mineralogical attributes, and exhibiting an additional aural component?"

Or, might it be something akin to the so-called Brocken Specter phenomenon? Weather Online says of this particular phenomenon: "The Brocken Specter (or Brocken bow) is an apparently greatly magnified shadow of an observer cast against mist or cloud below the level of a summit or ridge and surrounded by rainbow colored fringes resulting from the diffraction of light. The effect is an illusion. Depth perception is altered by the mist, causing the shadow to appear more distant and to be interpreted as larger than normally expected."

For many, the mystery of Ben Macdui's Big Gray Man lives on. For others, it's just a giant shadow. Albeit it's an imposing one!

Close Encounters with Alien Giants

For decades, within the annals of Ufology, countless types of apparent alien entity have been reported by startled witnesses to UFOs and their otherworldly crews. The list of extraterrestrial life forms is truly bizarre and includes beings that resemble (a) huge, flying jellyfish; (b) oversized bananas; (c) the Michelin Man; and (d) long-nosed, scrawny humanoids with glowing red eyes. But such beings are most assuredly not typical of those reported in the vast majority of close encounters of the Ufological kind. Indeed, they are firmly in the minority. Dominating the UFO scene are without doubt the human-looking Space-Brothers, the insect-like Grays, and the sinister Reptilians. But there are a surprising number of reports on file describing giant-sized aliens, too.

While the tales of alien giants most certainly do not attract the same sort of attention and acclaim as their long-haired cousins did way back in the contactee-driven era of the 1950s, and the emotionless Grays do today, that does not mean such issues are of no consequence. In fact, one could convincingly argue quite the opposite.

Two such notable cases emanate from within the British Isles; the details of one of which were given to Charles Bowen, a former editor of *Flying Saucer Review* magazine, and that were duly published in a classic book on alien entities that Bowen edited himself, *The Humanoids*. The year was 1958 and the location was very near to Balmoral, Scotland. As part of their basic training, an Aberdeen-based unit of the Territorial Army had been dispatched to the area in question to take part in a weekend of maneuvers.

During the course of the exercise, two of the group were deployed to guard a small hilltop and, fully equipped, set about digging themselves a trench for cover. On the first morning, just as dawn was breaking, both heard what they later described as a strange "gurgling" sound that seemed to originate from behind a dense group of trees, several hundred yards from their position. Unsurprisingly somewhat curious, they set out to investigate, when two giant, humanoid figures suddenly emerged from the shadows and proceeded towards them in ominous, lumbering fashion.

Naturally overcome with overwhelming terror, the pair hastily retreated. As they ran in panicked style, they heard a "swishing noise," and glancing over their shoulders saw a gigantic, disc-shaped object in the sky above which appeared to be following them. Reportedly "pulsating," the UFO swooped low over their heads and – to the complete and utter relief of the pair – quickly disappeared, curiously trailing a shower of sparks as it vanished from view.

A similar case, involving the Schwab family, who were then living in the English city of Bath, occurred late one weekend night in mid-March 1978, while they were attending a family get-together in the county of Wiltshire. While driving past the legendary Stonehenge around 11:00 P.M., they were shocked to the core by the startling sight of a "twelve-foot-tall thing, like a giant man," standing in the middle of the road.

Not surprisingly, Mr. Schwab brought the car to a rapid, screeching halt, and he, his wife and son watched amazed as a bright light from above suddenly enveloped the mighty being and "lit it up, and we could see it was like me and you, but twice as tall and in a silver suit and two big eyes [sic]."

Even more startling, the huge creature then began to slowly rise into the beam of light – which, the three could now see, was "coming out of the bottom of a big square-shaped object in the sky, and black [in color] that hummed so loud and made us all feel sick."

Within seconds, the giant and the beam of light were gone, and the mysterious craft duly soared into the heavens, leaving the Schwab family wondering what on earth – or, very possibly, off it – had just happened.

Rogue cases of Goliath-like aliens in decades past may not attract the same levels of attention and fascination as those of today's alleged DNA-stealing, pasty, skinny, denizens of Zeta Reticuli, but that does not mean they are without merit. After all, if extraterrestrials are visiting us, then perhaps – just like us, the Human Race – they come in all sorts of shapes and sizes.

Giants of the Solomon Islands

The Solomon Islands are located near Paupa New Guinea. They were named by a Spanish adventurer, one Alvaro de Mendana. He has gone down in history as the first European (so far as is known, at least) to have visited the islands, in 1568. And there are far more than a few of those islands. In fact, there are more than 900 of them, of widely varying degrees of size. Although no European visited the islands prior to the 16th century, archeological digging has demonstrated that primitive man inhabited at least some of them as far back as 29,000 BC. There are also good indications that before Europeans made their way to the Solomon Islands, the people regularly practiced cannibalism and were a violent and wild bunch. The islands are noted for something else besides a long and winding history: the presence of beasts that sound suspiciously Bigfoot-like.

We have a man named Marius Boirayon to thank for uncovering most of the currently available data on these marauding and not always particularly friendly creatures. A skilled engineer and helicopter pilot, he has unearthed witness accounts that describe creatures very much like Bigfoot: the majority of them are around ten feet in height, have flaming red eyes, hair that is a cross between brown and a deep red, and ape-like faces. But, not all of them.

Boirayon has made another parallel between the beasts of the Solomon Islands and the United States' Bigfoot: in the same precise way that there appears to be more than one kind of man-beast in the United States – the monster of the Pacific Northwest is manifestly different than the Skunk Ape of Florida – very much the same can be said about the Solomon Islands.

Boirayon's findings suggest that there could be as many as three varieties of hairy hominids on the Solomon Islands. One of them is a smallish creature that is far more like a hairy, wild man of old English lore than it is a cryptid ape. The second resembles the traditional Bigfoot. The third sounds like something akin to the gigantic Nyalmo of the Himalayas, in the sense that it is described as being a massive creature that typically reaches heights of fifteen feet, and maybe even twenty feet – despite how admittedly unlikely such a scenario sounds.

The Bigfoot of the Solomon Islands are hardly what one would call friendly: downright hostile would be a far better way of wording it. Kidnapping and eating the locals seem to be among their favorite past-times. As just one example of many, Boirayon uncovered the traumatic and terrifying story of Mango, a woman who was abducted from her village home by one of the creatures and held prisoner by it for around a quarter of a century, before she was finally able to escape. To the horror of her family and old friends, when Mango returned she was not the person she once was: living with the hideous beast for so long had driven her utterly insane and wild-like.

Rather notably, while held by the wild thing, Mango allegedly gave birth to its equally hideous-looking child after the creature forced itself upon her. Given that it is genetically impossible for humans and apes to interbreed, the likelihood is that the monsters of the Solomon Islands are not so monstrous, after all, but, in reality, are some form of ancient offshoot of the Human Race.

That the tropical jungles of the Solomon Islands could accommodate – and even conceivably hide – creatures up to around nine or ten feet tall is not at all unlikely. It's difficult, however, to imagine that towering monsters of fifteen to twenty feet in height could do likewise. There is, however, an intriguing theory to explain the reason why such immense things can't be tracked down, caught or killed. It's a theory that is chiefly focused around the island of Guadalcanal, the location of the 1942-1943 Battle of Guadalcanal, which saw Allied forces fighting the Japanese during the Second World War.

The people of Guadalcanal talk of longstanding legends of a vast underground world, far below their island, one which is only accessible if one knows where the secret entrance points can be found. So extensive are these massive caves, caverns, and underground realms that no less than thousands of the violent and giant beasts are rumored to inhabit their darkest corners. Much of the lore points in the direction of Guadalcanal's mountains, where, it is said, the tunnels and caves begin, and run so deep that one might be forgiven for thinking one had entered the nightmarish realm of Hell itself. It's not impossible that the descriptions of the massive sizes of the creatures are down to folkloric exaggeration and, in reality, we should be looking at beasts of a far more manageable eight or nine feet tall. As for the cave rumors, as this book shows, there are far more than a few cases of Bigfoot reportedly being a dweller of the wild and rarely explored underground.

Lest you think that these reports and stories might solely be the domains of "friend of a friend" tales and impossible to prove myths, it's well worth taking note of the on-the-record story of a man named Ezekiel Alebua. He was none other than the third Prime Minister of the Solomon Islands – a position he held from December 1986 to March 1989.

When he was a child, Alebua was taken by his father to a large cavern which was situated on the east side of Guadalcanal, where his father pointed out something incredible: huge, humanoid skeletons, somewhere in the order of fifteen feet long, lay scattered on the cave floor. How, exactly, Alebua's father knew of the cave and its eerie, long-dead inhabitants remains a mystery. Similar tales of massive, ape-like animals and deep, labyrinthine tunnels can be found on a number of other islands that comprise the Solomon Islands, including Malaita, Choiseul, and Santa Isabel.

And the list of strange, possibly even unearthly, giants goes on and on. As you will now learn as you dig further into the pages of this intriguing book…

Sources:

Boirayon, Marius. *Solomon Island Mysteries*. Kempton, IL: Adventures Unlimited Press, 2010.

Boirayon, Marius. "The Giants of the Solomon Islands and Their Hidden UFO Bases."

http://www.thewatcherfiles.com/giants/solomon-giants.htm. 2012.

Bowen, Charles (editor). *The Humanoids*. Chicago, IL: Henry Regnery Company, 1969.

Coleman, Loren. "Yeti Hunter Sir Edmund Hillary Dies."

http://www. cryptomundo.com/cryptozoo-news/hillary-obit/. January 10, 2008.

"David and Goliath." https://www.biblegateway.com/passage/?search=1+Samuel+17. 2017.

"Earth Chronicles." http://www.zetatalk.com/theword/tword08q.htm. 2017.

Epic of Gilgamesh, The. NY: Penguin Books, 2003.

Hall, Mark A. & Coleman, Loren. *True Giants*. San Antonio, TX: Anomalist Books, 2010.

Hawkes, Ernest William. *The Labrador Eskimo*. Ottawa, Canada: Ottawa Government Printing

Bureau, 1916.

"Nephilim and Giants in the Bible, The." http://beginningandend.com/nephilim-giants-bible/.

May 23, 2011.

Redfern, Nick. *The Bigfoot Book*. Canton, MI: Visible Ink Press, 2016.

Redfern, Nick. *Wildman*. Woolsery, U.K.: CFZ Press, 2012.

Roberts, Andy. "The Big Gray Man of Ben Macdui and Other Mountain Panics."

Strangely Strange but Oddly Normal. Woolsery, U.K.: CFZ Press, 2010.

GIANTS And The Lost Lands Of The Gods is a provocative examination of the real age of human civilization, which the author believes has been influenced by creatures from outer space. The mythical Atlantis, he claims, may well have been the cradle of a new type of man who penetrated the mysteries of nature and split the atom. Here is presented a wealth of information that indicates the existence of extraterrestrial beings on Earth in prehistoric times and, indeed, the possibility they may still be among us.

Man was earth, a vessel, an eyelid of quivering mud, a shape in clay,
A Caribbean jar, a Chibcha stone, an imperial goblet, an Araucanian flint.
Tender and bloodthirsty he was, but on the hilt of his weapon of damp
crystal the initials of Earth were inscribed.
—Pablo Neruda, Canto General

GIANTS AND THE LOST LANDS OF THE GODS

CHAPTER ONE
The Origins Of Mankind

One evening in the late summer of 1856, a team of workmen were enlarging a stone quarry in the Neander valley near Dusseldorf. As they were clearing away the layers of fine clay to get to the calcareous stratum beneath, they came across a pile of bones.

No one paid much attention to this: such finds were common enough, and the bones might have finished on a dung heap if the quarry's owner, Pieper by name, had not been present when they were discovered. Among Pieper's acquaintances was Professor Karl Fuhlrott, a secondary school teacher whose favorite leisure pursuit was looking for bones, from which he discerned strange tales of men who had lived in prehistoric ages. Seeing the splintered relics, Pieper thought of his friend; he had them put aside and sent them, a few days later, to swell the professor's collection.

This time it was three years before the latter came out with his "story," but when he did so, in the form of a modest essay, the Neanderthal bones caused an outcry in the scientific world, since he claimed that the bones were neither more nor less than the fossilized remains of a primitive type of man.

Some scholars were much impressed by Fuhlrott's theory, but the majority rejected it as absurd. This is hardly surprising, since practically nothing was known at that time of Darwin's view that the most complicated forms of animal and vegetable life had evolved from simple beginnings. Some believed that the bones must be those of a Celtic or Germanic warrior; others suggested that they were the remains of a Cossack who had fought in the campaigns of 1813-14 (and the upholders of this theory claimed that they could detect the marks of bayonet wounds), while others held that they were the bones of a deformed idiot.

Like many another pioneer of science, Professor Fuhlrott was regarded throughout his life as an amateur with a too vivid imagination. A few years after his death, however, he was triumphantly vindicated: remains closely similar to those of "Neanderthal man" were discovered first in a cave at Spy in Belgium and later

GIANTS AND THE LOST LANDS OF THE GODS

in France, Spain, Italy and Belgium again. Finally, a number of Neanderthal skeletons were unearthed, together with other bones, in a cave at Krapina in Yugoslavia, between Maribor and Zagreb.

The discoveries were a triumph for Darwin's theory. In the first years of the twentieth century, scholars no longer argued whether Neanderthal man was a representative of primitive humanity; the only point in dispute was where exactly he belonged in the story of evolution. As one find succeeded another, scientists felt able to paint a broad picture of the series of transformations which, they believed, led from the deformed ape of remote prehistoric times to the final appearance of homo sapiens. The gallery of our ancestors was enlarged to comprise an imposing collection of monsters, beginning with the Pithecanthropus of Java who was thought to have lived about a million years ago.

Then came the Peking Sinanthropus (from 1 million to 430,000 years ago), followed by Heidelberg man (430,000 to 240,000 years ago) and finally Neanderthal man, who supposedly lived between 240,000 and 140,000 years ago.

Can we safely accept this picture? The anthropologists, almost without exception, say that it is the true one, and give short shrift to doubters whom they regard as short-sighted conservatives or slaves of religious prejudice. True, in the 1930s some confusion was caused by the discovery in South Africa of the remains of an ape-man with completely different characteristics from those of the other known specimens of primitive humanity. But exceptions of this kind are usually glossed over as merely presenting a chronological problem, whereas in fact they ought to give ground for more serious reflection.

With the best of good will, we find it hard to understand how the prevailing theory has been accepted so lightly. Scholars of the greatest repute have upheld as a dogma what is no more than a vague and shaky hypothesis, and have constructed a whole history of human kind out of a few heaps of bones discovered in different parts of the world, without being able to point to any genuine links between them.

It would be easy to enumerate a host of questions and doubts concerning the bizarre theory of human origins which official science has accepted as holy writ. We do not wish to dwell on these unduly, but would only point out one fact.

The cranial capacity of one of our supposed ancestors was about 600-700 cubic centimeters, whereas that of homo sapiens is between 1,500 and 1,600. How is it that no one has unearthed any "missing links" in the form of skulls capable of containing, say, 800, 900, 1,000, 1,200 or 1,300 cubic centimeters of grey matter? Since the owners of these skulls are supposed to have lived in relatively recent times, it should be easier to find their remains than those of Sinanthropus or Pithecanthropus.

If the high priests of anthropology, after laughing Fuhlrott to scorn, had not then rushed to embrace his theories, we should not now have to call in question what appeared, only a few years ago, to be unshakeable conclusions. There was in fact some reason to doubt the official view as far back as the time of the Krapina excavations: among the twenty-odd individuals whose bones were found there, the majority were certainly of the Neanderthal type, but others were so slender and graceful that they clearly belonged to quite a different species.

One of the few scholars who expressed any doubt on this score was Professor Klaatsch of Breslau, an anthropologist who suggested that the remains found at Krapina represented two races which had coexisted there in prehistoric times. He was not far from the truth, for there is now good reason to think that Krapina was the scene of a cannibal feast at which Neanderthal men devoured the flesh of their victims. This habit is attested by a skull found at Monte Circeo, which was evidently cut open with a chisel-like object in order to scoop out the brains.

Altogether there was plenty of reason to doubt the accepted view of human evolution; but, as "Life Magazine" later wrote, anthropologists are not generally hospitable to new discoveries that conflict with existing theories.

Living Prehistory

Although common sense was not strong enough to dislodge orthodox evolutionists from their untenable positions, certain facts came to light which obliged them to give ground.

Over thirty years ago, Professor Leakey discovered at Kanan in Kenya, not far from Lake Victoria, a jawbone closely resembling that of homo sapiens, and soon afterwards he found, at Kanjera, two skulls which the jawbone might well have fitted. These finds were less ancient than the first discovery, but were nevertheless 400,000 years old. Skeptics who disbelieved in their antiquity were not lacking: they might still be heard from today if it were not for the fact that, in 1952, the anthropologist Carleton Coon and the geologist Louis Dupree discovered in some caves at Hotu in Persia the skulls of three indisputably human creatures who lived over 100,000 years ago.

This was discomforting enough for those scientists who insisted that homo sapiens could not date back further than a mere 50,000 years. But they were still further disconcerted when the American Ralph Solecki found in a cave at Shanidar in Iraq the remains of a Neanderthal man who had lived 45,000 years ago, when, according to the "classic" evolutionists, he ought already to have evolved into homo sapiens.

Then, by way of climax, Neanderthal man made a flesh-and-blood appearance in Morocco, was photographed by Professor Marcel Homet and mumbled in his own language something that might be freely translated thus: "Here I am, then, alive and well, though not perhaps very handsome. I am prehistory personified: I live in the same state as my grandpapa at Dusseldorf; I go about naked, I use clumsy tools made of wood or stone, and my vocabulary consists of a few dozen assorted grunts. Alas, I have not evolved in the very least: my species was born, you tell me, 240,000 years ago, a good while later than your kinsmen of Kanan and Kanjera, and it will die with me and my fellow-Neanderthalians who have managed, goodness knows how, to scrape along in north-western Africa up to the present time."

Finally, at the Rome conference on prehistory in 1962, the German archaeologist Walter Matthes presented some of the 500 stone figurines of men and animals which he had excavated on the banks of the Elbe near Hamburg. These are at least 200,000 years old and are certainly the most ancient works of their kind in the world; and, as the record of the conference duly notes, the features of the human faces in these carvings are those of homo sapiens, the most evolved and intelligent form of the human race.

Nowadays the majority of scientists are taking a different tack and are inclined to classify the Neanderthal creature as a type of gorilla: they believe also that, if mankind and the monkeys do share a common origin, it must have been many millions of years ago.

Professor Johannes Hürzeler has stated that "There is not one possibility in a thousand that men are descended from monkeys." His opinion as an anthropologist is worthy of respect: it was he who, in 1958, pronounced judgement on the skeleton dug up in 1872 at Baccinello near Grosseto in Tuscany. These bones were thought at the time to be those of a vanished species of tailed monkey, but they proved to be the remains of Oreopithecus, a pre-hominid which lived about 10 million years ago.

According to the latest scientific opinion, while this creature presents some "human" characteristics, it cannot be regarded as an ancestor of ours. This tends to confirm the existence of collateral branches of the species, among which we must rank the so-called "men" of Java, Peking, Heidelberg and so forth. These are henceforth to be regarded as representative of the monkey tribe which share some common features with us (as indeed do many extant species, including the proboscis monkey of Borneo) but are not, properly speaking, part of our family tree.

No doubt many of our cousins attempted, in the course of ages, to raise themselves above the animal level and to create artifacts of wood and stone. According to those scholars who have shaken off the dead weight of classic theory and endeavored to reconstitute, in its broad lines, the story of more or less rational species of bipeds, it was the Australopithecines, many of whose remains have been found in South Africa, that first began, two million years ago, to make use of hunting weapons such as stones, clubs and pointed sticks; some experts, from examination of their skulls, believe that they possessed a rudimentary form of

GIANTS AND THE LOST LANDS OF THE GODS

language.

As regards huntsmen in the dawn of prehistory, we may recall the chance discovery by Professor Leakey's son Richard, at Olduvai Gorge in Tanganyika, of huge animal bones, including the skull of a large ram with its frontal bones smashed in. The implements of the chase were found close by: beside the animal's right horn was an axe made of crocodile's teeth, and beside the left one a large stone which had evidently been hurled from a sling. These finds were about half a million years old, at that period there were already creatures in Africa who possessed effective hunting equipment. Yet, according to the classic evolutionists, it was not until about 30,000 years ago that our ancestors were capable of fashioning weapons of this kind.

The ancient inhabitants of Tanganyika may have come into contact with a race of hominids who lived somewhat further north, in Kenya, and who were skilled workers in stone 700,000 years ago: their discoverer, the American geologist Carter, actually believes that these dwarfish but enterprising creatures travelled as far as his own continent. This would be inconceivable if African geography were the same as it is today, but Carter explains his theory as follows.

"In the Pleistocene period, which began 700,000 years ago, the world went through an ice age. Huge glaciers covered millions of square miles of the earth to a depth, in places, of over 1,600 feet. This must have been due in part to a tremendous fall of snow, originating in seawater. The level of the sea would thus have been some 300 feet lower than it is now, and this would transform the face of the earth. Britain became part of the European continent, Florida was twice its present area, the South Sea Islands were joined to Asia and the mainland extended nearly as far as Australia; the Bering Sea disappeared and Siberia was joined to Alaska. The ice age also made a great difference to the African climate: the deserts turned into fertile plains across which the Kenya hominids were able to migrate."

Pithecanthropus and Sinanthropus must also have used crude implements of wood and stone; and it is interesting that some American and Soviet scholars believe that the yeti or "abominable snowman" (of whom there are apparently at least two species) is none other than a type of Sinanthropus (Peking man) which has survived in the inaccessible Himalayas and perhaps also in central Asia. A yeti with a bow and arrows was seen in 1913 by the British explorer H. Knight; during the 1961 expeditions the American professors Dhyrenfurth and Russel discovered beds of a primitive type in caves which the yeti were supposed to inhabit, while Soviet anthropologists deduced from their observations that the "monster" used some hard implement to dig for roots in the frozen ground and to cut steps in the ice. There is no reason why this should seem fanciful if we recall that the last Neanderthal men, in Africa, live at the same level, halfway between man and beast, to which their limited brain capacity restricts them.

GIANTS AND THE LOST LANDS OF THE GODS

Dinosaur Hunters

At this point we may ask ourselves what theory can be put forward instead of the discredited classic doctrine of evolution. The only scholar who tries to offer us a coherent alternative picture is Professor Carleton Coon, who until 1963 held the chair of anthropology at the University of Pennsylvania. In his monumental "Origin of Races" (1962) he tells us that the human race does not descend from a single ancestor but represents various types of homo erectus, species of primates which evolved independently of one another at different times and in different parts of the world. Homo sapiens is thus not the name of a single species, but a term denoting the stage at which each of the five main races developed from ape-like men into human beings.

According to Coon, this took place about 250,000 years ago in the case of the Mongoloids (peoples of East Asia, Polynesians, Amerindians, Chinese etc.) and Caucasoids (inhabiting Europe, North Africa and much of western and central Asia), but much later as regards the Congoloids (black Africans), Capoids (Hottentots, Bushmen) and Australoids (Australian aboriginals, Asiatic pygmies, Melanesians and Papuans); some of these, in fact, have evolved in quite recent times from homo erectus into homo sapiens.

Coon's theory is plausible in many respects, but it is hard to accept his dates even approximately, since we have seen that creatures definable as homo sapiens existed in Africa half a million years ago, and indeed there is evidence to justify pushing this date still further back.

Only a short while ago, official scientists rejected as a childish fantasy the idea that human beings once fought with "dragons of the prime," since they maintained that prehistoric monsters had died out long before the first men existed. But for the past few decades this view has suffered one blow after another with the discovery, especially in southern America, of graffiti and fossil remains which tell a very different story.

We need mention here only the excavations at Lagoa Santa and elsewhere in the Brazilian state of Minas Gerais, which have brought to light human skeletons buried under the bones of the toxodon (an ungulate creature about 9 feet long), the megatheriurn (a huge American tardigrade measuring some 20 feet) and the dinosaur.

We are left with the question, as yet unanswered: when did true man, essentially similar to ourselves, first make his appearance upon earth? All we can say in reply is that the human race is an extremely ancient one. In the canyon of Santa Maria, in the Brazilian highlands, traces have been found of troglodytes who lived about a million years ago: these were people who used stone clubs and flint-tipped arrows, bred livestock, probably tilled the soil, and embalmed their dead, whom they buried in jute sarcophaguses.

GIANTS AND THE LOST LANDS OF THE GODS

According to orthodox science, the first groups of European cave-dwellers came into existence about 200,000 years ago. But even if Professor Matthes' discovery, together with much other evidence, suggests that this figure should be increased by several millennia, we are still faced with an enigma: how is it that the American primitives, who seemed to have advanced quite a way towards civilization, did not develop any further in the course of a million years?

The answer must be that this is quite inconceivable. And the only explanation, therefore, is that the earth must have passed through more than one "prehistoric" period; that in some nameless, distant past mankind must have ascended a long way up the ladder of civilization, only to relapse into chaos and barbarism.

GIANTS AND THE LOST LANDS OF THE GODS

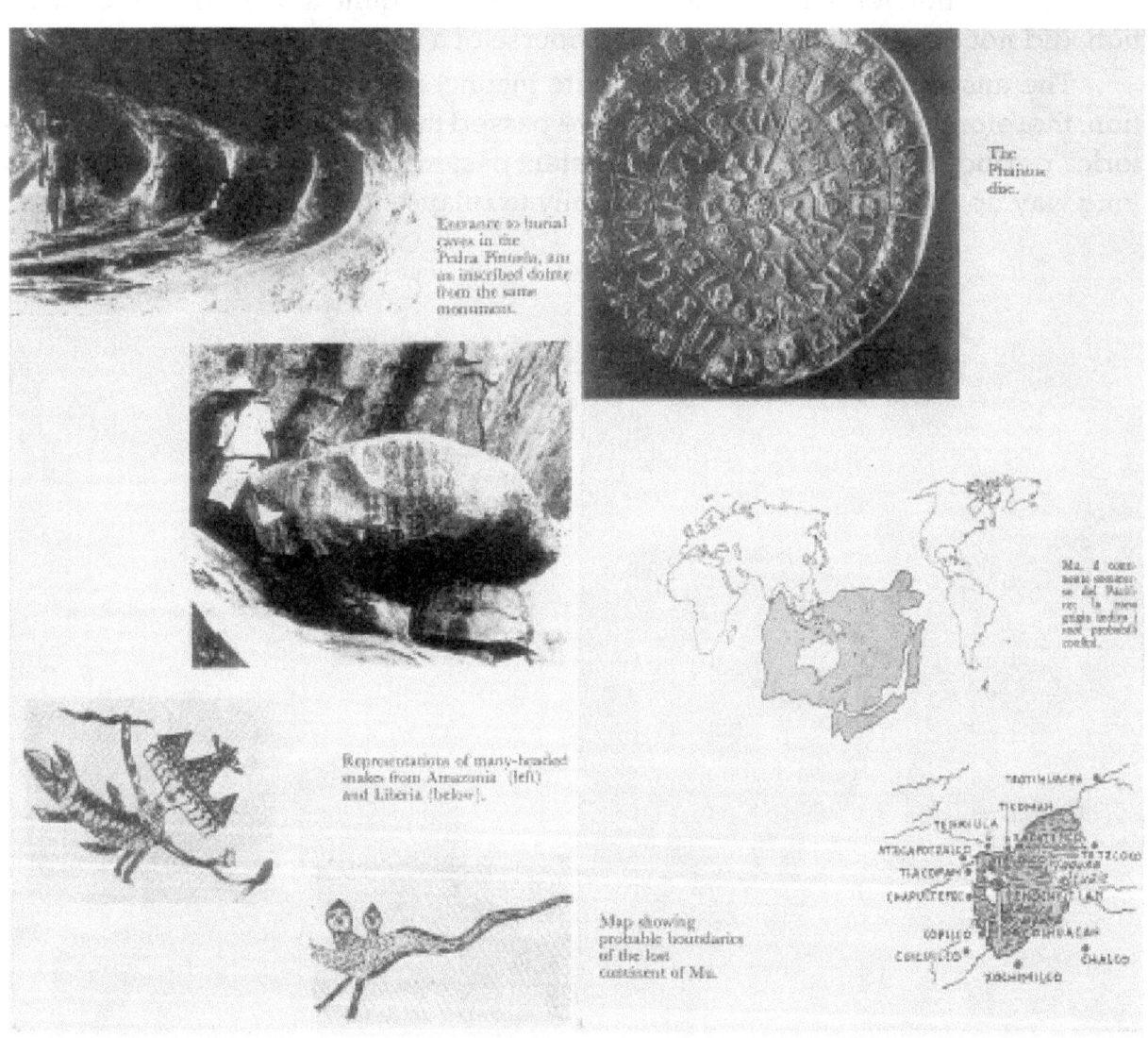

GIANTS AND THE LOST LANDS OF THE GODS

CHAPTER TWO
Cosmic Catastrophes

What force can it have been that wiped out flourishing civilizations at a single blow, decimating the population of the globe and condemning the survivors to take refuge in caves out of which their ancestors had painfully struggled thousands of years before? Clearly the cause must have been some fearful cataclysm affecting the whole of our planet.

There is much evidence that catastrophes on this scale did in fact occur. We may instance the discovery of the remains of mammoths throughout Siberia and the New Siberian Islands. The first discovery of a perfectly preserved mammoth was made in 1797 by a Cossack who unfortunately fed it to his sleigh-dogs; however, it would not have been of great value to science at that period. Those who found specimens in later years treated them with more care, and as the state of knowledge progressed it became possible to give an accurate description of this prehistoric beast.

However, according to the U.S. scientist, Charles H. Hapgood, although complete carcasses and skeletons are sometimes found, the remains usually look as if they had been thrown about by some gigantic force. In some places there are heaps of bones as high as a small hill, the remains of mammoths being interspersed with those of horses, antelopes, bison, huge felines and other smaller animals. These mysterious cemeteries have been known to man for ages past, and mammoth tusks up to 10 feet long have been objects of Asiatic trade for centuries if not millennia. Between 1880 and 1900 about ten million pairs of tusks were found in Siberia, and the supply still seems far from exhausted.

In Igor a sensation was caused by the discovery of a complete mammoth carcass near the Berezovka River, as this animal seemed to have died of cold in midsummer. The contents of its stomach were well preserved and included buttercups and flowering wild beans: this meant that they must have been swallowed about the end of July or beginning of August. The creature had died so suddenly that it still held in its jaws a mouthful of grasses and flowers. It had clearly been caught up by a tremendous force and hurled several miles from its pasture-ground. The pelvis and one leg were fractured; the huge animal had been knocked to its knees and had then frozen to death at what is normally the hottest time of the year.

Today, as we know, the Siberian tundra is a desolate expanse with a winter temperature lower than the North Pole: the annual mean is 16 degrees below zero Centigrade, with a maximum of 15 above zero in July and a lower limit of 49 degrees below (Fahrenheit 56 degrees below) in January.

The mammoth could not possibly have lived in such a climate: examination of its remains has shown that, contrary to what many still believe, it was accustomed to living in a temperate zone, like the horse, the bison, the tiger, the antelope and other mammals which were involved in the same general destruction. The foodstuffs found in the stomachs of these great proboscidea make it clear that Siberia in their day was a mild region of luxuriant vegetation.

We must conclude, therefore, that the whole mammoth species was killed off in an instantaneous tragedy, and that, immediately afterwards, large numbers of mammoth carcasses were immured in an icy sepulcher, failing which their bodies would have decayed. The effect of this catastrophe was to bring about an Arctic climate throughout Siberia, and in other parts of the globe as well. It is still the general opinion that what we now call Antarctica was embedded for millions of years under ice layers of more than a mile thick; but Admiral Byrd's expedition in 1946-7 produced evidence of a different kind, which was at first neglected but derived support from research undertaken during the International Geophysical Year.

American scientists fished up from the bed of the Antarctic Ocean specimens of a muddy sediment which showed that in comparatively recent times Antarctic rivers had borne down to the sea the alluvial products of an ice-free territory. This was apparently the case ten or twelve thousand years ago, i.e. just before the time when the mammoth suddenly became extinct; and there is much reason to think that it was one and the same cataclysm which brought about a total change of climate in the Antarctic and in Siberia.

A Cocoon Of Dust

Some geologists believe that the phenomenon which caused the mammoth to become extinct must have been similar, though on a much smaller scale, to those which precipitated the ice ages of the remoter past.

We do not in fact know the cause of the terrible, recurrent glaciation which covered the whole earth with a thick blanket of ice. Of the hundreds of theories, much the most likely is that a series of volcanic eruptions wrapped the earth in a cloud of dust so thick that the sun's rays could not penetrate it. This is not so farfetched as it may sound.

GIANTS AND THE LOST LANDS OF THE GODS

The explosion at ground level of a single hydrogen bomb stirs up a thousand million tons of earth which, in the form of minute grains of dust, is whirled up to a height of between 45 and 60 miles. Before these particles can fall back to earth again they are swept along by great winds which disperse them over enormous areas. While still in the air they constitute a kind of filter which impedes much of the sun's light and leads to sharp falls of temperature on the earth below.

We may also remember two famous volcanic eruptions of the past century. On 27 August 1883 the mountain of Rakata on Krakatau Island in the Sunda Strait erupted, hurling a cloud of ashes into the stratosphere. As these descended through the upper air they produced amazing visual effects: the sun and moon appeared in varying hues of purple, blue and green, and at sunset the earth was illuminated far and wide by fairy-like rays of pink and gold. But the farmers of the world paid dearly for this spectacle, and for three years or more, in almost every country, the normal amount of solar radiation was reduced by 15 per cent. Again, when Mount Katmai in the Alaska Peninsula erupted on 8 June 1912, temperature falls of 12 degrees Centigrade were recorded as far away as Algeria.

According to the meteorologist W. Humphreys, the effect of the eruption was, for a considerable time, to diminish by one-fifth the amount of heat received by the earth from the sun.

For the catastrophe to have brought about a permanent change in the climate of huge areas, dozens of volcanoes must have erupted simultaneously. As Hapgood says, "Storms capable of producing a 40-foot depth of snow or 40 successive days of rain are perfectly easy to imagine if we think of clouds of volcanic dust being cast into the air, cutting off the sun's radiance and chilling the atmosphere. A snowfall of this kind could kill animals over a vast area, freezing the corpses and covering them with a mantle of snow that would not melt in the following summer, but would increase in depth each winter."

In the American scholar's opinion, this fearful series of eruptions must have been caused by movements of the earth's land surface. According to Alfred Wegener the continents were originally formed by the disruption of a single primitive mass; parts of this began to move in different directions, sliding over lower strata which did not change their position. Hapgood appears to take the view that a series of similar displacements occurred about ten thousand years ago, as a result of which America moved south, while Siberia and Antarctica, which were formerly situated in temperate latitudes, became the coldest parts of the globe.

Wegener, on the other hand, believes that the breakup of the land mass started to take place some 250 million years ago, and that the continents have occupied their present positions for about a million years. We are not bound to accept this view, but it seems plausible enough. It is much harder, however, to accept Hapgood's theory, according to which the displacement of America, Siberia and

GIANTS AND THE LOST LANDS OF THE GODS

Antarctica took place within a relatively short time – so short, in fact, that it would have produced far more drastic convulsions than those he postulates – but went on for long enough to produce a continuous series of volcanic and seismic convulsions.

These might well have destroyed every form of life on our planet, but in any case they would have enveloped the earth in a cocoon of thick dust, with the result that every corner of its surface would have been plunged into a winter lasting many centuries. Not only mammoths, but all higher organisms of the animal and vegetable world would have succumbed to this catastrophe.

In actual fact, however, although the fearful offensive of "General Cold" was sufficient to devastate Siberia and Antarctica, it was not of long duration in the rest of the world; for reasons we shall try to explain later, it even led to a considerable rise in the temperature of Europe and America.

Encounters In Space

Casting about for other explanations of the apocalyptic events which ushered in the successive ice ages that have occurred on earth, we can only suppose that they must have had extraterrestrial causes.

It is easy to understand that, in the very distant past, the earth's crust was thin enough for the seething magma below to burst forth in violent eruptions; but it is hard to believe that an outburst of volcanic activity on a global scale could have happened spontaneously in later eras which are much closer to us from the geological point of view. Such an event could only be due to some external cause.

What can this muse have been? Without wishing to trespass into the realm of science fiction, we can only suggest that the cataclysm must have been due to some heavenly body colliding with the earth's surface. We may think of asteroids drawn from their orbit by unusual planetary conjunctions, enormous meteors from outer space, or previous satellites of the earth itself.

This hypothesis is consistent with the movement of the Arctic and Antarctic zones, which seems to have occurred more than once in the history of our planet. There are echoes of it in old Egyptian documents, in the Hermitage, Ipuwer and Harris papyri: the last-named speaks of a catastrophe following which "south became north and the earth turned round upon itself." Herodotus, moreover, tells us that according to the priests of Thebes (Luxor), "Twice in past ages the sun used to rise in a different quarter from where it rises now, and twice it was wont to set in the east instead of the west."

Scientific evidence is not lacking: according to Kreichgrauer, during the fossil coal era the North Pole was situated somewhere near Hawaii, while in later times it was at Lake Chad in Africa. The fact that this great reservoir of water possesses neither tributaries nor outlets proves, according to some American geolo-

GIANTS AND THE LOST LANDS OF THE GODS

gists, that it was formed by the melting of an enormous glacier.

Such extraordinary displacements may indeed have been caused by the violent eruption of many volcanoes, occurring more or less simultaneously around the globe. We may picture the effect by thinking of a firework which spins about and plunges as explosions take place successively on different parts of its surface.

A German geologist has reconstructed the effect of such a catastrophe as follows:

"To the northwest, a dazzling white streak of gas, some 1,200 or 1,500 miles long, shot up in a great arc across the sky. Silently and with lightning speed it approached, becoming wider and wider, and engulfed the earth like a huge serpent, while great conflagrations broke out on either side of it. Then death descended on the earth from outer space, in the form of a planetoid wrenched from its orbit. While still some distance from our planet, this body broke into two parts: both of them fell into the Atlantic with such terrific force that they burst through the earth's crust.

"With a roar, a fiery column rose into the sky, sweeping up with it gas, ashes, lava, stones and huge masses of incandescent magma. Destruction raged over thousands and thousands of miles; the ocean began to boil, vast quantities of water turned into steam which, together with the dust and volcanic ash, condensed into dark clouds that hid the sun. All the earth's volcanoes erupted with appalling violence."

This, as we shall see later, is a description of the catastrophe which extinguished the race of mammoths – a cosmic collision which may be dated 11,000 years ago, engulfing huge areas and raising harbor cities to an altitude of 13,000 feet; among other geological wonders, we owe to this event the creation of Niagara Falls. Stupendous as it was, it did not in itself bring on an ice age properly so called; but the resulting rains and floods constituted the deluge about which we read in Scripture.

Some scholars hold that the cause of the catastrophe was an asteroid attracted into the earth's gravitational field by an exceptional conjunction of the earth, the moon and Venus.

But, measured on a cosmic scale, it was a disaster of quite modest proportions compared to previous ones, including – as some scientists believe – the collision of three previous satellites with the earth, our present moon being the fourth of its kind.

Roaming Satellites

There are, as is well known, various theories of the moon's origin. Many believe that it was not part of the solar system but strayed in from a different part of space and was captured by the earth's gravitational field. As the Austrian Horbiger remarked, its composition is so different from that of the other members of our system that we are forced to think of stars and planets from unknown galactic regions.

The French author Denis Saurat, who, together with H. S. Bellamy, has evolved a fascinating theory based on Horbiger's investigations, writes in "Atlantis and the Giants":

"The moon is not the first satellite to go round the earth: each of the geological eras has had its own. And these periods are sharply distinct one from the other because at the end of each – and that is what brought it to an 'end' – its satellite crashed on the earth. The moon travels round the earth not in a closed ellipse but in a diminishing spiral, and this decreasing orbit will in the end – some 15 million years hence, according to Horbiger – cause it to crash in its turn. Thus a primary moon has already crashed; and a secondary moon and a tertiary moon.'

This theory may be indirectly confirmed from the work of Sir George Darwin, son of the great expounder of evolution, who held that our present moon was doomed to disintegration. When the earth was created, he explains, it revolved on its axis once in every five hours. As time went on, it slowed down, owing partly to the contrary pull of the tides which still affects its motion today. The loss of speed is only one second every 120,000 years, but the earth's motion through space is also retarded, so that the distance between it and the moon is continually increasing.

Fifty thousand million years from now the moon's distance from the earth will be about 340,000 miles; the earth's day will be equal to the month and to 47 of our present days. In this way the same face of the earth will always be turned towards the sun; the earth's days and nights will be unbearably hot and cold respectively, as the atmosphere will not suffice to protect it from the solar rays during such a prolonged period, or to store up enough daytime warmth to make the long nights endurable.

Then, when the earth comes to rotate even more slowly than the moon revolves round it, the pull of the tides will start to operate in the opposite sense, accelerating the earth's rotation. The moon will come closer to earth again, and at a certain point it will disintegrate. Some of the fragments will start spinning round the earth like Saturn's rings, while a destructive rain of meteors will fall upon the earth's surface.

Fearful earthquakes and seaquakes will follow, volcanoes will explode and vast areas will be engulfed by the sea. At best only a few wretched groups of human beings will survive, locked in a desperate struggle with such animals as have escaped the worldwide disaster and with monsters brought to birth by the altered environmental conditions.

GIANTS AND THE LOST LANDS OF THE GODS

The period within which Darwin predicted the disintegration of our moon is naturally related to its mass, its rate and direction of movement and its distance from the earth. We know little of any previous moons, but if they did exist, their end must have been more or less similar to the description quoted above.

As Saurat observes, there is a dream that suggests itself at one time or another to most people on earth: that of the moon falling from the sky. The heavens become blood-colored, the stars tremble, the moon begins to quiver; then it swells to giant size and rushes towards the earth, which is shaken by a devastating whirlwind. "This," Saurat continues, "is not a mere fantasy or premonition but reflects ancestral memories, transmitted unconsciously from generation to generation, in the same way as the account in the Book of Revelation is inspired by what took place in the remote past."

The "end of the world" has in fact already come about in the manner described by Scripture: "And lo, there was a great earthquake; and the sun became black as sackcloth of hair, and the moon became as blood; and the stars of heaven fell unto the earth, even as a fig-tree casteth her untimely figs, when she is shaken of a mighty wind. And the heaven departed as a scroll when it is rolled together; and every mountain and island were moved out of their places."

Is all this mere surmise? It is difficult to believe so, when myths, legends, sensational discoveries and rigorous scientific argument all combine to present a similar picture, full of uncertainty it is true, but agreeing in so many exact details that it cannot be ignored.

GIANTS AND THE LOST LANDS OF THE GODS

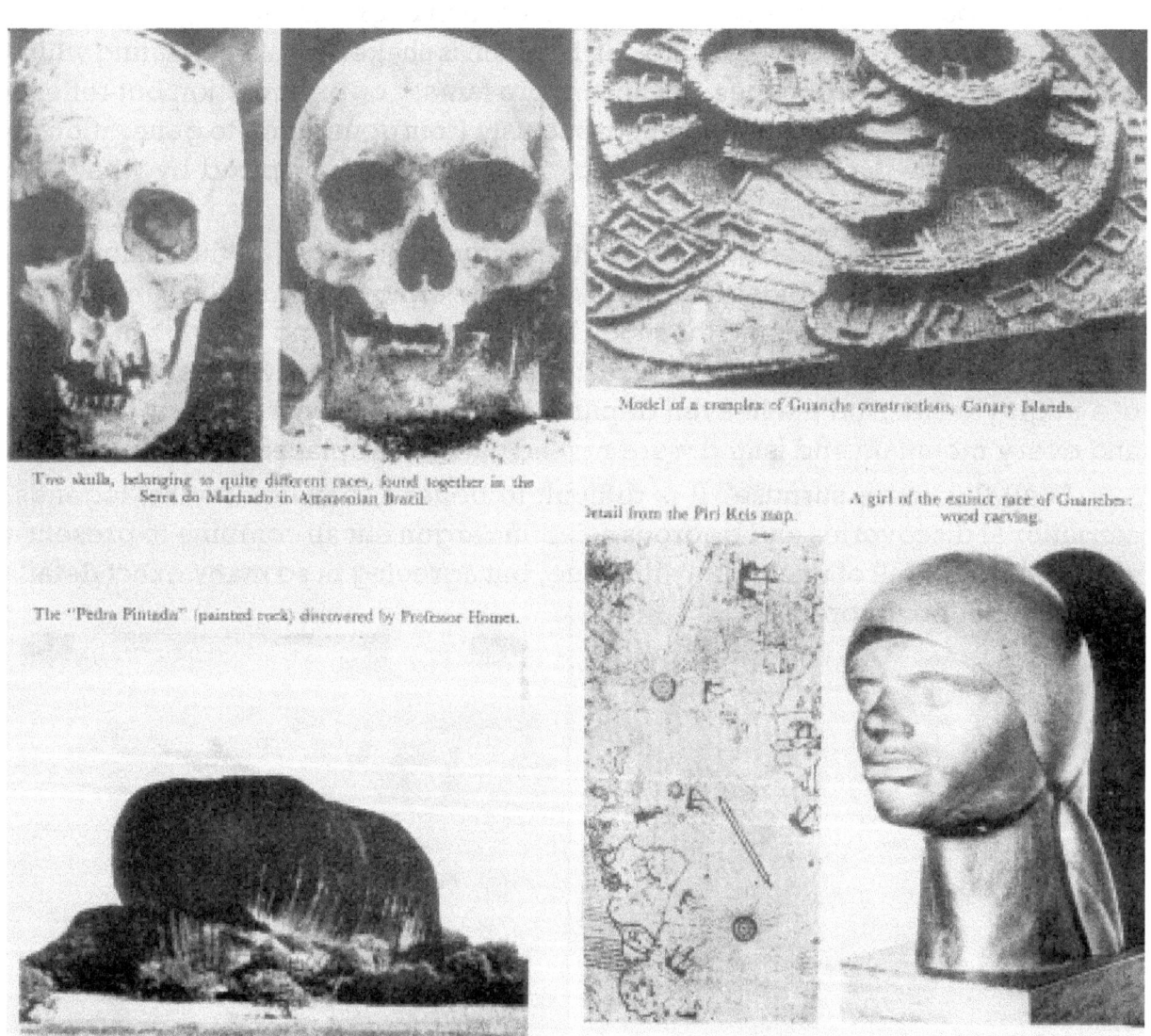

GIANTS AND THE LOST LANDS OF THE GODS

CHAPTER THREE
The Age Of Giants

Saurat and Bellamy put the question as to what is likely to happen when a satellite comes closer and closer to the earth. One effect is that the former's gravitational pull will become relatively greater. The tides will become stronger, thus flooding great continental areas, and, as a second consequence, human beings and creatures in general will become taller.

According to these two scientists, this is the only possible explanation of the huge species of plants and animals that have existed on earth, and of a race of men sixteen feet tall. The increase of men's stature, and likewise of their intelligence, is also due, according to this theory, to an increase in the intensity of cosmic rays.

There has been, and will continue to be, much animated discussion on the nature and effect of these rays. Years and years of experiment will be necessary before firm conclusions can be reached. Professor Jakob Eugster, the greatest expert on the subject, has remarked that "Like other radiations, such as wireless telegraphy, X-rays, etc., cosmic rays may have two types of effect: they may cause mutations, i.e. changes in inherited characteristics, and also damage or alterations in tissues."

If it is true that the earth has had moons that have been destroyed, and if the result has been to increase the intensity with which human beings are bombarded by radioactive particles, this may certainly be a contributory cause of the phenomenon of gigantism. To illustrate this we may recall the events of 1902 in the West Indian island of Martinique, when the eruption of Mont Pelé caused 20,000 deaths in the city of St. Pierre alone. Immediately before the disaster there appeared above the crater of the volcano a dark purple cloud consisting of gases saturated with aqueous vapor. This grew to an immense size and spread over the whole island, whose population still had no idea what was about to happen.

Suddenly a column of fire shot up from the mountain to a height of 1,300 feet, setting the gaseous cloud ablaze; the latter, burning at a temperature over 1,000 degrees Centigrade, exterminated the whole population except for one convict who was protected by the thick walls of his prison.

The devastated city was not rebuilt, but life on the island resumed sooner than could have been expected. Plants and animals returned to the scene, but all were of exceptional size: dogs, cats, tortoises, lizards and even insects were larger than had ever been known, and each generation grew bigger than the one before.

The French authorities established a research station at the foot of the volcano, and after a short time it was ascertained that the vegetable and animal mutations were due to radiations from minerals which had been thrown up by the explosion. These had their effect on human beings too: the director of the research center, Dr. Jules Graveure, became two and a half inches taller, and his assistant, Dr. Rouen, aged 59, grew about two inches.

Using cultures which had been sheltered from the radiations it was possible to observe, for instance, that a shoot exposed to the rays grew three times faster than normally, and that an irradiated plant developed in six months as much as it would otherwise have done in two years. Fruit ripened much faster and attained an extraordinary size, while cacti actually doubled in volume. Lower animals showed the effect of the rays also. A type of poisonous lizard called copa, which had previously measured up to eight inches in length, became a miniature dragon twenty inches long, and its bite, which had not always been fatal, was now more deadly than a cobra's.

This curious phenomenon of abnormal growth was no longer observed when the animals and plants in question were removed from Martinique. On the island itself, it turned out that the effect of radiation had reached its peak, and the "monsters" reverted to their ordinary size.

A Meeting With King Kong

Some scientists who reject the idea of lunar catastrophes still agree that cosmic rays are the cause of gigantism on earth, which has been clearly manifested in the plant and animal species. During the first phase of its existence the sun must have poured forth a stupendous volume of radiation on all its satellite planets: even today, the intensity of radiation goes hand in hand with the occurrence of sun-storms.

In this case, however, gigantism must have been a feature of life on earth from very early times, and not only in the Triassic period (from about 185 million years ago), which was that of the great prehistoric saurians. Cosmic rays, it is true, are filtered through the earth's atmosphere, which must have been much denser in early times. But it can hardly have been so dense as to affect radiation greatly, since at the present day rays of this type traverse the human body in in-

GIANTS AND THE LOST LANDS OF THE GODS

credible quantities – some 650,000 to the minute; they can penetrate massive walls of lead, or sea water to a depth of some 3,500 feet. The conclusion is, then, that cosmic rays would not in themselves have sufficed to create a race of giants, though they may certainly have helped to do so.

This is supported by the fact that large animals are known to have existed long after the disappearance of the saurians and giant members of the vegetable kingdom.

We have already mentioned the discoveries of Louis Leakey, and we may recall that his son Richard, now director of the National Museum of Kenya, was still a youth when he helped to discover hominid remains of extraordinary interest. He was climbing up the steep face of Olduvai Gorge, near Lake Victoria, when he stumbled and nearly lost his balance. Bending down, he saw a large bone protruding from the soil, which was a mixture of sand and gravel. He dug it out of the ground and found it to be a huge jawbone, with teeth as big as a human finger.

Young Leakey at this time was still a student with no special scientific knowledge, but he understood enough to run and tell his father of the discovery. When the latter came on the scene he had one of the greatest surprises of his career. The mandible was that of a huge baboon which had lived about half a million years ago; it was previously unknown to science, and was larger than any species known to have existed.

Inspired by this discovery, Professor Leakey at once made excavations in Olduvai Gorge, and his investigations were not without fruit. He unearthed some bones of uncertain provenance, which bore a resemblance to others in his museum. Having compared the two, he was astonished to find that they formed the skeleton of an animal of the pig family, similar to the African wild boar of today, but as large as a hippopotamus. In the course of further excavations in Tanganyika, Professor Leakey senior discovered the bones of another large boar and also two skulls, the first belonging to a ruminant of an unknown species and the second to a kind of large sheep.

The discovery of the "King Kong of Olduvai Gorge" is not particularly remarkable in itself. We already knew of the existence of huge prehistoric monkeys, such as the Gigantanthropus or Gigantopithecus which lived in the Chinese province of Kiang-Si about 550,000 years ago, and which is now thought to have been the ancestor of one species of yeti.

The Olduvai Gorge animal was 13 feet tall, or rather larger than the "Java meganthropus," to judge from the thickness of its jaw and the length of its muzzle. Sinanthropus Pekinensis was about ten feet tall, and the creature found at Swartkrans in South Africa measured about nine feet; this latter, it is known, was capable of lighting a fire and used to hunt with axes made out of the bones of animals of great size.

GIANTS AND THE LOST LANDS OF THE GODS

We now know that these enormous anthropoids did not represent an isolated case of gigantism among mammals, and the Olduvai Gorge finds are therefore of particular importance. Besides boars as large as hippopotami and sheep the size of horses, who knows what other giant representatives of the animal kingdom may have existed? In any event, the discoveries made up to now give a sufficiently clear picture of how all living beings have been growing progressively smaller since the era of the great saurians.

If we consider the animal kingdom at the present day, we find that the only remaining giants are the elephant, rising to a height of 13 feet (only just over 200,000 specimens are left in Africa) and the blue whale, 100 feet long, which is rapidly dying out. But even these are of modest proportions compared with the giants of remote eras such as the brontosaurus, which was 25 feet tall and 60 feet long and could, if it were alive today, drink with ease from the gutter of a two-storied house.

The present-day descendants of prehistoric monsters are absurdly small in size; what would the dinosaurs say if they could see the last scion of their family, the sphenodon of New Zealand – the only land animal possessing three eyes – which grows to a length of twenty-eight inches? Even greater would be the consternation of the scaly dragons of the past if they were to behold their descendant, the Australian moloch, a spine-covered lizard of the desert which lives on ants and measures eight inches.

It is a remarkable fact that all terrestrial animals are continuing to diminish in size. Unfortunately this has only been investigated for a short time, but it already seems clear that the largest members of the animal kingdom are either becoming extinct or shrinking as if touched by a magic wand.

Cyclopean Bones

Has this been more or less true of human beings also? Some believe that it has, and there is interesting evidence in support of their view.

A human skeleton 17 feet tall has been discovered at Gargayan in the Philippines, and bones of other human creatures over ten feet tall have been found in southeastern China. According to the paleontologist Pei Wen-chung, these are at least 300,000 years old. The same is true of the finds at Agadir in Morocco, where the French captain Lafanechere discovered a complete arsenal of hunting weapons including five hundred double-edged axes weighing seventeen and a half pounds, i.e. twenty times as heavy as would be convenient for modern man. Apart from the question of weight, to handle the axe at all one would need to have hands of a size appropriate to a giant with a stature of at least 13 feet.

Other stone implements of giant size have been found in Moravia and Syria, where the bones of their users have been discovered close by. In Ceylon explor-

GIANTS AND THE LOST LANDS OF THE GODS

ers have found the remains of creatures who must have been about 13 feet tall, and at Tura in Assam, near the border of East Pakistan (Bangladesh), a human skeleton measuring 11 feet has come to light. In this case, however, as with the bones found under a French dolmen whose owners must have been from 8 feet, 6 inches to 10 feet tall, we have to do with the descendants of giants rather than giants properly so called.

These traces of unusually tall human beings are not numerous, but there are at least as many of them as there are of the creatures who afford evidence for the evolutionist theories of classical anthropology. Moreover they have been discovered by pure chance, and the search for them throughout the world is still in its infancy.

As for non-archaeological evidence, it exists in abundance. Giants play an important part in the mythology of every people that has inhabited the earth, from the Mediterranean races of ancient times to the American Indians, from Tibet to Australia. We think chiefly of the Titans and Cyclopes of ancient Greece and their Nordic counterparts the Jotunn; but, looking further, we may cite the Izdubar of Chaldea, the Emin of Hebrew lore, the Danavas and Daityas of ancient India, the Rakshasas of the Hindu epic, and many more.

Turning to the Bible, we find in Genesis (chapter 6) the statement that "There were giants in the earth in those days" and that "The sons of God came in unto the daughters of men, and they bore children to them." In Deuteronomy 3: 11 we read that "Only Og king of Bashan remained of the remnant of giants" and that his bedstead measured nine cubits by four (a cubit being about 18 inches); and in I Samuel 17 of Goliath, whose height was "six cubits and a span." As Saurat observes (op. cit., p. 76), the Biblical references to giants are not necessary to the story from the religious point of view, and "they appear at the most diverse dates, in chapters unrelated to each other: Genesis 6, Numbers 13, Deuteronomy 3, Joshua 12, 13, 15 and 17, II Samuel 21, I Chronicles 20, Job 26, Baruch 2 and Revelation 20.

"These passages present every characteristic of historical authenticity: they are precise and concrete; they are introduced by no historical or mythological thesis; they prove nothing and are stated merely as facts; they occur in passages which have no apparent connection, and if they are taken away the narrative is not in any way interrupted; they are very short and apparently scattered about without any special importance or significance attached to them; they come from writers widely different from each other in both time and religious development."

Elsewhere Saurat points out that the phenomena of gigantic size and long life go together. The cells of the body become lighter, the organism wears out at a slower rate, and man therefore lives longer. This accounts for what the Bible tells us of the long-lived men of olden times, and for the association between gods and immortality.

GIANTS AND THE LOST LANDS OF THE GODS

Another French author, Michel Cargése, confirms this: "As the gravitational pull was less, objects in general were less heavy, the blood circulated more easily, and the whole organism was less subject to fatigue. Men were extraordinarily long-lived, with a more developed brain than ours and faculties that enabled them to acquire different forms of knowledge."

There is a curious parallel between our own scriptures and the Toltec legend which relates how the "First Age" was brought to an end by fearful destruction due to "floods and lightning," while in the "Second Age" our earth was peopled by giants called Quinametzin; most of these disappeared when the world was devastated by earthquakes, and those that survived were destroyed by men during the "Third Age," just as Goliath was slain by David.

But Aztec mythology is still more reminiscent of the Biblical story. As Ralph Bellamy tells us: "Xelua and his brother giants escaped from the world cataclysm by taking refuge on the summit of a mountain which they dedicated to the water-god Tlaloc. To commemorate the event and show their gratitude to the divinity, and also to provide themselves with a stronghold in the event of another flood, they built a 'zacauli,' a huge tower designed to reach the sky. But the gods, offended by their presumption, sent a fiery rain upon the earth, and many of the builders perished."

Then, as an American legend relates, mankind, which had previously spoken one language, was divided and began to speak many different tongues. We thus have here a Mexican version of the story of the Tower of Babel, based evidently on the Cholula pyramid of which we shall have occasion to speak further.

GIANTS AND THE LOST LANDS OF THE GODS

CHAPTER FOUR
The Mark Of The Titans

Some scholars are of the opinion that giants are mere figments of popular imagination, and that if they occur in every mythology it is because human beings like to personify the ideas of good and evil, extrapolating from their own image in accordance with a primitive mental process. But this does not suffice to account for the many giant structures which have been scattered about the earth since time immemorial.

These Titanic remains constitute a fascinating mystery by reason of their size and the transport problems they must have entailed. They range from the most ancient megaliths known as menhirs (Breton for "long stone"), which are single stones roughly hewn and planted vertically in the earth, to the dolmens ("table stone" or "hole of stone") consisting of two tall slabs with another huge stone poised on top. Both these types of megalith are common in Brittany, Wales, Cornwall, northern Germany, Switzerland, Corsica, Apulia and Spain, as well as in the Middle East, Turkestan, Mongolia, China, India and throughout South America.

Menhirs are regarded by some as phallic symbols, but for a long time now many archaeologists have taken them to represent human or superhuman figures. This is borne out by myths in various parts of the globe. The Greek legend tells how Deucalion and Pyrrha, after the Flood, threw stones behind their backs and saw them turn into men and women who were to repopulate the world; this is not too remote from the story of the African sky-gods who gave life to humankind by "blowing with the wind so that their souls entered into rocks." The Polynesians and ancient Peruvians, too, seem to have had Titanic beings in mind when they described how men, women and animals were created "from large stones."

Saurat believes that the megaliths were originally carved by giants in their own image and that men afterwards imitated them as a means of evoking and recalling to life the ancient beings whom their imagination had deified. More precisely, the menhirs signify man's Cyclopean ancestors, while the dolmens represent their tablets. In support of his theory Saurat quotes the findings of John Layard,

GIANTS AND THE LOST LANDS OF THE GODS

an ethnographer and psychologist who studied the inhabitants of a group of islands to the southeast of New Guinea.

In Saurat's words (op. cit., p. 64): "Normally, in front of the statue of the ancestor a dolmen is built up to three or four feet high: it usually consists of three stones, but is frequently more complex. This represents the giant's table on which pigs, specially bred for this purpose, are sacrificed; Layard discovered easily enough that not so long ago men were sacrificed instead of pigs as food for the giant." Saurat believes that this was a universal custom towards the end of the era of giants; he quotes a native legend according to which there were, first of all, benevolent giants who taught men the arts of civilization, but that these were followed by evil giants, cannibals, who had to have stone tables on which to eat men. Tagaro was a good giant and came from the sky.

Suque, who was evil, fought Tagaro but was thrown into the abyss – even as in Greece the wicked giants were thrown into the abyss by the "good" gods. Then all giants disappeared, but men, terrified, continued to protect themselves by keeping ready the statues, the tables, the victims (men or pigs) against their return.

It is remarkable that echoes of the Oceanic legend occur in the myths of many distant lands. The Greeks, for example, also speak of cannibalism: we remember the Titan Kronos who devoured his own children, and Homer's Cyclops fattening on human flesh. As Hermann and Georg Schreiber remark in "Vanished Cities" (London, 1958): "The legends of giants, which were widely disseminated in ancient America, form part of the Aztec creation myth; parallels to them are found in various parts of South America and even share the strange detail that these giants were homosexual cannibals who treated women merely as food, for which crime they were ultimately destroyed by heaven."

The evil giants were no doubt the builders or inspirers of cromlechs ("crooked stone" – menhirs disposed in a circle), dedicated to divinities or rather to giants who claimed divine honors. One of the most famous of these is Stonehenge in England, where a crowd assembles every Midsummer Day when the rising sun fills the aperture above the main altar with a magic circle of light.

One of the sects who meet there to perform their ceremonies maintains that Stonehenge was the cradle of the Druidic religion, but there is no scientific basis for this: Stonehenge had existed for many a century before the Druids began to celebrate their rites in Europe. It is known that in 1400 B.C. the inner "sanctuary" already had its present shape, while the outer ring was erected by 1800 B.C. at latest and is probably much older. It consists partly of local stone and partly of some quarried in Northern Ireland, and is of greater antiquity than the 345 prehistoric graves to be found nearby.

The mystery of Stonehenge is a fascinating one, but even more sensational is the fact that its builders seem to have had links with Homeric Greece. Archaeologists in southern England have come upon the representation of a sword which appears identical with that used by the warriors of the Iliad, and which hitherto was thought to be quite unknown to the rest of Europe. We may compare with this the fact that the French archaeologist R. Grosjean has discovered reliefs on Corsican menhirs depicting swords and daggers of exquisite workmanship and unusual design. In this way we begin to realize that all ancient civilizations had elements in common.

Megaliths of this kind are found in every continent, and another curious fact is that the stones of which they are made were often brought from a long way off. Slabs of African stone have been erected in Ireland, and those found in southern Russia and Siberia must have been quarried in some distant place, since there are no mountains for many miles around.

These simple yet startling monuments struck the imagination of the ancient Greeks and Romans: for instance Apollonius Rhodius, who lived in the third century B.C., appears almost to be writing science fiction when he says of the Greek megaliths that they are "living stones, possessed of such sensibility that they can be moved by mental force."

We cannot put an exact date to these Cyclopean Works, but the closer we come to the present day, the more they astound us. The prehistoric forts of Ireland and eastern Scotland are amazing enough, as are the calcined platforms of Iceland, as large and smooth as a missile launching site. Similar marvels can be found in the New World: in the state of Paraiba in eastern Brazil, for instance, there is a huge ruined fortress with walls over 80 feet high and 16 feet thick, and with an inner hall which, when intact, measured 164 yards by 50 yards. South America is full of stupendous ruins of this kind; but, as the French archaeologist and journalist Robert Charroux writes, "The great Peruvian monoliths are of small account compared to the stones of Baalbek. The ruins of this ancient Lebanese city with its huge sanctuaries display the building achievement of a people who discovered how to transport, cut and lift into position blocks of 750 tons' weight, at a time when there were no trucks or reinforced concrete and the keystone had not been invented."

Some of the foundation stones are 80 feet long, with a breadth and height of 15 feet. In the quarry from which they were taken, half a mile or so from the city, we may still see the biggest cut stone in the world, known as hajar al-hubla (the "stone of the pregnant woman"), which weighs about 2,000 tons. It seems incredible that human beings, at the dawn of history, should have been able to transport and erect such colossal pieces of masonry.

The Soviet scientist, Agrest, in fact believes that these stupendous constructions may have been the work of beings from outer space – the same visitors who, he thinks, may have caused the destruction of Sodom and Gomorrah by detonating part of the nuclear fuel of their spaceships. In this way, what we may call legends of the "astro-nautical era" come to us in the form of echoes of the remote past, amplified by the vaults of the mysterious "giants' galleries."

A Tunnel Under The Pacific

"If the Spaniards, when they entered Cuzco, had not behaved with such cruelty and slaughtered Atahualpa, who knows how many ships might have been needed to carry to Spain treasures which now lie buried in the bowels of the earth and which may remain there forever, since those who hid them have gone to their death without revealing the secret."

These words were written by the soldier-priest Pedro Cieza de Leon a few years after the murder of the last Inca emperor and the massacre of his subjects by Pizarro's murderous bands. The Spanish adventurers were so blinded by their lust for gold that they acted in the way most likely to defeat their ambition. Pizarro, it will be recalled, took Atahualpa prisoner and declared that he would only release him in return for all the treasure of the Incas. The emperor's wife, it is said, consulted the solar oracle and, having learnt that the Spaniards intended to kill Atahualpa in any case, took her own life after giving orders that the treasure should be securely hidden, as Harold Wilkin says, "in sealed caves to which mystic hieroglyphs, whose key is possessed only by one descendant of the Incas at a time, in each generation, give the open sesame; and in strange subterranean places, thousands of years old, which must have been made by a mysterious and highly civilized vanished race of South America in a day when the ancient Peruvians themselves were a mere wandering tribe of barbarians."

The story is quite a probable one: there are many underground passages of this kind, and not only in former Inca territory. The best-known, however, is the system of tunnels which is said to run from Lima to Cuzco, the Inca capital, and thence south-eastward to the Bolivian border. According to old documents one of these tunnels conceals a sumptuous royal tomb, and it is not only scientists who have been attracted by this speculation. The truth of it, however, is bound to remain in doubt for many years to come: it would be enormously expensive to clear the galleries of the rubble which blocks them to within forty yards or so of the entrance, and to dispel the mephitic fumes with which they have been filled for centuries. Other mortal dangers might well await the explorer: it is said that the Incas left booby-traps which would cause disastrous landslides if an intruder should set foot in the galleries.

Apart from the lure of gain, these tunnels present a fascinating archaeological problem. Scholars agree that they were not made by the Incas themselves, who used them but were ignorant of their origin. They are in fact so imposing that

GIANTS AND THE LOST LANDS OF THE GODS

it does not seem absurd to conjecture, as some scientists have done, that they are the handiwork of an unknown race of giants.

It is a strange fact, moreover, that tunnels of this sort are to be found in almost every part of the world. Besides South America they exist in California, Virginia, Hawaii (where they apparently link the islands of the archipelago), Oceania and Asia, as well as Sweden, Czechoslovakia, the Balearics and Malta. A huge tunnel, some thirty miles of which have been explored, runs between Spain and Morocco, and many believe that this is how the "Barbary apes," which are otherwise unknown in Europe, reached Gibraltar.

It has even been suggested that these Cyclopean galleries form a network connecting the most distant parts of our planet. The journalist John Sheppard, formerly correspondent of a well-known U.S. periodical in Ecuador, relates that in the summer of 1944, on the Colombian border, he came across a Mongol absorbed in meditation, with a praying-wheel of the kind used in Tibet. This, it is suggested, was none other than the thirteenth Dalai Lama, who was supposed to have died in 1933 but was never buried in the crypt designed to hold his remains; the reason given at Lhasa was that he did not in fact die but made the long underground pilgrimage to the Andes, where, according to certain priests, Lamaist religion was born and flourished before its association with Buddhism. This may seem a tall order, but lamas who have been questioned about the tunnels have usually replied: "Yes, they exist: they were made by giants who gave us the benefit of their knowledge when the world was young."

We might almost be convinced of this when we read what Charroux tells us of Eupalinos, who constructed a tunnel in ancient times on the island of Sarnos. "The works were begun simultaneously from both ends; the tunnel is 1,000 yards long, it is absolutely straight and the two teams met each other exactly according to plan. The French and Italian engineers who tunneled under Mont Blanc had at their disposal electronic measuring devices, radar, magnetic detectors and ultrasonic equipment. Eupalinos, as far as we know, did not even have the use of a compass."

Equally astounding from the technical point of view are the basalt sculptures of unknown age discovered in 1939 in the heart of the Mexican jungle – five enormous heads, recalling the well-known monuments of Easter Island – and other prodigious works of statuary found in the Andes, Asia and Oceania.

Another extraordinary phenomenon is a mountain at Havea in Brazil, carved in ancient times to resemble the head of a bearded man wearing a spiked helmet: the effect can still be seen despite the erosion of centuries. Moreover, on one side of the mountain which presents a smooth vertical face some 3,000 feet in height, an inscription has been carved in cuneiform characters some 10 feet tall. How this was done is a mystery for which not even the most tentative solution has been

GIANTS AND THE LOST LANDS OF THE GODS

offered.

The archaeologist Bernardo da Silva Ramos has found similar inscriptions in various parts of Latin America, and it was he who discovered the monumental ruins on the island of Marajo in the river Amazon, with imposing underground chambers connected by stone-walled tunnels. This discovery presented scientists with yet another puzzle in the shape of a collection of handsome vases with designs very similar to the Etruscan type.

We should not overlook the cuneiform inscriptions found in the Roosevelt plateau in Brazil, between the provinces of Amazonas and Mato Grosso. These records, which unfortunately cannot be read, are carved on enormous stone discs divided into six sectors and are thought to have been used for astronomical calculations.

The list could be extended indefinitely, but we will conclude by mentioning the ruins of Bamian, a small town in Afghanistan northwest of Kabul. The town stood in the center of a valley, surrounded by natural and artificial caves and guarded by five statues: the tallest of these is 150 feet high, the next 125 feet, the next two 60 and 13 feet, while the fifth is no taller than a present-day man. It was once thought that these were statues of Buddha, but it turned out that this interpretation was due to Buddhist priests who had lived in the caves around A.D. 100. The figures are in fact much older, as was proved by the examination of a sort of cement cloak in which the tallest of them was enwrapped, many thousands of years ago. What, then, do these statues represent? May it not be the decline of the race of giants, their gradual diminution in size and, finally, the pre-dominance of homo sapiens?

The Death Of Goliath

The views of Saurat and Bellamy concerning the race of giants are plausible in many respects, but obscure and unconvincing in others. Concerning the Andean civilization, Saurat writes as follows (op. cit., p. 16):

"Some thirty thousand years ago a highly developed civilization – utterly different from our own – was flourishing in the Andes, at 12,000 or 14,000 feet above the present level of the Pacific Ocean. At that period the sea there reached that height, and the Tiahuanaco civilization was on a seashore. The air was at a density normal for human beings, whereas now it is thin and nearly unbreathable.

"How did all this happen? Round the earth there revolved a satellite, in some ways comparable to our present moon (which was not then there) – though smaller than the moon – at a distance of five to six earth radii. Nowadays the tides rise and fall because our present moon is some sixty times the length of the earth's radius, i.e. some 240,000 miles, away from us and takes a comparatively long time to revolve round the earth. But the tertiary moon, being by then much nearer, revolved much more quickly and the waters attracted by its pull had no time to recede. A permanent tide kept all the waters of the earth accumulated in a great bulge right round the planet, roughly between the tropics."

Only what is now the highest ground would have emerged above this girdle-tide: some Andean peaks, the Mexican highlands, the mountains of New Guinea, Tibet and the Abyssinian plateau – the home of the Masai, who grow to a height of 6 feet 6 inches and are presumably of "Cyclopean" descent. But how is it then that colossal monuments are to be found in areas which were submerged by the tidal bulge?

Again, is it really possible that the approach of our previous satellite should have been marked by phenomena of such a simple and limited character, with the most spectacular effects confined to the races inhabiting islands of high ground? Granting this, we must assume that ordinary human life continued to develop in vast dried-up areas, subject to all kinds of atmospheric convulsions, until eventually, according to Saurat, a race of benevolent giants made their way on shipboard to the regions where our ancestors lived, bringing them the benefits of civilization.

All this is very perplexing; but it is certain that the giants existed, and it is hard to reject the Saurat-Bellamy theory completely. It is, however, possible to give a simpler explanation of the facts, if we accept the premise that the giants may have come from extraterrestrial space.

Some may think this pure fantasy, and we do not demand that the reader believe it, though it is a theory which continues to intrigue reputable scientists. As we shall see, there are many mysterious traces of the earth's remote past which seem to support the hypothesis of interplanetary links.

To conclude the story of the giants we may observe that, whatever the mode of their appearance, they must have established a rapid ascendancy over our dwarfish ancestors, but their rule was a short-lived one. We do not know for certain the reason for their decline: according to Saurat and Bellamy, it was due to the waning gravitational pull of the earth's satellite, while upholders of the "outer space" theory would put it down to their migration from a planet of less gravity to one of greater. At all events, the Cyclopes gradually died out. Latter-day giants may have continued to dominate the earth here and there, but the mutations in their physical and mental makeup laid them open to defeat by the new master-race of men. With the destruction of Polyphemus and Goliath, the reign of the Titans was over.

GIANTS AND THE LOST LANDS OF THE GODS

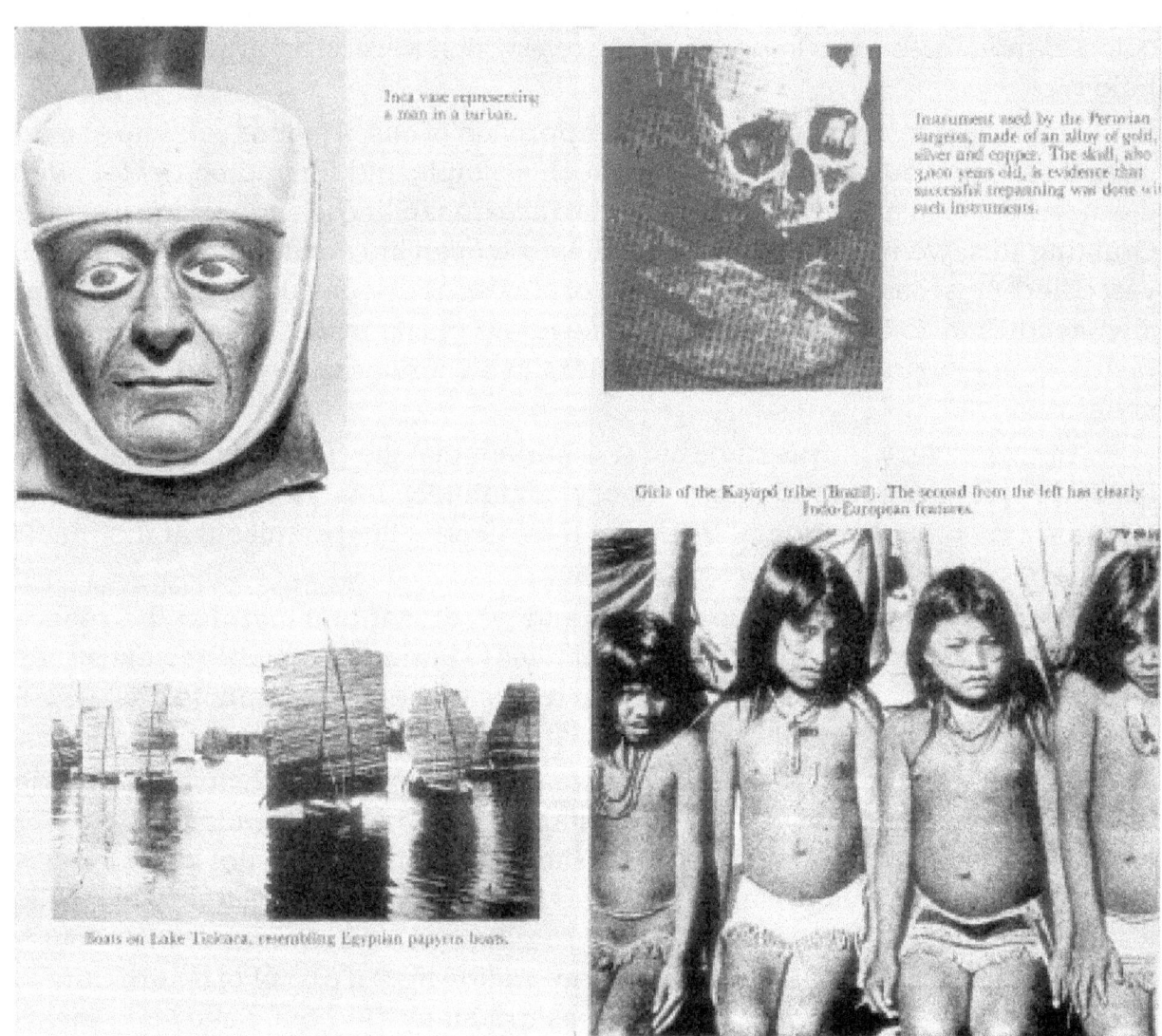

Inca vase representing a man in a turban.

Instrument used by the Peruvian surgeon, made of an alloy of gold, silver and copper. The skull, about 3,000 years old, is evidence that successful trepanning was done with such instruments.

Girls of the Kayapó tribe (Brazil). The second from the left has clearly Indo-European features.

Boats on Lake Titicaca, resembling Egyptian papyrus boats.

GIANTS AND THE LOST LANDS OF THE GODS

CHAPTER FIVE
Nightmares In Stone

We saw in our last chapter how, as many scholars have brought to light, statues and images in honor or in memory of the giants were erected by mankind all over the globe. But there is one place that contains a whole collection of such memorials, and that is Easter Island. This sinister, desolate rock in the eastern Pacific is a mere dot on the map, some 64 square miles of bare, inhospitable soil; yet what a rich problem it affords to scientists!

Who were the inhabitants of the island in the remote past? What is the origin of the race that was living there when it was discovered by Europeans? What are the "singing tablets"? Who carved and erected the famous stone images, how were they able to, and for what purpose? Who excavated the great subterranean tunnels that finish under the seabed, and what was the use of these? Such problems have baffled scholars for decades, and seem likely to continue to mock their efforts. But investigators do not give up easily, and there is some glimmer of light in what used to be thought impenetrable darkness.

An English adventurer named Davis is said to have reached Easter Island in 1687, but the "strange, squalid land" he speaks of is probably Mangareva, a considerable distance to the west. The credit for discovering the island is generally given to the Dutch admiral Roggeveen, who reached there on Easter Day 1722 and named it accordingly; the Polynesians called it Waihu or "land's end." The first serious studies of the island were made by Captain James Cook and the German naturalist Georg Forster, who landed there in 1774. Forster was struck by the curious appearance of the place: the ground was covered by huge rocks, evidently the result of a volcanic eruption, with scanty vegetation growing around them. The European visitors moved with difficulty over the rough ground, but the natives jumped with agility from rock to rock. Forster paints a gloomy picture of the island, surrounded by reefs and guarded by two rock points that emerge from the sea near its southern end; one of these, lashed by the waves, resembles a gigantic column of threatening aspect.

GIANTS AND THE LOST LANDS OF THE GODS

The natives whom Forster encountered were skinny and of middle height, with brown complexions and curly black hair; but there were among them other savages, white men with beards, who had apparently lived on the island for several generations.

Living conditions on the rock were miserably poor: there was, for instance, only a single spring of sweet water, at which the inhabitants took turns to drink and wash themselves.

A History Of Misfortunes

The strange, bleak landscape of the island, the stone heads and the mysterious tunnels have given rise to innumerable legends and have not been neglected by science fiction. An American writer, for instance, has suggested that the island may be a fragment of some lost world, disintegrated by an explosion in space. This, of course, is mere imagination, but there is indeed something about the lonely, nightmare island which makes one think that it could have been part of an asteroid.

When Roggeveen discovered the island, it boasted 5,000 or 6,000 inhabitants, who were soon given reason to think badly of the newcomers. The Dutch fired on the population without cause and killed twelve of them, and since that time the islanders' life has been one misfortune after another. In 1859-62 they were invaded by bands of Peruvian adventurers who enslaved and deported the whole population, including their king, Marata. Bishop Janssen of Tahiti protested strongly to Lima, and those of the unfortunates who survived were allowed to return; but the few who came back were ridden with smallpox, leprosy, syphilis and other diseases contracted in the unhealthy areas in which they had been forced to work.

When the first missionary, Father Eyraud, reached the island in 1864, he found only a few hundred wretched natives; nevertheless, the captain of the ship that brought him thought them good enough fodder for the plantations of Tahiti, and in this way another hundred underwent deportation for the second time. Those who remained encountered trouble of a fresh sort. An adventurer named Dutroux-Bornier claimed that he had bought the island from the ruler of Tahiti, who for some reason was supposed to own it; he seized the natives' miserable flocks and set up so tyrannical a régime that the islanders, timid and gentle as they were by nature, finally rose in revolt and killed him.

Afterwards the island became the property of a family named Brander; in 1888 they sold it to Chile, to which country it still belongs.

When we think of Easter Island, the first image that comes to mind is that of the enormous stone heads, carved from volcanic rock, which are among the strangest and most impressive monuments to be found anywhere. Three hundred of these were carved from a single crater; they were then hoisted and removed to

GIANTS AND THE LOST LANDS OF THE GODS

bases situated up to ten miles away.

Some of the colossi weigh as much as 30 tons; they vary in height, as a rule, from 11 to 66 feet, but there is an unfinished one which is no less than 164 feet high. When the natives were questioned about the origin and meaning of these statues, they were unable to answer. This was, no doubt, because their learned men were deported with King Marata: these guardians of tradition might have revealed many facts of the greatest interest about the past of their own society and also about the most mysterious of earth's civilizations.

Apart from the stone carvings there are some tablets made of a kind of wood not native to the island, with inscriptions reminiscent of the hieroglyphics of pre-Columbian America and also the script discovered in recent times in the Indus valley, which goes back to about 3,000 B.C. For a long time these were thought to be undecipherable; a key was in fact discovered by the same Bishop Janssen who rescued the natives from Peruvian bondage, but it remained unknown to science until further research was undertaken by the German anthropologist Thomas Barthel. In 1953 this scholar came across photographs of notes made by Janssen and realized that the latter, by questioning the Easter Islanders working in Tahiti, had succeeded in partially deciphering the so-called "singing tablets."

Barthel thereupon set out to discover the remainder of the bishop's notes. The Congregation of the Sacred Heart, to which Janssen belonged, had had its headquarters at Braine-le-Comte in Belgium, but when Barthel got there he was told that the fathers had moved elsewhere. Eventually his search led him to the abbey of Grottaferrata at the foot of the Alban Hills, where he found the remainder of the precious documents.

The "singing tablets" consist for the most part of the prayers inscribed in the fashion known as boustrophedon, i.e. with alternate lines from left to right and from right to left; the text begins at the bottom, and every other line is upside-down. One part of it reads: "They came from Rangitea, disembarked here and addressed prayers to the god of Rangitea." This goes to confirm that the Easter Islanders are of Polynesian origin; they must have come in about A.D. 1300 from the over-populated Society Islands, especially Raiatea (Rangitea). It would thus appear that the stone heads are less antique than was previously thought: the earliest of them may date from about 1350, and they are presumably representations of the natives' "august ancestors," honored with magic rites and human sacrifices.

It remains an enigma how the islanders could have transported these colossal statues for long distances and then hoisted them into position. Thor Heyerdahl, the leader of the famous Kon Tiki expedition, suggests that the statues were tugged over wooden logs with cables made of raflia and other vegetable fibers, and were hoisted by means of inclined planes made of rocks and sand. But the Easter Islanders in fact had no logs to serve as rollers, since the layer of soil covering the island's rocky surface is too shallow to permit the growth of trees.

In any case, no one can say why, alone among Polynesians, these migrants from Rangitea chose to erect monuments of this sort. Another mysterious fact is that many of the heads have been overturned, while others were left half finished. In many scholars' view the most likely explanation of this is that a religious revolution must have taken place, with the new creed forbidding ancestor-worship.

The Island Of The Apocalypse

Other mysteries of Easter Island will probably never be solved. Among these are the underground tunnels and the arrangement of the statues, recalling the magic circle of Stonehenge or the alignments (alleys of menhirs) in Brittany; the caves piled with ancient human bones, and the petroglyphs (carvings on stone) with motifs similar to those of the old civilizations of Central and South America, together with elements reminiscent of India, China and ancient Egypt.

For example, the "bird-men" of Easter Island are certainly akin to the fabulous "fire-bird" met with in India, the Americas and Mediterranean countries – a creature which seems to have been the symbol of one of the mother civilizations of our earth, the mythical Atlantis.

Are we to believe that the Atlanteans came to Easter Island? It might seem so from the legend which tells that "Many long years ago there came by sea, in two ships, king Hotu Matua, his queen and seven thousand of his subjects. They came from two islands, from the region of the sunrise, and when they reached here, their islands sank into the sea."

However, most scholars think that these were not Atlanteans but Americans, from some islands which may formerly have existed between Easter Island and the South American continent.

Centuries ago the population of Easter Island seems to have numbered between two and five thousand, divided into two classes: the plebs, with short ears, and the nobles, with long ears, i.e. with the lobes lengthened by means of hanging weights, as we also see in the statues. The plebs eventually revolted, and a civil war ensued which decimated the population.

The lengthening of the ear-lobes as a mark of aristocracy was also an Inca custom, and it would be strange for it to have flourished independently on Easter Island and in Peru. Moreover, many of the islanders' tools and works of art bear a striking resemblance to Peruvian ones. It seems likely, therefore, that the Incas may have reached Easter Island before the Polynesians and been exterminated or driven out by them. If so, the newcomers may have taken over from the Incas the cult of ancestors, thus explaining the famous statues – they may, in fact, have borrowed from Hotu Matua's subjects the notion of giant progenitors in times of yore. This would help to explain the extraordinary resemblance between the pedestals of the Easter Island statues and those of the Olmecs, of Pachacamac and the mysterious Tiahuanaco.

We must remember that the ancient Americans reckoned the giants to be among their mythical ancestors, and that some of the unknown animals found on carvings in the Peruvian desert are reproduced, on a smaller scale, on Easter Island. Another parallel is that we find on Easter Island the figure of a spiral, which the Incas, Egyptians and other peoples used to represent the number 100.

If, then, we regard the ancient Americans as the most direct heirs of Atlantis, it would seem that Easter Island is also linked with the famous "lost continent." But the island presents other relics of much greater antiquity than the Inca civilization, such as the ossuaries and the Cyclopean tunnels under the sea. Many geologists maintain that the island was never larger than it is now; but it is hard to believe that the inhabitants were given to digging large tunnels which led nowhere, for the mere pleasure of doing so. It has been suggested that the tunnels were part of a network of communication, as in Hawaii, between the islands of an archipelago which has now disappeared: Easter Island, on this hypothesis, may have been the common cemetery of the group, or a site devoted to religious sacrifice. Some go further and imagine that the island is under a curse for this reason, as shown by the many disasters that have befallen its people.

This is no better than superstition, though it must be admitted that the islanders have at all times had an unpleasant lot.

Others again see Easter Island as a kind of temple dedicated to humanity's endless struggle against cosmic forces of destruction, its fearful calamities and its moments of rebirth. They believe that the island formed part of each of the "lost continents" which have formed part of the earth's surface at different times: Lemuria, Gondwana, Mu and Atlantis. Still others claim to have found an account of the island in ancient Tibetan texts, from which they derive a prophecy that may not disturb our generation but, if it is true, will certainly afflict our descendants: the earth, they declare, will be subject to fresh convulsions which will devastate its surface and destroy all the works of man, thrusting him back into the Stone Age. Easter Island, they tell us, will survive many more catastrophes, but when it too is submerged beneath the waves, the world will come to an end. Such is the doom foretold by a Parisian group of explorers of the Easter Island mystery, who claim that it is confirmed by ancient Inca manuscripts which oral tradition has transmitted to our own day.

It is generally thought that the Incas were ignorant of writing, but the contrary has also been maintained. As Robert Charroux points out, "Francisco Toledo, the Viceroy of Peru, mentions that sometime around 1566 he had a bonfire made of Inca textiles and tablets with elaborate inscriptions concerning history, science, prophecy, etc. The existence of these Inca writings is confirmed by José

GIANTS AND THE LOST LANDS OF THE GODS

de Acosta (Historica natural y moral des las Indias, Seville 1590), Balboa and Father Bernabé Cobo. Fortunately they were partly rescued by the Jesuits and the Popes. Books by Garcilaso de la Vega, and some manuscripts containing precious information on South American mythology, were burnt in Spain in the sixteenth century; but the Vatican Library and Senior Beltran Garcia, a descendant of Garcilaso, have preserved the essential part of the tradition, recorded in unpublished manuscripts to which we have had access.

We may digress at this point in order to recall, with Charroux, what irreparable harm has been done by ignorance and fanaticism in destroying evidence of ancient times. Julius Caesar bears the heavy blame of first setting fire to the library at Alexandria, where Ptolemy I Soter had collected 700,000 volumes in which the whole knowledge and tradition of the time were recorded. Four centuries later the library was again set on fire and damaged by undisciplined bands, and in 641 it was burnt to the ground by order of the caliph Omar. It is said that, when asked by his captains what to do with the books, Omar replied: "If what they say is in the Koran, they are superfluous and may be burnt. If it is not, they are wicked and harmful and should be burnt." For months afterwards the precious manuscripts were used to help fuel the bath-houses of Alexandria, and in the end only a few escaped.

In A.D. 240 a similar auto-da-fé was carried out by the Ch'in emperor Chehoang, who ordered the destruction of all books in China dealing with history, astronomy and philosophy. At Rome, in the third century, Diocletian sought out and destroyed all books containing formulae for the manufacture of gold, since anyone who learnt how to transmute metals would be able to buy an empire.

The New Testament (Acts, chapter 19) relates that under St. Paul's influence, at Ephesus, "many of them which used curious arts brought their books together and burned them before all men." Jacques Weiss tells us that some ignorant Irish monks were responsible for burning 10,000 runic manuscripts on birch-bark, containing all the traditions and annals of the Celtic race.

Charroux also refers to the burning of the Uardan papyri and the Yucatan manuscripts, and his list might be indefinitely extended. Works destroyed in the past may well have included the "books of gods and men" which are said to have recorded the history of our earth "from the first dawn of intelligence," and in particular that of Lemuria and Gondwana. If so, there is little hope that we can throw light on the mystery of these two legendary continents, which imagination has peopled with a race of giants.

From Lemuria To Gondwana

If we try to imagine the first beginnings of our planet, the picture we get is that, after the first, partial solidification, the earth's face was constantly changing, convulsed and distorted by one catastrophe after another. Continents arose from the deep, were remolded as though by a giant hand and sank back into the ocean, while others took their place. Waters were channeled in fantastic crevices or formed into huge lakes, to be transformed into steam by a fiery blast from the bowels of the earth. Then, after long eons, a degree of calm supervened. About a thousand million years ago, as may be judged from various geological signs, the earth's land surface consisted of a single continental mass known as Megagea (Greek for "big land"). Three hundred million years later, however, there was another series of changes: violent convulsions once again destroyed huge areas and brought to birth new continents, destined like their predecessors to disappear or change shape time and again.

One of these land masses is thought to have covered a large part of what is now the Indian and Pacific Oceans, from Madagascar to Ceylon and from Polynesia, including Easter Island, to the Antarctic. Those who accept this theory call the lost continent Lemuria; they maintain that it existed in the Permian era, about 250 million years ago, and that after various changes it finally disappeared as the result of a fresh cataclysm at the beginning of the Tertiary period, some 60 million years ago.

Various islands in the Indian Ocean are thought to have been among the highest parts of the Lemurian continent: the Seychelles and Maldives, the Laccadive and Chagos Islands, the Saya de Malha Bank and perhaps the Cocos (Keeling) Islands. The evidence for Lemuria's existence rests partly on the fact that similar flora and fauna are found in areas now separated by vast expanses of water.

Even those scientists who assign a much earlier date to the human species than was, till recently, accepted by orthodox authority do not believe that Lemuria was inhabited by beings like ourselves. But there are Polynesian legends which speak of two "great islands" (continents?) of immense antiquity, inhabited respectively by black and yellow men who were continually fighting each other. The gods, it is said, tried to make peace between them, but finally decided that as they were incurably quarrelsome the only thing to do was to drown both islands beneath the waves.

There are, however, some exponents of esoteric lore who believe that they can penetrate further into the unwritten history of our planet. According to their ideas, the Lemurian scene may be described somewhat as follows. The continent is dotted with lakes and active volcanoes, thanks to whose fumes the sky is an eternal cloudy grey. The inhabitants are nightmare creatures resembling the giants spoken of by Saurat and Bellamy: grotesque caricatures of men, 10 to 15 feet tall, with a yellowish-brown hide like that of the rhinoceros or crocodile. Their arms and legs are very long and are permanently bent, as the knee and elbow joints do not permit of their being stretched out straight. Their hands and feet are very large, and the heel projects backwards.

Their heads are the most terrifying thing of all: the face is flat, the lower jaw elongated, the eyes small and wide apart, so that their owners can look sideways as well as forwards; moreover they have a third, functioning eye in the nape of the neck. They have no hair, and the shape of their forehead and cranium may be compared to the top half of a wrinkled orange.

Those who tell us all this about the Lemurians aver that with the passing of ages these appalling creatures evolved into something resembling a cross between primates and Bushmen. The latter race, we are told, are in fact descendants of Lemurians, together with Australian aborigines, the natives of Tierra del Fuego and some other African and Indian tribes.

The Lemurians are said to have lived at first in huts made of roughly hewn logs, and eventually to have built houses of stone and lava in the shape of windowless cubes, with a door and an opening in the top to admit light. A settlement of such houses is said to be on the ocean floor 30 miles west of Easter Island, while other ruins can be found in the jungles of Madagascar.

Clearly we shall never know the truth about Lemuria, and we are almost equally ignorant about the lost continent of Gondwana, concerning which we have a few documents and scientific facts swathed in a mist of legend. Did the ancient Greeks have this continent in mind when they bestowed on the Arcadians the name of "pre-lunar men" (proselenoi)? At all events, there are Tibetan texts which say that Gondwana was civilized before our present moon shone in the sky: its people, they claim, were wise and skillful and built "great houses of crystal," which we may imagine to be like our skyscrapers!

Among those who have studied the problem of Gondwana are the geologists Blandford and Suss, who believe that it had much territory in common with its predecessor Lemuria; including Easter Island, southern Africa, Madagascar and central India. We do not know whether Gondwana was a fragment of Lemuria, or whether one was thrown up and the other submerged by the same cataclysm. Here again, we have only crumbs of information and are obliged to conjecture from them as best we may.

GIANTS AND THE LOST LANDS OF THE GODS

CHAPTER SIX
The Lost World Of Mu

The stony expanse of the Gobi Desert (Shamo in Chinese), which covers much of Mongolia, is half a million square miles in area and about 1,200 miles long. It has been a fertile ground for archaeological discovery: here, in 1928-33, American paleontologists found the remains of the baluchitherium, a huge giraffe-like animal which seems to have lived only in Asia and in the Oligocene period; and here, too, were found the fossilized eggs of dinosaurs, proving that these creatures were oviparous.

A still more impressive discovery, however, was made by the Russian archaeologist Petr Kozlov (1863-1935), who, when exploring the ruins of the ancient city of Karakhoto, found in a tomb a mural painting 18,000 years old representing a young ruler and his consort: their emblem consisted of a circle divided into four quadrants with, in the centre, a sign corresponding to the Greek letter mu, which is also our M.

At the present day school pupils are still taught that it was the Phoenicians who invented the alphabet from which the Greek, our own and many others are derived; however, modern language studies have shown that they took it from the Egyptians. But how can we credit the Egyptians with the invention of letters if it turns out that systems of writing were in use all over the globe; or are we to regard the M of Kozlov's discovery as a mere coincidence? This leads us to the interesting theory of Colonel James Churchward, an unorthodox scholar who believed that Egyptian culture, together with those of the Chaldees, Babylonians, Persians, Greeks, Hindus and Chinese, were all derived from the culture of the lost world of Mu, the much-fabled 'Atlantis of the Pacific'. Long ages ago, according to Churchward, the superhuman race of Mu dominated the whole of Asia and southern Europe either directly or through its colonies, the chief of which was that of the Uighurs whose remains were discovered by Professor Kozlov.

To return to the mythical Lemuria, it appears that not all of this was engulfed by the sea, but that a portion of it continued to occupy a large part of what is now

GIANTS AND THE LOST LANDS OF THE GODS

the Pacific and Indian Oceans. We may imagine a huge island of roughly triangular shape with Australia at its centre, the base-line facing towards Antarctica and the other sides parallel with the east coast of Africa and the west coast of South America.

This, according to Churchward, was the original territory of Mu, the 'great motherland' of the human race. Legends concerning the existence of Mu are known in many countries and were certainly widespread before Churchward undertook his researches, but the evidence unearthed by him is regarded by many scholars as the most conclusive.

A Falling Star

In 1868 Colonel Churchward was in India and, it being a time of famine, was helping the high priest of a Buddhist seminary to distribute aid to the population. Being a keen amateur archaeologist he took an interest in some bas-reliefs which, the priest told him, were the work of two Naacals - 'holy brothers' who had been sent in ancient times from the motherland of Mu to bring wisdom to its colonies. The priest added that other tablets inscribed by these sages in the primal language of mankind were preserved as precious relics in the secret archives of the temple. Churchward asked to see them, and after long hesitation the high priest agreed, being himself curious to know what they might contain. With the priest's assistance Churchward deciphered them, and found that they described in detail the creation of the earth and of mankind. The set of tablets was incomplete; Churchward, fired with the idea that he might have discovered the oldest documents in history, went from temple to temple throughout India in search of the missing records, but in vain.

After retiring from the army Churchward continued to study dead languages and travelled throughout the world on what many thought a Utopian quest. He visited the south Pacific, Siberia, central Asia, Egypt, Australia, New Zealand and Tibet, picking up valuable items by the way. It was at Lhasa that he finally succeeded in discovering the missing portion of the record. Meanwhile the jigsaw was unexpectedly completed by the U.S. mineralogist William Niven, who discovered some tablets in Mexico inscribed in characters very similar to those inspected by Churchward.

Similar inscriptions afterwards came to light in Maya temples, pre-Columbian 'stone calendars', the Stone of Tizoc and the tablets, also of stone, at Azcopotzalco; while, several decades later, writing of the same type was found on Easter Island and on vessels dug up in 1925 at Glozel, not far from Vichy. Using these documents, Churchward reconstructed the geography of Mu on the lines we have indicated. He concluded that Mu had possessed seven great cities and many overseas colonies; its empire had arisen over 150,000 years ago and had

GIANTS AND THE LOST LANDS OF THE GODS

reached its peak some 75,000 years later.

Unfortunately Churchward afterwards embarked on arguments and hypotheses in which the dividing line between reality and fantasy was soon blurred. We may, however, note some of his specific conclusions. Mu, he believed, had a subtropical climate with vast forests and prairies inhabited by huge beasts including the mastodon and a primeval kind of elephant. The human population consisted of ten tribes, numbering 64,000,000 people in all, under a single government. The dominant race may be regarded as the ancestors of present-day Aryans; according to Churchward they were like us but taller, with bronzed complexions, blue eyes and black hair.

The 'motherland' is said to have been smitten by two calamities, the second of which, around 12,000 B.C., led to its destruction. The Lhasa tablets, it appears, describe this event as follows. 'When the Stal' Bal fell into the earth at a place where there is now nothing but sea, the seven cities with their temples and their golden gates were shaken; a great fire sprang up, and the streets filled with dense smoke. Men trembled with fear, and great crowds flocked to the temples and the king's palace. The king said to them: "Did I not predict all this?" and the men and women in the precious garments and bracelets begged and implored him: "Ra-Mu, save us." But the king told them that they were all doomed to die with their slaves and children, and that a new race of mankind would rise from their ashes.'

The 'star' referred to was, we may suppose, an enormous asteroid. We might know more about it if another catastrophe had not destroyed the archipelago which is believed to have survived the destruction of the rest of Mu for several millennia and which, according to Churchward, was the site of one of the seven great cities.

It may be mentioned here that during a cruise in 1686-7 by the British vessel The Bachelor's Delight, commanded by the adventurer Edward Davis, a Dutch officer sighted on the west coast of South America a 'fair high island' which looked like part of an archipelago and which the voyagers christened Davis Land. A year later, however, other ships which visited the area could find no trace of these islands. There would seem to have been a cataclysm in which all were engulfed except Easter Island. As the geologist I. Macmillan Brown wrote: 'It is impossible to account for the remains of the old Easter Island civilization except by the existence of a sub-merged archipelago at the place where Davis Land was sighted. Easter Island must have been the sacred cemetery of the islands in question.'

Other evidence affords solid support of Churchward's basic theory. For instance, before the advent of Europeans in the Pacific, the inhabitants of many of the scattered islands of Polynesia, Micronesia and Melanesia had never heard of one another, and with their primitive means of navigation it is inconceivable that they could have sailed such vast distances in the remote past. Yet they speak languages deriving from the same stock and have much in common as regards customs, mode of dress, tradition and religious beliefs. The area of Mu as defined by Churchward includes people of many races, not excluding the 'Aryans' who go back to prehistoric times.

The Italian scholar Egisto Roggero pointed out in his monumental work Il Mare (The Sea) that the peoples of the Sunda Islands (including Sumatra, Java, Borneo and Celebes), the Moluccas and the Philippines are quite different from either mainland Asiatics or Melanesians. They may be divided into two types, the (mongoloid) Malays of the coastal areas and a white race which has relapsed into barbarism and inhabits the jungles of the interior. Roggero also noted the existence of clearly Aryan groups in the Ryukyu Islands, Hokkaido and southern Sakhalin, where, as he put it, 'we may recognize the typical lineaments of our own family. The women, especially the girls, are extremely beautiful. Eighteenth-century navigators spoke with enthusiasm of the voluptuous grace of these women of "New Cythera", whose complexion is not darker than that of Sicilians or Andalusians.' And he goes on to say:

'There is thus a race in eastern Asia characterized by its resemblance to the white races of the West. Its first abode seems to have been on the islands of the Asian archipelago, where its most typical members are still to be found. This is the great "Oceanic race", an ancient people of whose story we know nothing. It may have had a great past, and modern science suggests that we may be its descendants. Can it be that there was once a great continent, and that these Polynesian archipelagos are all that is left after its disintegration?

This is only an hypothesis, but much can be said in support of it. In particular, the appearance and language of these islanders are essentially the same over hundreds and thousands of miles, all the way from North America to the shores of Asia? '

Further confirmation; as Churchward points out, may be found in the archaeology of the Pacific islands. The huge ruined walls near Lele in the Carolines, the slender pyramids at Tabiteuea in the Kingsmill group, the truncated red-marble columns in the Marianas, the huge stone arch of Tongatabu, the Fijian monolith with its indecipherable inscriptions, the majestic remains at Kukii on Hawaii Island, the great platform of red stone in the Navigators Islands (Samoa) - all these monuments have this in common, that they are built of material which is not native to the respective islands, but must have been brought from a place of origin which is now beneath the waves.

Cyclopean ruins, including the remains of great temples and vast terraces, have been discovered in the Carolines, and on Ponape in the same group (near the site, as Churchward believed, of another of the great cities of Mu) are the mouths of impressive underground passages. This puts us in mind not only of the

GIANTS AND THE LOST LANDS OF THE GODS

tunnels used by giants and their descendants, but also of many significant legends which are still alive in Asia.

The Venusians Of The Gobi Desert

'Thundering down from unsearchable heights, and wreathed in flames that filled the heavens with tongues of fire, came the chariot of the Sons of Fire and the Lords of Flame from the Resplendent Star. It alighted on the White Island of the Sea of Gobi, a green, marvelous expanse of fragrant flowers.'

These are the words of an ancient Indian text which relates how a mysterious being called Sanatkumara ('Everlasting Youth') visited our planet from Venus thousands of years ago and, together with his companions, awakened the intelligence of mankind, teaching our ancestors the arts of till- age and beekeeping and many other ways to improve their lives. The story has a strong appeal to lovers of the occult, who have embellished it with fanciful details. But there are also scientists of sober reputation, including some in the Soviet Union, who are disposed to give some credence to the idea that creatures from another world may have disembarked on earth. They are encouraged in this belief both by the profusion of mythological evidence and by the investigations of modern science.

Many of the Central Asian legends relate to the Gobi Desert, which in remote times - as human tradition and geology both inform us - was a great sea. According to Chinese sages, there was an island in this sea inhabited by 'white men with blue eyes and fair hair', who 'descended from heaven' and imparted the arts of civilization to their fellowmen—including, as some believe, the inhabitants of Mu, who thus attained a high degree of culture some 75,000 years ago. This receives support from an ancient Hindu tradition referred to by Wilkins, which relates that 'men from the great white star' (probably Venus) took up their abode on an island in the Sea of Gobi in the year 18,617,841 B.C.; they are said to have built a fortress, then a city, and to have constructed undersea tunnels linking their island with the mainland. The suggested date is based on erroneous 'Brahminical tables', but the account is a striking one and receives confirmation from many different and unexpected sources.

Some decades ago a map of the heavens was found in a cave at Bohistan in the Himalaya foothills. Its accuracy was confirmed by astronomers, who also noted that it diverged from our own maps in that it showed the position of the heavenly bodies 13,000 years ago. Another curious feature of the map, which was published in the National Geographic Magazine, was that lines were drawn on it connecting the earth and Venus.

Many years before, in 1778, a similar phenomenon had puzzled Jean-Sylvain Bailly, the mayor of Paris and French Astronomer Royal. Studying maps of the heavens brought back from India by missionaries, he found that they were many thou-

GIANTS AND THE LOST LANDS OF THE GODS

sands of years old but also that they showed stars which could not have been visible from their supposed place of origin. According to Bailly's calculations, the maps must have been drawn from somewhere in the Gobi Desert. He concluded from this that the Indians must have taken them over from some older and more civilized community, which he identified with the fabulous Atlantis - thus siting the latter, erroneously, in the region which formed the heartland of Mu and received visitors from outer space.

Many Soviet scientists are convinced of the existence of such visitors and have devoted much effort to finding their traces upon earth, and the Gobi Desert has been one of their favorite hunting-grounds. One such scientist is Professor Mikhail Agrest, an eminent mathematician and physicist, who has expressed the conviction that Sodom and Gomorrah were destroyed, a million years ago, by a nuclear explosion.

The Bible tells us how the inhabitants of these cities were punished for their vices by a rain of brimstone and fire from heaven; Lot and his family were spared, but Lot's wife transgressed the divine command not to look back on the scene of destruction and was turned into a pillar of salt. Scientists are agreed that the cities may have been destroyed four thousand years ago, but they do not accept the story of a consuming lire and cannot find evidence of a volcanic eruption or earthquake. Agrest, however, published an article in the Moscow Literaturnaya Gazeta at the beginning of 1960 which was much commented on by the Soviet radio and in which he emphasized that the ancient text speaks of the destruction having come from the heavens. The explanation he suggested was that visitors in a spaceship had had to get rid of part of their nuclear fuel and had exploded it in an area from which they first expelled the inhabitants.

At Baalbek in the Anti-Lebanon there is a giant platform, eroded by the weather, whose origin is wrapped in mystery. Agrest suggests that it may have been built to facilitate the landing and takeoff of spaceships from other worlds; his view is supported by many scientists who believe that myths and legends are not mere fantasies but derive from a basis of fact. The Biblical story, they suggest, reflects as faithfully as possible a catastrophe which had in fact occurred long before. 'The rain of fire and brimstone,' say Agrest, 'is a good description of the effects of a thermonuclear explosion. If the inhabitants of Hiroshima 'had been less civilized, they might well have spoken of the destruction of their city in these terms. Burning sulphur throws off intense heat and dissolves anything to which it adheres.' As for the story of Lot's wife, it recalls the vitrification of reinforced concrete which was one of the effects of the Hiroshima bomb. Given the quantities of rock-salt in the area, the blast of the explosion might well have covered her with a powder of minute of detritus, so that she would have resembled a pillar of salt.

Agrest's theory is further borne out by the tektites found in the Libyan desert.

GIANTS AND THE LOST LANDS OF THE GODS

The Soviet scholar is wrongly supposed to have described these as projectiles or the remains of destroyed spaceships; in fact, his theory is that they are fragments detached from spaceships by the heat generated by their contact with the atmosphere, and he points out that this was an accompanying phenomenon of the re-entry of Sputnik II. The fragments in question are glassy chips or shards, different from meteorites in composition; they have been discovered on or near the earth's surface in very restricted areas, and are most probably not of terrestrial origin.

Some scientists believe them to be fragments of a comet, others think they may have rained from the moon in consequence of volcanic eruptions or the impact of huge meteorites on that body. They appear to have rotated at high speed before reaching the earth, and thus to have become solidified. If they are really from spaceships, the quantity of them which can be seen in some areas is such that the ships must have been of enormous size.

Traces of vitrification such as are found on the site of Sodom and Gomorrah have also been discovered by Soviet explorers in a large part of the Gobi Desert and in the sinister Death Valley between California and Nevada. The adventurer William Walker, 'Commander-in-chief of the Republic of Nicaragua', wrote as follows of Death Valley in 1850:

'Around an imposing central building are the remains of a city that extended for about a mile. There are signs of a volcanic eruption, with carbonized or vitrified blocks, the result of some terrible catastrophe. In the centre of this city, a true American Pompeii, there is a rocky spur twenty to thirty feet high, on which the ruins of gigantic constructions can be seen. The buildings at their southern extremity look as though they had been in a furnace, and the rock on which they are built itself shows signs of having melted. Strange to say, the Indians have no tradition concerning the people who once lived there. The dismal ruins fill them with superstitious terror, but they know nothing of their history.'

If Walker had ever seen Pompeii or learned anything of vulcanology he would have known that there was never any such eruption in Death Valley and that no volcanic outburst, however violent, could have melted rocks, vitrified sand and made barren what was once a luxuriant area but is now a scene of contorted ruins expressing the torment of violated nature.

In the caves of Turkestan and the Gobi Desert the Russians have discovered what may be age-old instruments used in navigating cosmic vehicles. These are hemispherical objects of glass or porcelain, ending in a cone with a drop of mercury inside. Science has no explanation for these, but it is remarkable that mercury played an important part in propelling the 'heavenly chariots' which are so often described in Sanskrit texts. According to the Ramayana and the Dronaparva (part of the Mahabharata), the 'aerial car' (vimzina) was shaped like a sphere and borne along at great speed on a mighty wind generated by mercury. It moved in

GIANTS AND THE LOST LANDS OF THE GODS

any way the pilot might desire-up or down, forwards or backwards. Another Indian source, the Samar, speaks of 'iron machines, well-knit and smooth, with a charge of mercury that shot out of the back in the form of a roaring flame', and another work, the Samaranganasutradhara, actually describes how such vehicles were constructed.

The great Sir Isaac Newton may have had an inkling, or more than an inkling, of such matters when he wrote, in a letter of 1676 on the transmutation of metals: 'The way in which mercury may be so impregnated has been thought it to be concealed by others that have known it, and therefore may possibly be an inlet to something more noble, not to be communicated without immense danger to the world, if there should be any verity in the Hermetic writers.' At all events, it is interesting that the modern science of astronautics is turning its attention to mercury as a fuel. At an international space congress, in Paris in 1959 there was talk of an 'iono-mercurial engine', and in 1966 the French were planning to launch an artificial satellite powered by a 'mercury solar furnace' (the 'Phaeton Project').

The Amazing Kappas

Louis Pauwels and Jacques Bergier, in Le matin des magiciens (Paris, 1960), refer to the phenomenon of 'cup-marks' on rocks, concerning which the American amateur scientist Charles Hoy Fort wrote as follows:

'They look to me like symbols of communication; but not communication between some of the inhabitants of this earth and other inhabitants of this earth. My own impression is that some external force has marked, with symbols, rocks on this earth, from far away.

'I do not think that cup-marks are inscribed communications among different inhabitants of this earth, because it seems too unacceptable that inhabitants of China, Scotland and America should all have conceived of the same system.

'Cup-marks are strings of cuplike impressions in rocks. Sometimes there are rings around them, and sometimes they have only semicircles. Great Britain, America, France, Algeria, Circassia, Palestine: they are virtually everywhere - except in the far north, I think. In China, cliffs are dotted with them. Upon a cliff near Lake Como, there is a maze of these markings. In Italy and Spain and India they occur in enormous numbers.

'Given that a force, say, like electric force could, from a distance, mark such a Explorers from Somewhere, and an attempt, from Somewhere, to communicate with them: so a frenzy of showering' of messages toward this earth, in the hope that some of them would mark rocks near the lost explorers.

'Or that somewhere upon this earth, there is can especial rocky surface, or receptor upon which for ages have been received messages from some other world; but that at times messages go astray and mark substances perhaps thou-

GIANTS AND THE LOST LANDS OF THE GODS

sands of miles from the receptor.

'That perhaps forces behind the history of this earth have left upon the rocks of Palestine and England, and India and China, records that may some day be deciphered, of their misdirected instructions to certain esoteric ones: Order of the Freemasons, the Jesuits.'

The mysterious cup-marks are plentiful in the mountains which bound the Gobi Desert on the north, where strange rites are performed by the shamans, the priests or witch-doctors of the ancient animistic cult that still lives on in Mongolia.

The shamans fall into a trance induced by the monotonous beating of a small drum or tambourine, and claim that in this state they are in communication with a nightmare world of spirits. Some of the latter—black, hunchbacked, with long claws—have the power to 'cast their skin' and assume human form. Thus transformed, they go about unrecognized; but when clad in their 'dark skin' they are said to be invisible and to sail or fly in great shells, over the waters or through the clouds 'summoning the dead'. These shells are mentioned in the Ghal Sudur ('Book of Fire') in which ancient traditions are handed down; as for the source of the other details, we may perhaps look for it in Japan.

Some years ago the Mainichi Graphic, a serious weekly, put to question whether strange beings might not have come to Japan from outer space and lived there till about 3,000 B.C. This speculation was defended by the eminent archaeologist and historian, Professor Komatsu Kitamura, who wrote:

'I was led to this hypothesis in the first instance by a print illustrating an old work on the history of the legendary Kappas or "men of the canebrake" who are said to have inhabited Japan in the Heian period (ninth to eleventh century A.D.). They are described in the old texts as web-footed bipeds with three hooked fingers on each hand, the centre digit being much longer than the others. Their skin is brown, smooth, silky and lucent; their heads are elongated, they have large ears and strange eyes of triangular shape. According to all reports they wear a curious kind of hat "with four needles in it;" their nose is like a proboscis and is connected to a casket-shaped hump on their backs. The old writers add that they could move with equal rapidity by land and sea.

'Until recent times this description could only have suggested to us creatures of legend, vaguely resembling monkeys. But we now know that many "fabulous" creatures existed in reality, e.g. the so-called giants, or "dragons" which were really saurians of the Cenozoic era. Considering the Kappas more closely, I suddenly realized their startling resemblance to modern frogmen. Their "smooth, brown skin" could have been a close-fitting waterproof suit; their webbed hands and feet, and the hooks on their fingers and toes, would be suitable equipment, and the "proboscis" and "hump" would, of course, be breathing apparatus, complete with oxygen bottles. As for the "four needles", I am tempted to believe that

GIANTS AND THE LOST LANDS OF THE GODS

they were radio antennae.'

We may rule out the idea that the mysterious Kappas are a mere fantasy, since there is a large body of evidence tending to confirm that they existed. On the other hand, given the state of Japanese culture a thousand years ago, we cannot suppose that they were merely a branch of the Japanese race with a special talent for diving. The only alternative conclusion is that they came from outer space; and, as Professor Kitamura observes, the tales about them seem to confirm this view, since they speak of vehicles 'like great shells, able to move swiftly over the waters or through the heavens'.

We are thus led in imagination from Mongolia to Japan and back, following the enigmatic Kappas who, after the land of Mu was engulfed, flew about in search of survivors among their countrymen. As we shall see, there are traces of spatial visitors in many parts of the globe. We may mention here a curious, ageless statue in the Japanese island of Honshiu, which looks like a semi-human diver: the helmet is too small, the goggles are enormous and stick out sideways, the arms barely reach down to the waist, the flanks are massive and very low, while the stumpy legs resemble a pair of goblets.

As for space-helmets, the masks used by witch-doctors among many primitive Asian tribes look as if they derived from them. As Zorovsky says, 'May not these be imitations of space-helmets, to which magic powers have been ascribed through the ages? The makers of strange funeral masks with- out definite features, such as we End among many ancient peoples, may have designed them in memory of mythical astronauts, in the hope that with their aid the departed would ascend rapidly to heaven or return to earth again, or perhaps enjoy a sweet sleep before reincarnation—this hope being inspired, perhaps, by the artificial hibernation which was observed to be a custom of the visitors from outer space.'

GIANTS AND THE LOST LANDS OF THE GODS

CHAPTER SEVEN
Legends Of The Stars

Certain unusual phenomena, embroidered by local superstition, attracted the attention of Soviet scientists to a 'bottomless well' in Azerbaijan. A bluish light seemed to emanate from its walls, and it gave forth strange groaning and whistling noises. There was, as the scientists knew, nothing supernatural about these; some of the investigators went a certain distance down the well, while others explored crevices in the neighborhood to see if they communicated with it. They found more than they expected: a whole network of tunnels, which turned out to be linked with others in Georgia and throughout the Caucasus.

These were at first thought to be prehistoric caves: near their mouths were found graffiti and human remains, but on inspection it turned out that the bones were of much later date than the drawings. It was also discovered that most of the caves led to tunnels carved in the mountain-side. These were too much blocked by rubble to be explored properly, but even so they formed an impressive system of broad passages, circular 'concourses', empty niches, wells and channels so narrow that not even a child could have passed along them.

One large tunnel which it was possible to follow for a considerable distance led to a spacious underground hall or piazza, more than 65 feet high. Clearly this was the work of intelligent beings, but for what purpose? No clue has yet been found; the answer to the mystery may lie further on, in the blocked portion of the tunnels.

The main entrances to these tunnels are regular in form, with handsome straight walls and narrow arches. The most curious fact about them is that they are almost identical with similar tunnels in Central America. The caves which are often found near the Caucasian tunnels contain graffiti which also represent universal motifs: the swastika, symbolizing infinity, and the spiral. As to the purpose of the tunnels, some Soviet archaeologists believe that they are part of a huge network stretching out towards Iran and perhaps linked with those discovered near the Amu Datya (in Turkmenistan and on the Russo-Afghan border) or even the underground labyrinths of central and western China, Tibet and Mongolia.

Some of these tunnels were found in 1920-1 by the explorer Ossendowski, who suggested that they had served as hiding-places to Mongol tribes harried by Genghis Khan. The orientalist Nicholas Roerich refers in this connection to the belief that there is in Asia an immense underground kingdom called Shambhala from which a new saviour of humanity is to appear in the person of the hero Maitreya.

The Tibetans believe that the tunnels are citadels, the last of which still afford refuge to the survivors of an immense cataclysm. This unknown people is said to make use of an underground source of energy which replaces that of the sun, causing plants to breed and 'prolonging human life. It is supposed to give out a green fluorescence, and it is curious that we also meet with this idea in American legend. An explorer in the Amazon jungle is said to have found his way into an underground labyrinth illuminated 'as though by an emerald sun': he retreated hastily to avoid the clutches of a monstrous spider, but before doing so saw 'shadows like men' moving at the end of a passage.

The descendants of the Incas tell frightening tales of their ancestors who dwell 'in the heart of the mountains' but come out occasionally to walk in the starlight. It is hard to tell whether these are real people or ghosts. According to Tom Wilson, an Indian guide in California, they are substantial enough; he relates that fifty years ago his grandfather, who knew nothing of the South American tales, chanced to find himself in a great underground city where he lived for a time among strange people 'dressed in something that resembled leather but was not' (plastic materials in 1920?), speaking a strange tongue and eating unnatural food. Could these be the 'immortals of Mu'? The occultists will readily tell us so, but the reader would do well to be cautious.

Fifteen years later a gold prospector named White came upon an underground cemetery where, in a large hall or open space, he found hundreds of naturally mummified bodies, some reclining on chairs made of rock and others lying on the floor in distorted poses, as though death had caught them unawares. These too wore garments like leather and were lit by a sinister green fluorescence; around them, in the same green light, sparkled enormous gold statues.

An expedition set out to investigate White's story, but failed to reach its destination. Another old miner, however, who had apparently kept silent out of superstitious fear, finally avowed that he himself could have found the way to the underground cemetery at any time; he described details of it that White had noticed but had never mentioned to anyone.

The Apache Indians tell stories of tunnels between their lands and the mythical city of Tiahuanaco, and claim that some of their ancestors, fleeing from other tribes, travelled for years by this route until they reached South America. We may

GIANTS AND THE LOST LANDS OF THE GODS

doubt such tales, but we cannot fail to be struck by the assurance of Indian chiefs that the tunnels were 'carved out by rays that destroy the living rock' and that their creators were 'beings that live near the stars'.

Missiles In The Temple

Returning to Asia, we find alongside the myth of Shambhala that of another secret kingdom known as Agarthi, Agartha or Agharti, with a central sanctuary somewhere under the Himalayas. According to Ossendowski, this 'centre of wisdom and the human mind' was founded at least 600,600 years ago.

Some of the descriptions given of it are too fantastic to waste time on, and from time to time various charlatans have presented themselves as 'grand priests of Agarthi'. But the references to spaceflights and superhuman powers possessed by its inhabitants are so frequent and correspond so closely to the tales told of gods and heroes in Sanskrit texts that many scientists have considered the myth worthy of close study. As Miller, an American scholar, puts it: 'Agarthi and other cosmic riddles, the mysteries of Tibet and the para- psychological gifts of many Asians are all chapters of the same book-that of the lost civilization of Mu. Some day perhaps we may be able to get some idea of the remaining contents, but when and how?'

Looking for a needle in a haystack is child's play by comparison, as would be confirmed by all those who have tried to throw light on the mysterious race of star-worshippers called the Hsing Nu. Of non-Chinese origin, this people inhabited what is now an empty and little-known area in northern Tibet, south of the Kun Lun range.

It is thought they may have come from Persia or Syria, as the finds that have been made are reminiscent of the Ugaritic culture, especially figures of Baal wearing a long conical helmet, his body covered in silver.

When the French explorer, Father Duparc, discovered the ruins of the Hsing Nu capital in 1725, its people were only a legend, having been destroyed by the Chinese many centuries before. Within the city Duparc found over a hundred monoliths which had apparently belonged to a temple and had been covered with layers of silver, some of which had been overlooked by plunderers and was still to be seen. He also discovered a three-storied pyramid, the lower part of a tower of blue porcelain, and the royal palace with thrones surmounted by images of the sun and moon. There was also a 'moonstone', a large object of an unearthly white color with bas-reliefs of unknown animals and flowers.

In 1854 another French explorer, Latour, discovered tombs, weapons, copper vessels and silver and gold necklaces adorned with swastikas and spirals. Later expeditions, however, found only some carved slabs of stone, as the ruined city had meanwhile been buried by sandstorms.

GIANTS AND THE LOST LANDS OF THE GODS

In 1952 a Soviet expedition made an attempt to unearth part of the ruins. The work was long and arduous, as they had to do without proper instruments which could not be brought to the spot. All the Soviet scientists were able to retrieve was the tip of a pointed monolith with inscriptions, the stone bearing a close resemblance to that found in the prehistoric African city of Zimbabwe, however, Tibetan monks showed the scientists various pieces of evidence concerning the Hsing Nu, including ancient documents giving a minute description of the three-storied pyramid. According to these, its three stories represented, reading upwards, 'the Ancient Land, when men rose up to the stars; the Middle Land, when men came down from the stars; and the New Land, the world of distant stars'.

Are we to understand from these enigmatic words that in some remote past human beings were able to visit one of the heavenly bodies, that they afterwards came back to earth and lost the power of space-travel? This, at all events, is what the Tibetans believe: according to them, Hsing Nu space-travel was linked with religion, and this ancient people taught that the souls of the dead rose to heaven and were turned into stars.

The Soviet experts brought back a description of the temple which agrees with Duparc's to a large extent. According to the Tibetan chronicles, there reposed on the altar a 'stone brought from the moon' (not 'fallen from the moon', like e.g. a meteorite), described as a milky white stone surrounded by exquisite drawings of the flora and fauna of the 'star of the gods' and by slender monoliths coated with silver. Could these be the animals and plants of a planet colonized by cosmonauts of ancient times, with the monoliths symbolizing their spaceships?

It is said that before they were engulfed by a 'fiery cataclysm' the Hsing Nu were a highly civilized people and cultivated arts still known to the Tibetans, including 'speech at a distance' and thought-transmission through space. How- ever, the survivors of the catastrophe lapsed into barbarism and superstition. The report of these preternatural powers aroused interest among Soviet scholars, whose studies of parapsychology had to be carried on in secret because Stalin had forbidden them to pursue such 'magico-religious fooleries'.

During the thaw after the dictator's death the subject was still treated with some skepticism, but its exponents were able to convince the authorities that it was not 'magic' but a serious branch of science, the investigation of which would bring its own contribution to human progress. Leonid Vasilyev of the Soviet Academy of Sciences revealed that in Stalin's lifetime he had conducted secret experiments at Leningrad which had proved that certain subjects could receive and transmit thoughts telepathically even when immured in underground cells lined with lead. Another psychologist, Professor Kazhinsky, produced supporting evidence, and a research group was set up in Moscow composed of psychiatrists, physiologists, neurologists and physicists, under the direction of the young Doctor E.

GIANTS AND THE LOST LANDS OF THE GODS

Naumov. Khruschev personally encouraged these studies, which it was thought might prove useful in the astronautical sphere: telepathy would enable the pilots of spaceships to contact one another if their instruments should fail, and also perhaps to communicate with extraterrestrial beings. Many Soviet universities are experimenting with drugs thought capable of increasing telepathic powers, and at Moscow University work is being done on the construction of apparatus to improve extrasensory perception, These studies are being pushed forward by scientists who have to their credit such devices as the 'sleep machine' to cure insomnia and the 'robot hypnotizer' which enables the human brain to absorb and retain a quantity of knowledge beyond its normal capacity.

Since the study of parapsychology ceased to be taboo in the Soviet Union, Vasilyev and his followers have examined a large amount of material from disciplines other than their own, including archaeology and its findings concerning Hsing Nu and the Tibetans. It had long been known that the lamas possessed extrasensory powers, but it seemed a bold speculation to imagine that they, like the Hsing Nu of old, were able to communicate with other planets. However, nothing is ruled out of court by the leaders of Soviet science. As the great astronautical expert, Leonid Sedov, enjoined upon his fellow-workers: 'You must investigate everything and neglect nothing, however out-of-the-way it may seem. There is always time to discard afterwards."

For years now the Russians have been following this advice in every branch of science. Their expeditions to Tibet have been instructed to bring back useful knowledge in every field, including the mysterious phenomena of lung-gom, the mental and physical discipline which confers extraordinary powers of resistance and weightlessness, and tu-mo, whereby an individual can generate such body heat as to be able to survive, naked, at an altitude of 15,000 feet. Certainly the Russians will not have neglected to look for evidence of telepathy and telekinesis.

In 1959 a Soviet mission visited several Tibetan monasteries to discover what they could concerning 'routes to the stars', which might seem to belong purely to science fiction. A report on the expedition was made by a Scandinavian scholar at an astronautical congress in Moscow. The explorers met with grave difficulties: two of them fell into crevasses and were seriously injured, while three others had to be left, in a state of exhaustion, to be tended in hospitable villages.

Finally, however, in the great monastery of Galden, the Soviet scientists were able to meet an aged lama with a thorough knowledge of astronomy and astronautical problems. The lama claimed that in certain conditions he was able to enter into visual contact with the inhabitants of another planet. For a long time he refused to allow the Russians to witness such an experiment, but finally he agreed that two of them might do so.

After the team had been offered rest and refreshment, the two chosen mem-

GIANTS AND THE LOST LANDS OF THE GODS

bers were made to perform exercises of mental concentration, accompanied by yoga 'gymnastics', and to observe a special diet. They then assembled in the austere cell where the experiment was to take place. The lama took the two scientists by the hand' and all three concentrated their minds according to previous directions, while at regular intervals a curious apparatus gave out a muffled note, the echo of which was immediately deadened. Then, in the depths of the cell, a cloudy image came into view: it gradually took the shape of a creature somewhat like a man, but with indiscernible features and jointed limbs like those of an insect or crustacean. The creature stood upright and motionless, and in front of it was seen what appeared to be a moving reproduction of the solar system, with Mercury, Venus, the earth and other planets revolving round a large gleaming ball. Counting the tiny spheres, the Russian scholars found to their surprise that instead of nine planets there were ten—an additional member of the system was revolving outside the orbit of Pluto.

The lama refused to answer any questions as to the source of the image, and would only tell the scientists that there was indeed another planet outside Pluto—possibly a former satellite of Neptune which had gone into orbit of its own—and that before many years elapsed it would be discovered by astronomers. The experiment bore no other fruit; one of those who took part described it as follows: 'Neither I nor my colleague will ever know whether the image was really before us or only in our minds, whether it was projected through space or imposed on our senses by the lama himself. We can describe approximately what it looked like, but it had some- thing unearthly about it, and it hardly seems possible that anything so extraordinary could be conceived by the human mind alone.'

The political dispute between the Soviet Union and China has put an end to the former's explorations in Tibet, but Soviet scientists continue to take a lively interest in the subject. They have turned their attention to India, where the great masters of yoga are said to possess secrets that will help astronauts to endure conditions of space travel.

A Cubical Space Vehicle

The Indian subcontinent is another inexhaustible mine of ancient lore, cosmic legends and strange extrasensory phenomena. Saint-Yves d'Alveydre, a somewhat overimaginative authority on Agarthi, believes that India owes the discovery of yoga to this underground kingdom. Some of the extra- ordinary powers conferred by yoga are enumerated in the Yogasutra, a pre-Christian text. This claims that man can make his body larger or smaller, weightless or invisible; can travel anywhere including to the stars, overcoming natural obstacles by willpower (e.g. penetrating walls and rocks or sinking underground); can create, transform or annihilate any object, and can enter into the body, mind and soul of another

GIANTS AND THE LOST LANDS OF THE GODS

person. All this, we are told, can be attained by means of samzidhi (absorption, sublimation); the gods possess such powers by right of birth, but 'giants and ordinary mortals can acquire them by the use of herbs'.

There are occultists who would have us believe that the naacals, the 'great brethren' of Mu who were also the rulers of Agarthi, confided the secrets of yoga to the chief men of Tibet. But skeptics point ironically to the mention of 'herbs', recalling the many drugs that confer the illusion of flight, invisibility and other strange powers. At the same time we should remember that the ancient Indians had an advanced knowledge of pharmaceutics: together with other nations they seem, for example, to have used something very similar to penicillin. Over 5,000 years ago Imhotep, the Egyptian Aesculapius, is said to have used a miraculous substance 'derived from earth and decomposition', which presumably was some kind of antibiotic. The ancient Chinese modes of healing are still in use today, and the Indians, under the guise of a religious ceremony, practiced inoculation against smallpox. The Ayurvedic system of medicine was based on the use of vegetable products of great efficacy, showing that they knew much more than modern man about the healing properties of trees and plants.

In our day, Oriental doctors have turned over the leaves of ancient books and discovered new and effective ways of treating circulatory disturbances and various forms of tuberculosis. Professor Angelo Viziano, who has made a close study of Indian medicine, has for example described the powers of a herb named balucchar, the juice of which, rubbed on the scalp, acts as a tranquilizer and soporific; he also mentions secret vegetable products whereby Indian doctors cure diabetes 'as effectively as with insulin'. '

The Russians, at all events, think it worth while to investigate all these matters, not excluding the legendary space vehicle known as the dhurakapalam. In this they are following in the footsteps of the last Tsar, Nicholas II, who took much interest in a book entitled Initiations: the author of this, a French occultist named Sédir, described a meeting between one of his masters and the constructors and pilots of this mysterious vehicle. The Tsar maintained close and friendly relations with Sédir, and further details may well have been buried in his private papers.

The 'Cape Kennedy' of Indian space flights was situated, it appears, in what is now a dead city in the Deccan, accessible only by a steep tunnel leading from the base of a mountain to its summit. The monks who dwell in this strange retreat are said to possess the secret of freeing metals from terrestrial magnetism and endowing them with transparency and preternatural energy, by striking them incessantly with little hammers: the transformation is effected by the sound thus produced. The dhurakapalam itself is a diaphanous cube with golden reflections, its side measuring about 5 feet. The pilot, according to Sédir, is seated inside the cube on a box filled with laurel-ashes, which have an insulating power; in front of

GIANTS AND THE LOST LANDS OF THE GODS

him is a disc of burnished gold. He controls the vehicle by means of two crystal knobs, connected with silver wires to a battery of sonic energy. This mysterious element provides the power supply; the machine takes off from the ground with a deafening roar, travels through the stratosphere (described as 'a grey nothing, traversed by streaks of light and dotted with the white puffs of explosions) and into outer space, where it moves with incredible speed from planet to planet, from sun to sun, perhaps from galaxy to galaxy.

We do not believe that Soviet scientists give too much credence to the dhurakapalam, but it is quite possible that they intend to find out whether the story has any core of truth which might, if properly understood, lead to an important scientific discovery.

Inca agriculture in the Urubamba valley near Pisac, Peru: fields still under cultivation today and ancient terraces.

Three stages of an operation performed by a Peruvian surgeon with instruments at least 3,000 years old.

Machu Picchu, said to have been built on the ruins of a still earlier city.

GIANTS AND THE LOST LANDS OF THE GODS

CHAPTER EIGHT
The Colonies Of Mu

Five or six thousand years ago, when the pyramid of Cheops had not been built, Greece was overrun by wild hunters and Troy was not even a distant dream, the city of Mohenjo-daro flourished in what is now southern Pakistan, between Larkana and Kandiaro.

This metropolis, of whose very name we are uncertain, greets us across the ages in an unusual manner: seeds found among its ruins have awoken from their long sleep and ripened into an unknown type of grain, more nutritive than any species known today. It was this tiny miracle, compressed into a short news item, which first made the public aware of the existence of Mohenjo-daro; but most readers probably did not know that the excavation of its ruins filled an important gap in archaeological knowledge, while at the same time posing a host of questions.

Up to forty years ago, students of Indian civilization were faced by a curious enigma. On the one hand they possessed the Rig-Veda ('Veda of Hymns'), a text dating back about 2,000 years and belonging to a people of high culture, While on the other there was no evidence of a single work of art or building of earlier date than the third century B.C., when Greek and Persian influence had already made itself felt. The intervening period was a mystery, the more puzzling because of occasional discoveries relating to it: remains of walls, bronze weapons and furniture, and a strange seal representing a horned animal of unknown species, with an indecipherable inscription. This last was found at Harappa in the Punjab, about 125 miles southwest of Lahore.

In 1921 the Indian archaeologist Daya Harappa carried out excavations which brought to light the remains of an ancient city whose inhabitants made no use of iron but apparently only of stone and bronze, yet had reached a high degree of civilization, as was shown by the ruins of a massive structure resembling a silo in the shape of a truncated cone, and also a male torso of extraordinary perfection. A year later, other archaeologists were engaged in excavating the ruins of a Bud-

GIANTS AND THE LOST LANDS OF THE GODS

dhist temple of the second century A.D. on an islet in the Indus about 450 miles from Harappa, in a hilly area called by the natives Mohenjo-daro, the 'hill of death'.

To their surprise, they found under the temple walls the remains of a still older structure which showed features in common with the 'Harappa civilization'. The work of excavation continued in the 1940s and brought to light at Mohenjo-daro a complete city with a regular network of streets running east-west and south-north.

The city must have been inhabited for hundreds or thousands of years; it was no doubt rebuilt many times after destruction by war, flood or earthquake. Altogether eight strata of ruins have been discovered, and more would probably be found if it were possible to dig deeper: it is not, because the water-level has now been reached. '

One striking fact which throws light on the social structure of the unknown people of Harappa and Mohenjo-daro is that in the latter city there is no trace of a royal palace or temple, such as are found in all other ancient cities known to us. What Mohenjo-daro lacks in splendor, however, it gains in rationality. Its most impressive building is a bathhouse, formerly covered, with a pool measuring 40 feet by 23 feet; alongside it is a steam-bath and a hot-air heating system.

The main street, running north and south, is over half a mile long and 33 feet wide. The houses were of one or two stories or sometimes three, and were expertly built in bricks similar to ours. Each bedroom had running water and a bathroom and lavatory: this, as the plumbing system shows, was also true of the upper floors, now destroyed. The municipal sewerage was so efficient that British engineers declared they could do no better at the present day. Pipes and drains under every street carried off refuse and rainwater, of which there must have been a great deal.

As a German archaeologist writes, 'There are many signs that at the time when Mohenjo-daro was at its zenith, the local climate was much colder and damper than it is today. Here in Sind, for instance, use is now made almost entirely of air-dried bricks, which make the air cooler than baked ones. Today the area is so dry and deforested that it would be impossible to collect a quantity of wood equal to that used to bake the huge number of bricks used at Mohenjo-daro.'

An elegant silver casket was found to contain jewels, rings, bracelets and necklaces of gold, silver and ivory. Another contained the remains of a fine cotton fabric, the oldest so far discovered. Hitherto the earliest traces of cotton were found among the ancient Americans, while in the Mediterranean basin it first appears at the time of Alexander the Great, about 300 B.C.

As we noted, the inhabitants of Harappa do not seem to have known the use of iron; or perhaps, as believers in the lost continent of Mu would suggest, they

GIANTS AND THE LOST LANDS OF THE GODS

once knew it but then forgot it. Halfway between Harappa and Mohenjo-daro, where the Panjnad flows into the Indus, there is said to have been a find of ancient metal objects including an iron thimble and a very light cup, apparently of aluminum. We cannot vouch for this report, which comes from a periodical that sometimes leaps to conclusions, but we think it should be mentioned since, in this field, too, Asia is full of surprises.

The famous 'pillar near the Qutb Minar at Delhi, for instance, which is over 4,000 years old, consists of pieces of iron soldered or knit together in some other way and showing no signs of rust, though it has been exposed for centuries to heat and rain and every variation of climate. This, moreover, is pure iron, which can be produced today only in tiny quantities and by electrolysis.

The Smithsonian Institution and the Bureau of Standards in Washington have brought to light objects proving that, 7,000 years ago, some peoples were producing steel in furnaces at a temperature of 9,000 degrees Centigrade. We may also recall that coins such as those minted by Euthydemus II (222-187 B.C.) of Bactria, now in Afghanistan, contain clear traces of nickel, a metal which can only be extracted from its ore by complicated procedures. .

A belt found with other objects in the tomb of the Chinese general Chou Chu (A.D. 265-316) was analyzed in 1958 by the Institute of Applied Physics of the Chinese Academy of Sciences: it proved to contain 85 per cent of aluminum, 10 per cent of copper and 5 per cent of manganese. As the French review Horizons commented, 'Although there is plenty of aluminum to be found in the world, it is a difficult metal to extract. The electronic method of obtaining it from bauxite has only been known since 1808. The fact that Chinese metallurgists were capable of extracting it from bauxite 1,600 years ago is an important discovery in the history of science.'

Toys were also found at Mohenjo-daro: little clay figures of animals, some with movable heads, other figurines on wheels, tiny carts, whistles in the shape of a bird, dice and a game resembling draughts. Cattle-breeding was much developed; zoologists tell us that the inhabitants bred zebu, also a short-horned European type of animal, buffalo, bison and another species now extinct; different strains were bred with great care, as were dogs and several kinds of sheep. They do not seem to have had horses, but remains of the period, found close to Mohenjo-daro, suggest that they domesticated not only elephants but also the rhinoceros. The possibility of taming this animal has been discovered, or rather rediscovered, in recent years by modern zoopsychology.

The centre of Harappa is probably much older than that of Mohenjo-daro, but the two cities are regarded as belonging to a single empire which reached the height of its splendor thousands of years ago. It is in fact unthinkable that a civilization such as that depicted in the Indian texts should have limited its radius

GIANTS AND THE LOST LANDS OF THE GODS

of action to 600 miles or so. We may recall that the Ramayana describes Rama as traveling on his vimana over the whole subcontinent, from the mountains and rivers of the north all the way to Ceylon. If such an empire had still existed at the time of the most recent Mohenjo-daro remains there would certainly be other traces of it, considering its size and the fact that the two centres that have been discovered were not necessarily the most important ones.

But everything has disappeared as though the earth had swallowed it up. Perhaps indeed it did, for only a cataclysm of the sort we have imagined could annihilate a culture so completely.

Believers in the existence of Mu maintain that Harappa and Mohenjo-daro represent two of its colonies: saved from the cataclysm but cut off from the source of their civilization, they entered on a period of decline but preserved traces of their old greatness until they were finally destroyed. However this may be, the unknown Indian race must have been impressive to look at. But we have no delineation of its features, no evidence as to where its people came from or where they went.

No tombs have come to light in the excavations; perhaps the dead were cremated, or buried in distant and long-forgotten cemeteries. Nor do we know how Mohenjo-daro met its end. It was not destroyed suddenly, for in that case there would certainly be remains of human beings. But the population cannot have been deported or simply abandoned their city in good order, considering the precious objects and implements that were left behind.

Science has no answer to this puzzle, but some believe that the answer is obvious: men, women and children were literally removed from the face of the earth, 'atomized' by some terrible means of disintegration; This may seem a far-fetched hypothesis, but those who advance it do not do so on wholly fantastic grounds.

Super-Atomic Power

As we saw, the vimana appears to have been some kind of aerial vehicle, but it would take many pages to quote and analyze all the references to it in Indian and Tibetan texts. The Ramayana, the great Indian epic which relates the adventures of Rama, is attributed to the poet Valmiki (fourth to third century B.C.), but no doubt derives in part from earlier work. It speaks of the 'fiery chariot' as follows: 'Bhima flew along in his car, resplendent as the sun and loud as thunder . The flying chariot shone like a flame in the night sky of summer. It swept by like a comet. It was as if two suns were shining . Then the chariot rose up and all the 'heavens brightened.'

In the Mahavira of Bhavabhuti (eighth century) we read: 'An aerial chariot, the Pushpaka, conveys many people to the ancient capital of Ayodhya. The sky is

GIANTS AND THE LOST LANDS OF THE GODS

full of stupendous flying-machines, dark as night, but picked out by lights with a yellowish glare.

Until recent years such accounts may have been considered mere fables, but in the nuclear age we cannot help recognizing in the ancient descriptions reactors, rockets and spaceships. The Vedas, moreover, tell us of vimanas of various types and sizes: the agnihotra-vimana with two engines, the 'elephant vimana' with more, and other types named after the kingfisher, ibis, etc., very much as we now christen various types of aircraft and missile.

The Mausolaparvan (part of the Mahabhwrata) says: 'It was an unknown weapon, an iron thunderbolt, a gigantic messenger of death that burnt to ashes all the descendants of Andhaka and Vrishni. Their corpses were featureless, the hair and nails fell away, vessels broke into fragments without cause, the birds turned white. Within a few hours every food be- came unwholesome.' And again: 'Cukra, flying in a 'vimana of great power, hurled at the triple city a missile weighted with all the force of the universe. An incandescent smoke, like ten thousand suns, rose in all its splendor.'

Are these mere myths the product of the ancient writers' fantasy? The column of blazing smoke, an explosion brighter than the sun, hair and nails falling out, contaminated food, animals and birds losing their color—none of these details would be out of place in a description of atomic warfare. The Vedic authors may indeed have had strong imaginations, but this seems to go beyond coincidence.

There is thus solid reason to believe that Asia, and perhaps the lost continent of Mu, was once the scene of frightful wars, massacre on a scale otherwise unknown, and perhaps ruthless mass deportations.

On the basis of research carried out jointly by scholars from the USA, the USSR and India, the Smithsonian Institution in 1958 suggested that the Eskimos might have migrated northwards to their present homes from central Asia, Mongolia and Ceylon, more than 10,000 years ago. In this connection, Pauwels and Bergier write (op cit., p. 202):

'How could a primitive people have decided, suddenly and of one accord, to leave their original homes for the inhospitable regions where they now live? And how did they make the journey? Even today, they know nothing of geography or that the world is round. Why should they leave the earthly paradise of Ceylon? The Institution does not offer any answer to these questions. We do not claim that ours is the right one, but we put it forward as a test of mental flexibility: supposing that, 10,000 years ago, the world was governed by a more developed civilization which established a deportation area in the Far North? . . . Now turn to Eskimo folklore, and what do we find there? It tells us that certain tribes were flown to the far north, at the beginning of time, on "gigantic birds made of metal".

GIANTS AND THE LOST LANDS OF THE GODS

In the last century archaeologists dismissed these birds as an absurdity; but should we do so today?'

The Indian sources, moreover, do not confine themselves to ordinary atomic weapons. There is the Saura, a kind of giant H-bomb, the Agniratha, a remote-control jet bomber, the Sikharastra bomb with napalm-like effects, the Avidiastra, which attacks the enemy's nerve system. Again we read in Bhavabhuti's account: 'The sage, putting his confidence in Brahma, instructed him in all secrets and in the use of powerful weapons inducing sleep (prasvépana), and of a fire that would reduce to ashes the great army of Kurnbhakarna. As though the conventional armament of those days was not enough! Or here again is the description of a super-bomb from the Dronaparvan (Mahabharata, book vii): 'They launched a huge missile of burning fire without smoke, and thick darkness fell upon the armies and on everything. A terrible wind arose, and blood colored clouds swept down on to the earth: nature went mad, and the sun revolved upon itself. The enemy fell like shrubs consumed by the fire, the rivers boiled and those who had dived into them perished miserably. The forests burnt; horses and elephants plunged wildly through them, neighing and trumpeting. When the wind had cleared away the smoke we beheld thousands of corpses burnt to ashes.'

Here, finally, is the account of the Dronaparvan of 'Brahma's weapon': 'The son of Drona hurled the weapon and great winds arose; the waters rushed upon the earth. The soldiers were deafened by peals of thunder, the earth shook, the waters rose up, the mountains split asunder.' Here again we cannot suppose that this is pure mythology without a basis of fact: imagination, however lively, could not have described vehicles and weapons with such accuracy.

The Valley Of The Seven Dead Men

Many parts of the globe have yet to be fully explored, and it is quite possible that We may discover other regions where strange, terrible destruction has taken place. In India there may well be many of these, to judge from references in ancient books. One locality that comes to mind is the 'valley of the seven dead men', the exact whereabouts of which is kept a secret by New Delhi for fear that some foolhardy person, lured by tales of treasure, may meet his death there as happened, eighty years ago, to the companions of Graham Dickford. '

Dickford was one of the innumerable nineteenth-century adventurers in far-flung countries who set out to get rich by every possible means, at the risk of their own lives or, more often, those of others. He came to the notice of the British Indian authorities in 1892, when he was picked up in a state of collapse and taken to hospital in a small town. There he stammered out a frightening tale. Along with some companions of his own persuasion, he had discovered a mysterious valley in the heart of the jungle where, according to the natives, there was a temple filled with amazing treasures; but instead of a heap of gold and jewels the party came upon a scene of horror. All his companions had been killed, and Dickford himself was half-dead: he was wracked with fever, completely bald and covered with terrible burns. In his delirium, interrupted by strangled screams, he spoke of a 'great flying fire', 'shadows in the night' and 'ghosts that kill by looking at you'. His story grew more and more in- coherent, and within three days of being found he died in agony, crying out and struggling with such violence that the Indian attendants fled in terror.

Dickford's tale was not taken seriously until 1906, when the Government of India sent an expedition to the spot: this confirmed Dickford's account, and the 'witches' cauldron' claimed two more lives. The valley proved to be infested by all the most poisonous snakes and plants of India. As for the 'flying fire', the leader of the expedition reported that if one struck a match, there was a terrific roar and flames shot from one end of the valley to the other'.

The two explorers who lost their lives had gone down into a funnel-shaped hollow when they suddenly began to stagger and fall to the ground. Their comrades rushed to their aid but found them already dead. They were able to retrieve the bodies, but themselves felt a dizzy, choking sensation as long as they remained in the hollow. That night they suffered from fearful nightmares, and for days afterwards they felt an unnatural sense of oppression.

In 1911 a second expedition of jungle veterans set out for the valley. Of its seven members, only two returned. The others had been in an open area surrounded by higher ground when they suddenly began to spin round and then collapse as though struck by lightning, deaf to the cries of their friends who were standing at a distance.

Eight years later a third group of intrepid explorers made their way to the valley, where they found 17 human skeletons. The valley took its toll of this expedition also: three of its members, who had been laughing and joking with their fellows, suddenly jumped for no apparent reason over a rocky cliff and were dashed to pieces on the ground below.

Some scientists have suggested that these strange and dreadful phenomena may be due to natural gases of an inflammable or nerve-paralyzing kind, or blasts of carbonic acid gas, or to some feature of the climate which causes the proliferation of snakes and poisonous plants. As Einstein said in a different context, this savors of 'too many things in too little space'. The explanations offered are not particularly convincing, and they do not account for Dickford's story of 'ghosts that kill by looking at you'.

If, on the other hand, we are prepared to admit the space- travel theory, we may recall the ancient Indian texts with their hints of the fearful effects of thermonuclear weapons and others still more destructive. We may also remember Death

GIANTS AND THE LOST LANDS OF THE GODS

Valley in the USA with its misshapen trees and its population of reptiles, the fumes that make it fatal to human life and the weird lights described by Dr. Martin which 'leap up out of the ground, sometimes in shapes resembling human beings; they move through the darkness, sometimes slowly and sometimes with the speed of lightning; they twist and turn, shoot up like flames or claws; and rush skywards in columns of white fire'.

A member of the flat-headed race? Peruvian rock-carving.

Figures from the Gate of the Sun at Tiahuanacu. Some think they represent a solar ion motor and a space-traveller respectively.

Two statues from Tiahuanaco showing Semitic features.

Fire-bird totem from Alaska.

West Indian sculpture of a unidentified being.

GIANTS AND THE LOST LANDS OF THE GODS

CHAPTER NINE
Secrets Of The Pyramids

If all the Works on pyramidology that have been written since the Middle Ages were piled one on top of another, the result would no doubt be an edifice nearly as high as the pyramids themselves. By 'pyramidology' we refer here not to the factual description of these monuments, but to the endeavors that have been made to extract from them information that transcends ordinary Egyptology.

The tenth-century Arabic writer Masudi, for instance, is not much spoken of by 'official' scientists, though they may occasionally mention a manuscript of his which is preserved at Oxford. But to the pyramidologists he is a major prophet on account of his statement that the Great Pyramid was not, as is generally thought, built in about 2900 B.C. as a tomb for the fourth-dynasty pharaoh Cheops (Khufu), but was erected by a ruler named Surid some 300 years before the Deluge (of which he is said to have had a prophetic vision) in order to preserve the memory of Egypt's great achievements in every field and the occult powers of its people, especially that of divining the future. 'In the eastern pyramid,' says Masudi, referring to that of Cheops, 'the king caused to be inscribed the celestial spheres, the chronicle of times past and future and of all that was to happen in Egypt.'

The historian Abu Zeyd el Balkhi claims that the pyramid is older still, and that an inscription declares it to have been built 'when Lyra was in the sign of Cancer', 'twice 36,000 solar years before the date of Egypt', or about 73,300 years ago. There are many other theories too; some believe that the pyramid is 150,000 years old, others regard it as a compendium of astronomical science or a history of the Egyptian race from its remotest origins. But Masudi's version, in one form or another, has always exercised the strongest fascination.

About the middle of the last century John Taylor, a London publisher who had never seen the Great Pyramid but had made an exhaustive study of facts concerning it, wrote a book expounding his theory that it was built under divine inspiration by an ancient Hebrew, perhaps Noah himself; that the basis of its dimensions was the 'sacred cubit' of about 20 inches, and that the structure expressed all kinds of mathematical truths. A few years later Charles Piazzi Smyth, the Astronomer Royal of Scotland, enlarged upon Taylor's theory and discovered all sorts of measurements embodied in the construction: for instance, the height of the pyramid divided by twice the length of one of its base-lines gave a value close to that of pi; the height multiplied by a thousand million was approximately the distance from the earth to the sun, and the base-line divided by the breadth of one of the stones gave the figure 365, the number of days in the year. But, as Sir Flinders Petrie tells us, one of Smyth's disciples was disillusioned when he found him one day trying to file away a projecting piece of granite in the royal antechamber so as to make its dimensions correspond with his theory.

A scholar who has gone to some trouble to investigate these absurdities remarks that it is really not difficult to arrive at what seem extraordinary results. 'If anyone takes the trouble to measure such a complex structure as the pyramid, he is bound to come across various "basic" measurements which he can apply at will to produce a desired conclusion. Given sufficient patience and versatility, he is sure to be able to arrive at figures that coincide with important scientific data and formulae. In fact the quest could hardly be unsuccessful, since it is not subject to the discipline of any rule.

'Take, for instance, the height of the Pyramid. Smyth multiplies it by 109 to obtain the distance from the earth to the sun, but this figure 109 is quite arbitrary. If no such simple multiple had met the case, Smyth could have chosen some other that would have given the distance from the earth to the moon or the nearest star, or any other known measurement. The only "discovery" of this sort that is somewhat harder to explain is that involving the value of pi. The Egyptians may have used this ratio on purpose, but it is more likely to be the incidental consequence of a different plan of construction.

A 'grand master' of pyramidology duly appeared in the person of one Menzies, who declared' that every 'pyramid inch' (Piazzi Smyth's unit, equal to 1.001 inches) of the internal corridors represented one year of the earth's history, and that, as Masudi wrote, the corridors give a faithful account of the world's past and future. Accepting that the world was created in 4004 B.C., and having noted that the stones record the Flood, the Exodus from Egypt and the birth, death and resurrection of Christ, we discover with alarm that, according to Menzies, the period from 1882 to 1911 was that of the Great Tribulation, terminated by the second coming of the Saviour.

This may suffice to demonstrate the absurdity of the ideas put forward by Taylor, Smyth, Menzies and their disciples and imitators. The only reason we have mentioned them at all is that before dealing with the true mysteries of ancient Egypt, we wished to ensure that the reader was not distracted by baseless fables masquerading as scientific truths.

Sirius Rose Over The Nile

The history of ancient Egypt is known to many in its broad lines, beginning with the First Dynasty, around 4241 B.C.; the previous period is wrapped in mystery. Some scholars believe that the Egyptians attained the civilization we know, beginning more or less from zero, and that they were inhabitants of the Saharan plain (not yet completely a desert) who settled along the Nile. However, most Soviet historians and archaeologists hold that they could not, at a single stroke, have developed the flourishing culture which characterized them at all periods known to us. Attention should be paid, moreover, to the evidence of ancient writings which have been wrongly dismissed as fables. Herodotus, the 'father of history', relates that he saw at Thebes (Luxor) 341 wooden statues of high priests who had successively held office since the foundation of the great temple, 11,000 years before.

Nevertheless, up to a few decades ago it was supposed that not much remained to be discovered in Egypt. Opinions changed, however, when excavations were resumed after the Second World War, bringing to light objects that could not previously be known but which it was felt could not be unique. In 1954, for instance, the Egyptian expert Zeki Y. Saad discovered at Helwan textiles of extraordinary strength and delicacy, such as could only be produced today in highly specialized factories. As Dr. Saad observed, it seems impossible that they could have been made by hand; while the American scholar W. B. Emery remarks that the excavations show archaic Egyptian civilization to have been far more advanced than was previously thought.

The corollary to this, in the opinion of Soviet scholars, was that Egyptian culture must have been developing for a long time previously, and that there must have been a still more archaic civilization of which we know nothing, but which might account for the Egyptians' profound knowledge of astronomy.

Acting on this theory, and with the aid of experts from Cairo, the Russians have thrown light on one of the most fascinating secrets of archaeology. The full results of their investigations in the Nile Valley in the early 60s have not been published, but from advance reports it is clear that Egyptian civilization is in fact much older than was previously suspected. It is true that the objects so far brought to light have been shown, by radiocarbon dating, not to be older than some 6,200 years. But there are other tombs and objects buried deep beneath the sands of Saqqara, Abydos and Helwan, and it is on these pre-dynastic finds that the Soviet conclusions are based. According to reports from Moscow they include inscriptions that prolong the Egyptian calendar for a long span of years, celestial maps of great accuracy and many objects whose purpose is still unknown.

Among the finds are spherical crystal lenses of the utmost precision, used no doubt for astronomical observation. Similar lenses, it is interesting to note, have been discovered in Iraq and also in central Australia; today they can be manufactured only by means of a special abrasive based on cerium oxide. This substance is derived from an electrochemical process and cannot be isolated without the use of electric energy: so we are faced with the intriguing question, did the ancient Egyptians have knowledge of electricity?

As regards their calendar, the French scholar Jacques Vernes writes: 'We know that the Egyptian year began on what we call 19 July. On that day Sirius stands in the heavens at the same altitude as the rising sun, and it is also the day on which the Nile waters begin to rise. There is no connection between the two phenomena, but the coincidence evidently struck the Egyptians, and they made it the basis of their calendar.

After a lapse of 4 years Sirius rises on the second day of the Egyptian year, after 8 years on the third day, after 12 years on the fourth and so on. The Egyptians corrected this by adding one or more days to their year, in the same fashion as our leap-year. Such corrections were made during a cycle of 1,461 years, after which Sirius again rose with the sun on 19 July. Now the inscriptions found by the Russians in the newly discovered graves correspond to 25 such cycles, and 25 times 1,461 is 36,525 years. Since the calendar as we know it begins in 4241 B.C., it follows that Egyptian civilization dates back 40 centuries before the Christian era.

The positions of the fixed stars in the maps found by Soviet archaeologists agree with those they are known to have occupied thousands of years ago. The maps confirm that the Egyptians had a vast knowledge of astronomy, and they show what we did not know before, that this included knowledge of the 'dark' companion of Sirius. Curiously enough, the Dogon tribe of central Africa are also aware of this star's existence, of which they may have learned from prehistoric Egypt.

Soviet scholars suggest, though with hesitation, that the Egyptians originally came from Indonesia. Is it possible that they belonged to the realm of Mu, and that the check which their development underwent, as the Russians maintain, 10 or 12,000 years ago was due to a cosmic disaster such as the fall of an asteroid? In this way Egyptian culture as we know it, going back barely as far as 4,000 B.C., would have been only a pale reflection of a world of unknown marvels.

GIANTS AND THE LOST LANDS OF THE GODS

The Radioactive Curse

The statement that we 'know' Egyptian culture of the dynastic period refers, of course, only to its broad features. There are many mysteries still to be cleared up, and above all, as with other ancient civilizations, there are ever-recurrent hints that the earth was previously the scene of great mother-cultures which were destroyed in some primeval cataclysm.

There are, as we shall see, many enigmatic links between Egypt, Asia and pre-Columbian America. To study these from the Egyptian end we should pass on from Giza, where the Great Pyramid is situated, to nearby Saqqara, where the Third-Dynasty pharaoh Zoser decided to improve on the mastaba (rectangular tomb) of his predecessors, and built the first of the majestic series of pyramids. This was a step pyramid, exactly like those of Asia and America, and we may ask ourselves whether Zoser was not in fact renewing the practice of a more ancient civilization which had been that of all three continents.

Pyramids of the well-known Giza type are of later date, and it is at Saqqara that we can best look for the key to Egypt's fascinating secrets, many of which will only be unlocked at the cost of much toil.

Buried in the sand a short way from Zoser's tomb is another huge step pyramid, or rather the base of one which for some reason remained unfinished. For decades the entrance could not be found, and scientists had given up the problem in despair; it was finally solved by the Cairo expert, Professor Zakaria Goneim, by the sole use of mathematical calculations based on Zoser's pyramid. The excavations were extremely difficult; on two occasions the path was blocked by masses of rubble (under the second of which was found a superb collection of gold bracelets), and a large part of the corridor vault gave way, killing a workman and injuring two others.

Finally Goneim and his companions reached the tomb-chamber, some 130 feet below ground; but this was not the end of the mystery. Inside the marble sarcophagus, closed by a sliding panel, there should have been a wooden coffin containing the pharaoh's mummified remains, but in fact nothing was found.

If the tomb had been pillaged centuries before, then presumably the precious objects would have been taken also. It seems therefore that the sarcophagus was placed empty in the chamber, either to foil predators or because it was regarded as containing the Ka - the vital spirit or soul - of the dead ruler. The mummy of this pharaoh, who belonged to the third dynasty but whose name we do not know, must be elsewhere in a second tomb-chamber. Professor Goneim in fact discovered another entrance to the tomb, but operations had to be suspended during the Suez crisis of 1956, and he died before conditions returned to normal. We have tried without success to ascertain the circumstances of his death, with some claim to be due to a 'curse' of the kind that has allegedly afflicted other

GIANTS AND THE LOST LANDS OF THE GODS

Egyptologists.

Are we to believe such stories? Many tales have been told of strange and sinister events following on the exhumation of mummified pharaohs, but the reality is different from what occultists and journalistic sensation-lovers would have us think. Take, for example, the story of the remains of Rameses II, who was ruler of Egypt during the captivity of the Israelites and has reposed since 1886 in the Cairo Museum.

One damp, sultry afternoon, a crowd of visitors to the museum heard a loud creaking noise followed by the sound of breaking glass. Turning towards the tomb, they saw an incredible sight: the mummy which had been reclining in the sarcophagus sat up, opened its mouth as if to shout, turned its head sharply to the north, spread out its arms and, smashed the glass with its right hand.

Some of the crowd fainted, others rushed downstairs towards the exit or jumped out of the window. Dozens were injured, the attendant on duty threw up his job and no one else could be found to take it; the Egyptian government paid large sums in compensation and for a long time the public boycotted the museum, fearing lest the roof should collapse over their heads. But no further prodigy occurred, and the experts decided that all that had happened was that the mummy, used to the cold, dry air of the tomb-chamber, had reacted in this startling but natural way to the humidity of Cairo. Nevertheless, since one cannot be too careful, it now reposes with its head facing north as enjoined by the funeral prayer.

As for the famous Tutankhamun, it must be said that the story of a tablet having been found on the mummy, pro- claiming a curse on all who should disturb it, is pure fantasy. The only inscription on the sarcophagus of this young pharaoh is one invoking peace on the departed. Nor is it by any means the case that all those who had anything to do with the excavation of the tomb died in mysterious circumstances.

Professor Howard Carter, the head of the 1923 expedition, died sixteen years afterwards at the age of 66; others concerned also died of old age or natural causes. It is true, however, that a number of people connected with the expedition died within a short period after it. These included Lord Carnarvon, the promoter of the work (said to have been killed by an insect bite), his half-brother Aubrey Herbert, a nurse who had attended him, Howard Carter's former secretary, three other members of the team and Lord Carnarvon's stepmother.

Thirty-five years later, by a curious chance, Dr. Geoffrey Dean of the hospital at Port Elizabeth in South Africa discovered in one of his patients symptoms of the mysterious disease which had killed many Egyptologists, known as histoplasmosis or 'cave disease' and spread by microscopic fungi to be found on the bodies of animals (especially bats), in organic detritus and dust. This may account for the death of Lord Carnarvon and others to whom he may have passed the infec-

GIANTS AND THE LOST LANDS OF THE GODS

tion, but not for the deaths of many other scientists since the pyramids came to be excavated on a large scale.

Since the destruction of Hiroshima and Nagasaki we are able to identify the cause of their death as atomic gangrene. As Professor Goneim observed, summing up the researches of a large number of Egyptian scientists, it has been found that the pitch used to preserve corpses for mummification comes from the shores of the Red Sea and parts of Asia Minor and contains highly radioactive substances. Moreover, the cloth used for swathing is radioactive, and the burial chambers were probably full of radioactive dust. There is every reason to think that the Egyptian priests made use of this fact not only to preserve the remains of their rulers but also to punish desecrators of their tombs. They may have seen in radioactivity a manifestation of Ra, the sun-god: according to Goneim this is borne out by numerous obscure passages in ancient documents.

We may recall here a curious event that took place about the middle of the fifteenth century, when the tomb of Cicero's daughter Tullia was opened. The girl's body lay, intact, in an unknown transparent liquid, and a lamp at her feet burnt for some time after the tomb was broken into. The notion of an all-preserving liquid, and of a lamp that could burn for over 1,500 years, is bound to make us think of atomic energy.

The American archaeologist A. Hyatt Verrill has put forward a still bolder hypothesis: he suggests that the stones of the pre-Columbian pyramids were not hewn by means of a chisel, but that the builders used a kind of radioactive paste which was capable of eating into granite. He claims to have seen for himself remnants of this substance in the possession of an Indian witch-doctor.

The Voltaic Monster And The Defeat Of Gravity

We do not know how much the ancient Egyptians knew of atomic energy, but Professor Goneim was convinced that they were no strangers to scientific mysteries. As he pointed out, there are chambers so deeply hidden away in the pyramids that no fresh air penetrated to them until they were discovered forty centuries after being sealed. Yet the walls, floor and ceiling of these chambers are painted with delicate hieroglyphics in several colors, and this work was certainly carried out within the chambers after their completion, What did the artists use for light? Work of this delicacy and precision requires the equivalent of daylight; lamps or torches would not do, and in any case these cannot have been used, as there is no trace of smoke or soot.

It may seem hard to believe that the Egyptians used some form of artificial light; but the idea has been advanced, even before the Soviet discovery of lenses made in ancient times by an electrochemical process. Indirect confirmation is forthcoming from Baghdad, where a German sewage engineer found in the mu-

GIANTS AND THE LOST LANDS OF THE GODS

seum, labeled as 'religious objects' of the Sassanid period (A.D. 226-630), a number of electric batteries in working order. Investigation showed that a sect had existed two thousand years ago which jealously preserved electrical secrets, including galvano-plastic techniques. What is more, a few miles south of Baghdad, in the heart of ancient Babylon, accumulators were found which are believed to be 3,000 or 4,000 years old and to have been made, so to speak, under Egyptian license—thus recalling the view of some French archaeologists that Moses learned his magic arts in secret from the Egyptians after he was rescued and adopted by Thermutis, the daughter of Rameses II. According to Maurice Denis-Papin (descendant of a celebrated French physicist), as quoted ,by Robert Charroux, the Ark of the Covenant (Exodus 25), Containing the Tables of the Law, Aaron's rod and a vessel full of manna, was in fact an electrical appliance capable of producing discharges of 500 or 700 volts. To quote Denis-Papin more fully:

'The Ark was made of acacia wood, lined with gold inside and out (on the same principle as an electric condenser, two conductors separated by an insulating material) and surrounded by a "wreath of gold". It was kept in a dry place, where the natural magnetic field is normally 500 - 600 volts per meter of height. It may have contained batteries like those in the Baghdad museum; the "wreath", in that case, would have been used to charge the batteries or the condenser.

Custody of the Ark was reserved to the Levites, and it was transported by means of gold-covered staves which were passed through rings on either side of it. The electric charge would thus be grounded without danger to the bearers. The insulated Ark would at times be surrounded with flames and lightning, and if an unauthorized person were to touch it he would receive a violent shock; in short, it behaved exactly like a Leyden jar.

Denis-Papin goes on to say that the other miracles attributed to Moses are explicable on the assumption that he shared the Egyptians' knowledge of physics, chemistry, geology and meteorology. Some believe, too, that he used explosives to quell the rebellion of Korah, Dathan and Abiram (Numbers, 16), when 'the ground clave asunder that was under them, and the earth opened her mouth and swallowed them up, and they . . . went down alive into the pit . . . And there came out a fire from the Lord, and consumed the two hundred and fifty men that offered incense' or again when he punished the sacrilege of Nadab and Abihu (Leviticus 10), and 'there went out fire from the Lord and devoured them.'

The eighteenth-century physicist Francois Arago suggested that the Temple of Solomon was protected by twenty-four lightning conductors, and this device may have been known to other ancient peoples. For example, the Greek doctor and historian Ctesias (fourth century B.C.) brought home from his travels in Greece and Egypt two 'magic swords' which, if stuck in the ground with the points upward, would 'drive away clouds, hail and tempests'. Their powers were probably exaggerated, but it is quite possible they were lightning conductors. Many authorities think the Etruscans possessed electricity, and that the kings of Rome may have learned of it from the Etruscan sages. According to Livy and Dionysius of Halicarnassus, Numa Pompilius was able to 'let loose the fire of Jove', i.e. the lightning, and they relate how Tullus Hostilius, less skilled than his predecessor, was struck by lightning during a religious ceremony at which he had tried to display similar powers. Lars Porsena, on the other hand, is said to have used electricity to free his kingdom from a monster whose name, by an extraordinary coincidence, was Volt.

To return to the pyramids, another scientific puzzle is presented by the fact that they cannot possibly have been built without an exact plan and appropriate machinery; the manual force of slave labor was not in itself enough. For instance, the blocks of which the Great Pyramid is constructed mostly weigh between 15 and 100 tons, and the ceiling of the 'king's chamber' is made of slabs of red granite weighing 70 tons. To raise a structure of this kind nowadays one would have to build around it, on the sand, plat- forms of reinforced concrete capable of bearing the weight of 40-wheel trucks, not to speak of other devices of modern engineering. The same is true of the great monuments of pre-Columbian America, and all over the world we find examples of building materials having been transported for incredible distances. The Austrian archaeologist K. Lanik, for instance, tells us that on the Magdalensberg near Klagenfurt, over 2,500 years ago, there was a metropolis with walls 23 feet thick; the stone blocks were quarried from mountains a considerable distance away and somehow brought to the summit, where they were riveted with huge slabs of marble.

This is not the only example of its kind in Europe alone: many Roman and Celtic strongholds confront us with the same mystery.

Some have suggested that the pyramids were built by means of inclined planes, the blocks being rolled into position on tree-trunks. But this will not do, since each block would need at least five hundred pairs of hands to hold it, and how could five hundred men get near enough at the same time? We are forced to conclude, therefore, that the ancient Egyptians and Americans had lifting devices of at least equal efficiency to those of modern times. Why has there never been any mention of these? Because techniques changed and building became less ambitious, so that the massive apparatus fell into disuse, was gradually destroyed and eventually lost to memory. This has in fact happened with various devices known to man. For instance, if an archaeologist a thousand years hence should come upon the remains of street-lamps dating from a time prior to the discovery of electricity, he might well form a plausible theory to account for them, but how could he prove it by producing a gas lantern such as those with which the streets of all civilized cities were lit until a few decades ago?

GIANTS AND THE LOST LANDS OF THE GODS

Some people advance still more sensational theories as regards the Egyptians, e.g. that they knew how to eliminate the force of gravity or to cut and transport blocks of stone by ultrasonic means. As Charroux says, 'Prehistoric man understood the power of vibrations and used it as a means of carving flint.' Or, to quote Lenormand's book on Chaldean magic, 'the priests of On were able to conjure up storms and to build their temples with stones that would have been too heavy for a thousand men to lift.' According to an Arab legend, the Egyptians used scrolls of papyrus with magic words written on them, on which blocks for the pyramids came flying through the air. Jacques Weiss perhaps remembered this when he wrote: 'The huge blocks of up to 600 tons weight are slightly convex on certain sides, so that they fit perfectly into others which are concave and the resultant structure is of perfect solidity. They can only have been got into place by means of levitation."

Charroux tells us that the priests of ancient Egypt were distinguished by their power to rise into the air at will, and he quotes interesting references to levitation in ancient authors. Thus Pliny the Elder states that the architect Dinocrates, a contemporary of Alexander the Great, constructed the vault of the temple of Arsinoe with 'magnetic stones' so that idols could be suspended in mid-air. Ruflnus of Aquileia, around A.D. 400, refers to magnetism in describing from his own experience the ascension of a disc representing the sun in the great temple of Serapis, near Alexandria; while Lucian (second century A.D.), who was noted for his skepticism, relates that he saw the image of a Syrian deity being raised into the air by its priests.

Other cases of levitation can be quoted from different periods and peoples. Cassiodorus, the fifth century statesman and writer, speaks of an iron Cupid suspended between the ceiling and door of a temple of Diana; and in Tibet, the embalmed body of the reformer Tsong Kaba was seen, poised a span from the ground, by thousands of pilgrims to the Khaldan monastery. Mahomet's coffin remained for a long time without support high up in the mosque at Medina, and for centuries a 'flying rod' was seen, motionless in mid- air, in the church at Bizan in Abyssinia. This was verified in 1515 by Father Francisco Alvares, secretary to the Portuguese embassy, who assured himself that there was no secret support, and also by the French physician Jacques Poucet two centuries later. 'Suspecting that there might be some invisible artifice,' he writes, 'I asked the abbot's leave to perform an experiment. I moved a stick around the object, above and below and to either side of it, and thus confirmed that it was indeed poised without support.'

Are these examples of magnetism or of ultrasonic devices? On either hypothesis they are hard to understand; some consider the latter more probable, and it must be admitted that acoustic science was well advanced in ancient times. To quote Charroux again: 'According to some Egyptian palimpsests, the priests of Karnak, Abydos and Thebes were chosen for the strength and harmony of their voices. By pronouncing a certain word in a prescribed tone they could cause the heavy portals of the temple to open wide. Such stories as this, and the many Oriental tales of magic doors giving access to temples, crypts and caves, might be explained in terms of ingenious devices or trickery; but the frequency of such reports, and the mystery of the pyramids, incline us to look for a scientific explanation, which may be either straightforward or technical. That is to say, we may think of sounds emitted at a certain pitch and touching of a spring mechanism, or else of sounds or ultrasounds acting upon an electric cell, as light would do.

'The phrase, "Open sesame", is not an arbitrary one; the capsule containing the seed of this plant bursts from the ground when it is ripe, but the emission of a low-pitched note can cause it to open before its time. This fact was known to the Egyptians, the Hebrews and other Orientals, and it may well be that they had a profound knowledge of the physical effects that can be achieved by vocal means.'

Heron of Alexandria (first century A.D.), a mathematician, engineer and inventor, and his master Ctesibius, are said to have made much use of devices causing huge idols to rise from below ground, making priests and statues stand in midair, opening doors by 'magic', producing rain of perfumed water and causing harmonious sounds to issue from the beaks of birds made of metal. As the occultist Eliphas Levi writes: 'They could cause the temple to be wrapped in clouds or bathed in unearthly light; darkness might supervene in daytime, or the night be suddenly lit up; lamps would burn of their own accord, the images of gods would blaze, claps of thunder would ring out - and woe to the impious man who brought on himself the curse of those who administered the sacred mysteries!'

GIANTS AND THE LOST LANDS OF THE GODS

Fine carvings of the "fire-bird" from the vicinity of Malinalco, Mexico.

Stylized spider and "canals" at Nazca (Nasca), Peru.

The "landing-field" at Nazca, with a representation of the fire-bird.

The "virgin of the rocks" and "man's profile": carvings at Allumiere near Rome.

Gate of the Sun, Tiahuanaco.

GIANTS AND THE LOST LANDS OF THE GODS

CHAPTER TEN
An Empire In The Sahara

At a depth varying between 1,000 and 4,000 feet below the surface of the Sahara there is an expanse of sweet water known as the underground sea of Albienne: its area is at least 230,000 square miles, or four times that of England and Wales. This is only one of many natural reservoirs concealed under the rocks and burning sand: the water resources of north Africa are immense, and we may hope that one day they will be used to transform the desert into an area of prosperity and comfort.

Several scientists, and notably the German geologist Hoffmann, have maintained that in comparatively recent times nearly the whole of north Africa lay under the Mediterranean Sea, out of which what are now its mountains and plateaux rose in the form of great islands. This appeared likely enough, but the discovery of the sea of Albienne goes to confirm the contrary theory advanced by W. Scott Elliot (an investigator who combines genuine science with absurd esoteric doctrines) to the effect that what is now the Sahara was formerly not part of the Mediterranean but a huge inland lake, which some earth convulsion in remote times transformed into a jungle. Elliot relates this to the cataclysm of 11,000 years ago, but the lake must in fact have disappeared earlier, as it has been proved that in 8000 B.C. the Sahara was covered with forests which must have originated several millennia before.

Ancient writers describe the Sahara as a wooded area with great rivers, supporting a dense population and various fauna including antelopes, giraffes, elephants, lions and panthers. The change in its appearance was brought about by sharp variations of temperature and later by the action of the winds and waters. Pastoral lands encroached more and more on what had been a jungle, and the process of drying up was accelerated by livestock: horses were bred by Libyans, camels by the Romans and goats and donkeys by the Arabs.

But, thousands of years before this, the Sahara had been the home of a civilization unknown to us - probably the same which, according to Soviet scholars,

GIANTS AND THE LOST LANDS OF THE GODS

came from Asia and gave birth to the Egyptian and perhaps other cultures of the Mediterranean basin.

Proofs of the link with Egypt are being unearthed by science: for instance the discoveries of Fabrizio Mori, the Italian painter and archaeologist, who has found in the Acacus massif between Libya and Algeria a series of graffiti dating from the time when the area was still a garden of delight, as described by Suetonius Paulinus. These rock carvings of men, women, animals, boats and waterways bring us tales of a world whose existence we had not suspected.

The mummified body of a child which died 5,400 years ago shows that the prehistoric inhabitants of the Sahara practiced a cult of the dead, and there is good reason to suppose that their society flourished well before that date. Apart from the resemblance to Egypt, some of the figures show features reminiscent of ancient Greece,

Links with ancient Egypt are also found in the rock paintings of the Tassili-n-Ajjer in southeastern Algeria, which seem to embody the memory of legendary giants: a woman nearly seven feet tall, and a male colossus of 11 feet 6 inches, are receiving the homage of smaller beings. In a scene which seems to- represent a ritual dance, the hair of those taking part is dyed red in the fashion customary among the Masai of Kenya and Tanganyika, who are thought to be the last descendants of the Titans. Many figures wear on their heads an elegantly shaped object resembling a basket: its actual significance is unknown. One extraordinary carving has been christened by the French ethnographer Henri Lhote 'the great god of the Martians'. It resembles a man in a space-suit: the 'helmet' is round, with two eyeholes and a row of elliptical marks above. The articulation of the neck can be clearly seen, and the rest of the garment might be mistaken for an astronaut's overalls. A photograph of this curious figure was published in the newspapers with Yuri Gagarin's signature superimposed, as though the Soviet space-hero were inscribing it to his unknown predecessors.

The finds in the Acacus massif and at Tassili-n-Aijer are the most important, but the prehistoric race has left traces all over the Sahara. We may mention the carvings of men with horses' tails and the pictures of mummies, alongside an actual one, at Wau-Muhuggiac, also the pictures discovered by Captain Coche over 6,000 feet up at Martutech in the central Sahara: these are charming country scenes with peasants and oxen, and are very similar to those of Egypt.

Thirty years ago the archaeologists Di Caporiacio and Almasy discovered in the Arkenu massif between Libya and the Sudan carvings of giraffes, ostriches, buffalo, bulls, zebu-like animals, and men with bows and arrows. The German explorer Leo Frobenius in 1931, and the Societa Geografica Italiana in 1933, made a study of similar carvings in Fezzan; they came to the conclusion that the elephants, rhinoceroses, ostriches and crocodiles had once been part of the local fauna and

GIANTS AND THE LOST LANDS OF THE GODS

that the area must have presented a similar aspect to present-day central Africa.

Written In Sand

The authors of these carvings, remarkable though they are, cannot have reached a particularly high level of civilization. Some scholars, however, believe them to be the survivors of a race that underwent a series of natural calamities. Léon Mayou actually suggests that the Sahara may have been the Biblical Eden; while some exponents of esoteric doctrine believe that, like many other parts of the world, it was embellished by cities inhabited by wonderful blond creatures, with a light complexion and dark eyes. The occultists even tell us that there was an imperial palace with alabaster-covered walls, decorated inside with gold leaf and exquisite enamel tiles, while the interior of the temples was entirely gold except for the ivory floor. We are told much of the religion of this ancient people, its ceremonies and vestments.

It appears that they worshipped the planets, and wore in honor of the sun 'a garment of fine silk shot with gold'; Vulcan's color was a 'rich, violent red', that of Mercury varied from bright orange to lemon-yellow, and so forth.

Naturally all this is pure fantasy. There was probably a worldwide catastrophe, and there may have been a great civilization before it. The investigation of the latter, however, is not a mere pursuit of airy mirages: it resembles an advance across an unknown land in which a few mysterious tracks can be perceived.

In 1815-19 Giovan Battista Belzoni, a monk and archaeologist from Padua, visited Egypt and Nubia several times: he discovered ruins, catacombs, sarcophagi and mummies of great antiquity, but the technical resources of his day did not enable him to leave us a full account of them.

Near the village of Cassar he came across a well 66 feet deep, which, the natives told him, had the useful property of providing cold water by day and hot water by night. This, he recalled, was mentioned by Herodotus in the fifth century B.C.: the Greek historian added that there was in the neighborhood a huge temple dedicated to Zeus Ammon. Belzoni made excavations and in fact discovered the ruins of great walls, pillars and statues of great beauty.

Another Italian scholar, Centunviro, found in an old manuscript an account of a city on the southern edge of what is now the Libyan desert. He set out to find it and discovered the ruins near Waw al Adani, including pillars surmounted by strange figures of two-headed animals. He also found the entrance to an underground passage which apparently belonged to a temple of the sun. He explored this with a Turkish guide and, at the risk of his life, brought to light a gold cup adorned with figures of human beings, animals and flowers, and a vase on which an unknown artist, thousands of years before, had depicted scenes of aquatic fauna and flora.

GIANTS AND THE LOST LANDS OF THE GODS

It is a great pity that we have no fuller information on the work of these two pioneers. If their discoveries had been followed up, we might have material for comparison with other bygone civilizations, and our ideas on the remote past of Africa might be less vague than they are.

The 'Saharan empire', like Atlantis, has its ardent partisans, who believe that it was so large and powerful as to leave its mark on most of Africa and the Mediterranean basin. Some of the theories on this subject are mere fancies, while others are based on solid facts; we are not certain, however, that these facts are rightly interpreted. The puzzle is capable of being read in different ways. Where, for instance, does the Benin civilization fit in, and also that of Zimbabwe?

Benin, the capital of the Nigerian province of that name (formerly a large native kingdom), is today a town of some 22,000 inhabitants, about 50 miles inland from the Bight of Benin. Its modern story begins in 1897, when the London firm of Hale and Son put up for auction a number of objects such as carved elephants' tusks, bronzes and exquisitely worked sheets of metal. All the finds were more or less damaged, and dealers and connoisseurs showed a reluctance to buy. By pure chance, however, the collection came to the notice of Felix von Luschan, the director of a Berlin museum, who bought it outright and telegraphed to the German consul at Lagos: 'Buy all Benin antiquities you can get hold of, on my responsibility and regardless of price.'

The objects whose value was thus recognized had been discovered some months before by British troops sent on a punitive expedition against the Benin tribe, members of which had murdered a high colonial official and his staff. As the troops penetrated into the jungle they found that the murder had been on a much larger scale. Not only the British officials but thousands of slaves and captives, men, women and children, had been put to death by the natives in honor of their king's dead father, as required by the revolting cult of Juju. Near the royal hut were five enclosures full of mutilated corpses. The whole village, in fact, was a ghastly cemetery: common graves, over three hundred feet deep, were piled with the remains of generations of victims of the cult of ritual slaughter. The British decided to set fire to the charnel-house, but searched it first in the hope of finding treasure. They came upon neither silver nor gold, but 'only' the ivories and bronzes whose value was at first not appreciated even by experts of repute.

When von Luschan's action became known, explorers from all over the world rushed to the destroyed village and brought back other relics for which the museums bid high prices: bronze plaques that had been affixed to doors and posts, balconies and other fragments of a ruined palace, elaborate weapons and furniture, reliefs depicting trees, fruit, flowers and animals, black and white men and Asiatics, and various scenes of peaceable and warlike activity.

The study of Benin's past presented much difficulty, as the natives did not

GIANTS AND THE LOST LANDS OF THE GODS

possess the art of writing; but it was traced back as far as 1140, when the Juju cult was introduced by a king named Eweka. There must, it was thought, have been an advanced culture prior to that date; but where had it flourished, and what was the explanation of features in Benin art that were reminiscent of Greece and India? A curious fact is that Esige Osawe, believed to have been the tenth king, prided himself on having been born a 'white man'. According to tradition he sent messages and gifts to the land of the whites 'beyond the great water' and invited them to visit his country; some of them did so, and remained as traders.

The Latvian ethnologist Ivar Lissner writes in The Silent Past (London, 1963): 'The bronzes of Benin attracted the attention they did because they represented a unique exception among the sculptures produced by other African Negro races. To those endowed with a Western sense of form they appear more intelligible and less alien than the Negro art of the rest of the Dark Continent.

'We now know that the Yoruba, a tribal group of Sudanese 100,000 inhabitants before the First European colonizers arrived on the scene, and that they were not only skilled hoe-farmers and breeders of small livestock but also traders on an extensive scale. Their highly developed handicrafts, cotton weaving, dyeing, pottery, and bronze and brass founding techniques spread beyond the borders of their own territory.

'The chief centre of Yoruba art was Ile-Ife, religious capital, cultural centre and seat of the spiritual head of all the Yoruba. Ile-Ife, which lies about 50 miles from Ibadan in Nigeria, means "land of the origin" and has a present population of 50,000. The only surviving works of the "Ife period" are made either of stone, quartz, granite, bronze or baked clay, because wood carvings have fallen prey to the climate in the course of centuries, Yoruba sculptures found during the past twenty years occupy a unique position in the art of Africa as a whole. In 1938 and 1939 some splendid works of art were unearthed in the palace precincts of the Oni of Ife, most of them sculptures in brass. Brass varies from red to pale gold in color according to the proportion of copper employed. So amazingly lifelike in every detail is one bronze male figure from Tada on the Niger, and so subtle and expressive are the Negroid faces of the Ife Ends, that experts are continually searching for signs of more ancient influence.

'Foreign artists may well have taught in the foundries at the court of the Benin kings... From the purely technical aspect, the brassworks of ancient Benin will stand comparison with the finest European examples, for the works of art in bronze and brass that came from the hands of these native artists were nothing short of masterpieces. Yet, the inexplicable, incomprehensible problem of interrelationship remains.'

The art of the Yoruba and of Benin may be connected with that of the mysterious Nok culture, which flourished over twenty centuries ago and is represented

GIANTS AND THE LOST LANDS OF THE GODS

by a life-size terracotta head dug up in 1954 in Zaria Province, northern Nigeria. The Nok people used primitive stone weapons, and implements and also more sophisticated iron ones, a contrast often found in antique civilizations. It is conceivable that the Nok, Benin and Yoruba cultures were all founded by colonists who intermarried with the natives in ancient times, and that this explains Esige Osawe's dim recollection of his white ancestors. This leads, once again, to thoughts of Mu and Atlantis, and reminds us of another archaeological enigma, that of Zimbabwe.

The Towers And The Phoenix

The ruins of Zimbabwe, in Rhodesia, near Lake Victoria, were accidentally discovered in 1868 by a Boer named Adam Renders. He did not pay much attention, but in 1871 the German geologist Carl Mauch visited the spot and announced that he believed it to be the remains of a citadel of Ophir - the wild country, governed in the tenth century B.C. by a vassal of the Queen of Sheba, which was supposed to have contained the fabulous gold mines of King Solomon.

This view was supported by such scholars as Quatremére and Heeren. It is interesting that the Arab traveller Ibn Batuta, born at Tangier in 1304, refers to the country behind the Sofala coast as Youli, which sounds very like Ophir: his words are: 'From Youfi they bring gold dust to Sofala' (Lissner, op. cit., p. 287). '

Other archaeologists agreed with the British scholar Richard Hall that Zimbabwe was more likely to have been a Phoenician mining centre. However, the Egyptologist David Randall-Maciver brought evidence to show that the ruins were medieval in date, and this conclusion was supported by the archaeologist Gertrude Caton Thompson. The name itself is too recent to shed any light: it is a compound of the Bantu words zimba (houses) and mabgi (stone). But al- Masudi, who visited Africa in 916 or 917, confirms that the city existed then: he declares, 'It is a land that produces gold in quantity and other marvels as well.'

Those who built the walls of the elliptical temple, which are 13-16 feet thick, and of the conical tower (33 feet thick) were clearly not ignorant of civilized arts. They may have come from north Africa, but in the absence of inscriptions it is impossible to be sure. On the other hand, there have been found in' and near Zimbabwe precious objects from many distant lands: pearls and gold bracelets from Arabia, Chinese porcelain at least a thousand years old, implements and works of art from India and East Asia, and jewels whose origin cannot be determined. ,

In the light of discoveries at Umtali and Inyanga, Dr. Caton Thompson and Father Paul Schebesta believe that the people of Zimbabwe were identical with the founders of the Monomatapa empire (the title of the dynasty was originally a name signifying 'lord of the mines'), which ruled from Rhodesia to Mozambique until about 1500. The people were sun-worshippers and their ruler was called 'son of the sun'; he had about 3,000 wives and concubines, but could beget a legitimate heir only on one of his sisters. Many other details bring irresistibly to mind the civilizations of Egypt and pre-Columbian America. The animals depicted on the steatite monuments of Zimbabwe recall the bas-reliefs of India and the New World; the bird carved on top of a pillar, formerly the emblem of Monomatapa and now that of Rhodesia, is none other than the Thunderbird of the Red Indians, the Fire-Bird or the resurgent phoenix of worldwide mythology.

The 13-foot monoliths inside the temple recall the enigmatic monuments of the Hsing-Nu. As Charroux writes: 'Among the ruins, but in a good state of preservation, we find, as at Machu Picchu in Peru, high oval towers like silos, with no aperture in their walls, as though they could only be inhabited by winged beings. At Machu Picchu they are in fact called the "abodes of winged men". We believe these were human beings who possessed the secret of levitation and movement through space, as tradition attests in America, Asia and Africa. It may be that Zimbabwe and Machu Picchu were both inhabited by a race of mankind endowed with knowledge which is a sealed book to us.'

The Malagasy Enigma

We now come to Madagascar, an island which many regard as one of the most significant natural features that have survived from an earth of very different aspect to the one we know. We have already referred to the less than plausible theory that Madagascar is part of a lost continent of Lemuria. We may now briefly consider the theory of Gondwanaland, which in some scholars' opinion provides, inter alia, a link between Madagascar and Zimbabwe.

According to the Italian geologist F. De Agostini, 'Gondwana, a region in the Central Provinces of India, has given its name to palaeo-mesozoic schist and sandstone formations which that region has in common with southern and eastern Africa, Madagascar, Australia and South America. On account of this similarity it is believed that in the palaeo-mesozoic age these areas were united with the Indian subcontinent in a single land mass, which for convenience is called Gondwanaland.'

Studies on the ethnic character of the Malagasies and the fauna and flora of their island suggest that it was once linked to what are now very distant parts of the world. We cannot go into this in detail, but will note that the anthropoid apes, pachyderms and other wild beasts which are found throughout Africa, including Mozambique, do not occur in Madagascar, while species that are found there are characteristic of other continents. The proponents of Gondwanaland believe that it broke up into Africa, Australia and the Deccan (southern India), which was formerly linked with Madagascar. To quote De Agostini again: 'During the Pliocene,

GIANTS AND THE LOST LANDS OF THE GODS

the last period of the Tertiary age, the strip of land between India and Madagascar apparently broke into several pieces; the island broke away from the rest of the Deccan, which floated on oil to join the Asian continent. This is suggested by the chain of small archipelagos between Madagascar and India: the Mascarene Islands, including Réunion, Mauritius and Rodrigues, the Chagos Archipelago, the Maldives and Laccadives.'

Gondwanaland is thus thought to have existed during an era which lasted from 520 to 60 million years, B.C. The German scholar Thor Nielsen believes that America, Africa, India and Madagascar assumed something like their present shapes about 130 million years ago. This was long before Man made his appearance on earth, and we can therefore reject out of hand the theory of Madame Blavatsky, the foundress of theosophy, that there were three-eyed human beings whose joints enabled them to walk forwards or backwards and who, for good measure, were hermaphrodite and oviparous. Ideas of this sort generally rest on ill-digested fragments of scientific knowledge, eked out with a wild imagination. The 'third eye' was no doubt suggested to Madame Blavatsky by the fact that all fossils of Gondwanaland reptiles have a depression, known as the pineal cavity, which undoubtedly points to the existence of such an eye.

This is true at the present day of a 'living fossil' which exists in small numbers in New Zealand, in certain islands of the Cook Strait - a lizard, twenty inches long, known as the hatteria or sphenodon (also tuatara), which has other strange characteristics: it shares its abode with a burrowing seabird, and lays eggs in a parchment-like membrane out of which the young ones hatch some fifteen months later.

There does not seem to be much ground for believing that Gondwanaland had a civilization of its own; but it should be noted that ethnically the Malagasies are clearly of Asiatic origin. This suggests either that Gondwanaland was succeeded by another lost continent, i.e. that known as Mu, or else that the Malagasies came from Asia by sea. The latter alternative seems less probable, since they could not have brought their fauna and flora with them.

GIANTS AND THE LOST LANDS OF THE GODS

CHAPTER ELEVEN
Pangs Of Rebirth

Until a fairly short time ago, there seemed to be no great mystery about the origins of mankind: scientists believed that existing discoveries enabled them to reconstruct in broad lines the story of human evolution and the progress of civilization from the Stone Age to those of Bronze and Iron.

Subsequent research, however, has shown that this was too simple. The new discoveries have complicated the puzzle instead of filling it in, and have made it more incomprehensible than ever. We find evidence, for instance, of high culture in eras which were supposed to have been completely primitive, and other outcroppings of civilization in unexpected places. Running through all this evidence are mysterious traces of similarity and correspondence. The prehistoric scene is forever complicated anew by points of resemblance, contrasts and anachronisms; and the only way to simplify it is by entertaining hypotheses which differ widely from traditional views but are not necessarily absurd for that reason.

If, for instance, we accept the supposition that there were once continents or great archipelagos, now submerged in the Atlantic and Pacific Oceans, we may understand the presence of common features in the history of lands far distant from one another. We may imagine high civilizations destroyed by a natural disaster, the survivors wandering in search of a new home, their efforts to rebuild or to use the remnants of former culture, their attempts to civilize barbarian neighbors - and in this way we may find the answer to many paradoxes.

We are not surprised, at the present day, if we come across a rifle, a gramophone or a pair of field-glasses amongst a group of South American Indians who are still in the Stone Age; nor does it astonish us if these primitive people scratch on a rock-surface the outline of an aircraft that has struck their fancy, or copy as best they can some tool produced in a Western factory, a single specimen of which has fallen into their hands. Why then should we refuse to believe evidence of extraordinary scientific knowledge among the ancient Egyptians, cosmic symbols among the Maltese, hydraulic works at Tyre, skyscrapers' in Carthage

GIANTS AND THE LOST LANDS OF THE GODS

and the amazing structure of prehistoric Jericho?

Jericho Without Trumpets

The Biblical Jericho, whose ruins are about 14 miles northeast of Jerusalem, is one of the most ancient cities of the Near East. Joshua, it will be remembered, stormed and destroyed it after the famous trumpet-blast had overthrown its walls. This story has given rise to theories of secret or ultrasonic weapons, death-rays and the like, but it is more probable that Joshua's ally in the battle for the Promised Land was in fact an earthquake.

The American archaeologist William F. Albright believes that the city was sacked by the Israelites between 1375 and 1300 B.C. This was not the first time, however, that it was visited by a natural disaster: it was already an ancient city, with 7,000 or 8,000 years of stormy history behind it.

We do not know who founded the first city with its walls 16 feet high, or who, when they had fallen, replaced them by others at a height of 23 feet, or who, 4,000 years before the first pyramid, built the huge tower 30 feet in diameter, the oldest known tower in the Mediterranean area. The work must have been done by highly skilled engineers, since even today it is impossible to dislodge a single brick from the ruins. But here is the paradox: this people of master-craftsmen knew nothing of the potter's art - instead of crockery they used stone vessels like our most primitive ancestors.

Their plates and dishes were made of flint; their knives, saws, augers and scrapers were made of carefully shaped flint or obsidian. This is the more remarkable since their houses were not only solidly built, but more comfortable and better designed than those of later periods. They were shaped like halved eggs and probably had two stories, the walls being of oval bricks and the floor of burnt stucco; the corners, as in some ultramodern rooms, were rounded to avoid collecting dust.

The absence of pottery is very unusual. We know that nomadic peoples did not use it because it was too breakable, but it has been shown time and again that as soon as a community became sedentary it began making domestic utensils out of clay. But Jericho is an exception; men dwelt there for thousands of years, baking bricks in the sun, making stucco and using wood for decoration, but without inventing crockery.

The most ancient inhabitants of Jericho, nevertheless, did have a knowledge of clay or plaster. This is shown by the most important finds of the pre-Biblical city, namely ten human skulls on which the features of the dead were modeled, with traces of color that are still visible and with shells for eyes. The skulls were buried under the floors of houses, testifying to ancestor-worship and a belief in life after death. The only other parts of 'the world where this custom is known of is New Guinea, where it is practiced to this day among many tribes. As a means of keeping the dead man's soul alive they cut off his head and draw his features on the skull with chalk, embellished by ritual designs or the warrior's war-paint; here too the eyes are represented by shells.

To explain the absence of ceramics in the highly developed city of Jericho, and other paradoxes of the same sort in different parts of the world, we may resort to an imaginary example. Let us suppose that our world has been torn asunder by nuclear war and that the survivors are painfully struggling to rebuild society. They possess a fair amount of scientific and technical knowledge, but are unable to put much of it into practice; they build houses and towns like the old ones, but it is beyond their power to create gas, electricity and heating systems. Then, as one generation succeeds another, such things are forgotten even in theory, and centuries elapse before men rediscover and reinvent the devices that improved their ancestors' lives. If, then, 9,000 or 10,000 years hence, the archaeologists of a new civilized society come upon the ruins of one of the first rebuilt communities, they will be just as amazed by the absence of electrical appliances as we are by the lack of ceramics at Jericho.

It is clear from this that conventional scientists are in error when they assume that the course of history has been a more or less steady progress from the Stone Age to the nuclear age, with no major interruption or setback.

Assurbanipal, the last great ruler of Assyria (669-626 B.C.), owned a library which, some scholars believe, contained documents dating from before the Flood. One day, pointing to the desert, he is said to have told some sages: 'In ancient times there were powerful cities out yonder; their walls no longer stand, but we have tablets inscribed in their language!'

The tablets in question have not been wholly deciphered. The historian Gérard Heym believes that they contain important secrets, but so far all that has been read from them consists of mathematical data; multiplication and division tables, square and cube roots etc.

Around 1800, the astronomer and mathematician Laplace called into question the accepted view that all science was originated by the Greeks. 'It is curious,' he wrote, 'that the Egyptians did not choose to communicate their astronomical ideas and observations to future ages. But we know the reputation of their priests who imparted knowledge to Thales and Pythagoras, Eurodoxus and Plato.'

In 1962, at Tell Dibae near Baghdad, Iraqi archaeologists discovered a tablet inscribed with what we call Pythagoras's theorem, the work of Babylonians who lived fifteen hundred years before the Greek philosopher's time.

We have already pointed out that, owing to the destruction of so many ancient libraries, it is impossible to form a clear picture of the history of human progress. It must be added that much of the existing evidence has been wrongly interpreted, and that part of it is as obscure to us as a magnetic tape would be to a savage who had never heard of the recording process. As Pauwels and Bergier remark: 'In a timetable issued by U.S. airlines we read: "You may reserve a seat from wherever you like: the booking is recorded by computer, and another computer makes the reservation on the flight of your choice. Your ticket will be perforated to indicate . . ." etc., etc. What would become of a text like this if it were translated, at two or three removes, into an Amazonian dialect by people who had never seen an aircraft or a computer and who did not know the names of American cities?

We must also recall that ancient technology may have achieved results similar to ours by quite different processes. The strange hemispheres of glass and earthenware found by the Russians in Turkestan and the Gobi Desert may be examples of this. The electric batteries of Baghdad remained for years in an obscure corner of the museum, classified as religious objects of minor importance.

To quote Pauwels and Bergier once more: 'Nazi Germany was progressively isolated from the rest of the world from 1933, a period of 12 years only, but in that time German technology diverged remarkably from that of other countries. The Germans were behindhand in research on the atomic bomb, but they developed giant rockets that had no parallel in the United States or Russia. They had no radar, but they developed infrared detectors which were no less efficient. They did not invent silicones, but they created a completely new branch of organic chemistry. In addition to these radical differences of technique, we find differences in the realm of theory that are more extraordinary still . If a gulf of this kind can develop in a mere twelve years, in the modern world with all its means of communication, what must it have been as between ancient cultures? and how can our archaeologists form any idea of the sciences and techniques, the philosophy and state of knowledge among the Mayas or the Kyhmers?'

If, in addition, we take into account the fearful cataclysms that have occurred on earth in past ages, our position may be compared to someone trying to reconstruct a complicated game and possessing only the torn and charred remnants of a pack of cards whose values and significance are unknown to him.

Baalbek, The Sea Of Porphyry

At Baalbek in the Lebanon, it will be remembered, there is a colossal stone which the Soviet scholar Mikhail Agrest believes to have been part of a space travel station. A series of earthquakes, culminating in a fearful disaster in 1759, reduced what was once a metropolis to 'a chaos of ruined splendor, a great sea of marble and porphyry, columns and capitals'. Even the ruins are prodigious; the outer ramparts, for instance, are composed of huge stones 400 feet long, each weighing some 8,000 tons. Viewing them, we can understand the Arab legend

GIANTS AND THE LOST LANDS OF THE GODS

that Nimrod, the 'mighty hunter' and king of Lebanon, sent a tribe of giants after the Flood to rebuild the citadel. According to another legend, the original founder of Baalbek was none other than Cain himself, who built the city as a refuge from the wrath of God and created a race of giants to live within its walls.

At all events, Baalbek is a most ancient city, and the mystery of its origin is not solved by the Roman, Greek and Phoenician tombs that surround it. We know a little more of Ugarit in Syria, which was destroyed by a mysterious catastrophe in the fourteenth century B.C., but here again the subject is full of riddles. Abimilki, king of Tyre, wrote to the pharaoh Amenophis IV: 'The royal city of Ugarit has been wasted by fire. Half the centre is burnt, and the other half is no more.' The traces of fire are clear enough, but this cannot have been the sole cause of the ruined houses and walls, the chaos of stone blocks, some of which have been hurled for considerable distances. The havoc does not appear to be due to an earthquake either, and as for war, ancient Mediterranean weapons could not bring about devastation on this scale. It is curious, too, that Troy, Knossos and other great cities were destroyed at the same epoch.

The ruins of Ugarit, at Ras Shamra near Latakia, were discovered in 1929 by the French professor Claude Schaeffer. It was one of the oldest strongholds of the Canaanites, who lived in the Promised Land before the children of Israel, and whom the Greeks later called Phoenicians. Ugarit must have been a city of great splendor. As Lissner tells us (op. cit., p. 31), 'Extensive residential areas were laced by straight streets intersecting at right angles. There were multi-roomed houses equipped with baths and elaborate sanitary installations.

Rainwater flowed into the city along fine stone canals and there was an admirable drainage system. Walled fountains installed in the courtyards were faced with handsome stone tiles and their central access sheltered by small roofs supported on four legs. Large stone tubs were placed by the fountains to receive water. Living and sleeping quarters were probably situated on the second story, and were approached by stone stairs of considerable width.'

At Ugarit, too, we find religion associated with monoliths (representing spaceships, according to some theories): the god El is seated on a stone pillar, and his consort Asheratian is symbolized by a sacred post of a type found among many prehistoric peoples.

A divinity who played a prominent part in Canaanite religion is Baal, after whom Baalbek is named and whose cult was fiercely attacked by the Old Testament prophets. His name became equated with 'Lord' and figures in that of the demon Beelzebub (lord of flies).

The Canaanites preserved such a lively memory of the catastrophe which befell the earth 11,000 years ago that, as one of their tablets reveals, they never felt certain that winter would be followed by spring.

GIANTS AND THE LOST LANDS OF THE GODS

At Ugarit, too, we find evidence of remarkable geographical links. At a depth of 25 feet (there are five strata of ruins corresponding to as many civilizations, the oldest being of measureless antiquity) there have been found pins, bracelets and necklaces from the Caucasus, Crete and the Balkan peninsula, and also from further afield in Asia and the Rhine valley. All things considered, we would not dismiss the theory that the Canaanites and their successors the Phoenicians were the most favored heirs of some great civilization of the remoter past. As time went on their buildings became less monumental and more practical, but they remain worthy of admiration.

Tyre, one of the most famous Phoenician cities, was situated where the Lebanese town of Sur now stands at the tip of a small peninsula. The ancient city extended further west and was separated from the mainland by a strait over a mile wide: this was ascertained in 1934 by the French scholar Poidebard, whose theory, based on aerial photography, was later confirmed by underwater exploration. Tyre was transformed from an island into a peninsula by Alexander the Great, who besieged the city in 332 B.C. and, for the purpose, built a mole 200 feet wide across the strait; in course of time this was joined to the seabed by the accumulation of sand and other deposits. The mole, impressive though it is, was less majestic than the architecture of Tyre itself. The soldier and historian Anianus (second century A.D.) tells us that the walls were 165 feet high and that, owing to the lack of ground space, men lived in houses of four or five stories. This was confirmed by the submarine observations, which also showed that the moles on the south side of the harbor were extremely modern in construction. One of these still lies intact on the sea bottom; it is 26 feet wide and 250 feet long.

Three thousand years ago the Phoenicians diverted the stream of Ras el-Ain, which rose at Palaetyros on the mainland (a city stretching for 8 miles, opposite the island), so as to irrigate their fields at the far end of the peninsula. Water from the spring was taken by boat to the island, where huge reservoirs were built, as it had no sweet water of its own. There must also have been an underwater passage between Tyre and the mainland, since otherwise the city could not have withstood a 13 year siege, from 585 to 572 B.C., by Nebuchadnezzar II (the Great) of Babylonia and Nineveh. However big the reservoir, it could not have sustained a population of 25,000 for that length of time.

The Phoenicians and their successors created other marvels at Carthage, where they also built six-story houses. At the height of its prosperity, according to the Greek geographer Strabo, this city had a population of 700,000. The Carthaginians were the first people in history to mint coins of metal, to float joint-stock companies and to issue public loans. They possessed a formidable army noted for its 'artillery', and by way of defense against enemy catapults there were huge underground bunkers, each capable of sheltering 300 war elephants.

GIANTS AND THE LOST LANDS OF THE GODS

CHAPTER TWELVE
The Wandering Masters

Harking hack to still more ancient times, it will be worth our while to give a rapid glance to the impressive ruins which bear witness to the work of 'wandering masters', primitive craftsmen and architects who spread throughout Europe the arts of civilizations that are lost in the dawn of history.

We may begin with Malta, as there is no part of the world richer in megalithic remains than this tiny island. They include titanic monuments, innumerable tunnels with three-story underground chambers, the purpose of which is not known, and wells that descend into the bowels of the earth. There are also mysterious tracks, from three and a half to five inches wide; these are certainly of great antiquity, as some of them underlie tombs of the Phoenician period and deposits that date back further still. It has been inferred from studying them that Malta must once have been larger than it is now and connected - together with its neighbor islands of Gozo, Comino and Filfla - to Italy or Africa: otherwise the tracks would not lead out to sea, or break off at the edge of precipices that must have been caused by some convulsion of nature.

This conclusion is confirmed by geology and by excavated bones of deer, hippopotami and elephants. Men were living in Malta 100,000 years ago, as is proved by human teeth discovered near Valletta with the remains of dwarf hippopotami (a long extinct species); yet no human skeleton has been found on the islands dating from the same period as the great megalithic works. It was hoped that some remains might have come to light in 1915, when Sir Themistocles Zammit first began to excavate the typical Maltese system of semi-oval chambers built in pairs and divided by a corridor.

But no traces were found of the unknown engineers, either between the walls or under the flooring of these Cyclopean temples (if such they were). However, as Lissner tells 'us (op. cit., p. 63):

'In the Mnaidra sanctuary, which consisted of two massive oval buildings, mountains of neolithic vessels were found. Seen from the air, this veritable miracle

GIANTS AND THE LOST LANDS OF THE GODS

in stone looks like a half-finished game played by giants.

'A similar impression is created by the Gigantia, which comprises the ruins of two enormous temples on the neighboring island of Gozo. Blocks and slabs of stone must have been brought there from miles away, for heavy building materials were not available in the immediate area. Many of the Gigantia's upright stones are over 16 feet high, and one is more than 26 feet long and 13 feet wide.

'Equally astonishing is the size of several monolithic pillars and slabs in the ruins of Hagiar Kim ("standing stones"). One of the pillars there is over 16 feet high, and one of the slabs nearly two and a half feet thick, 10 feet high and 23 feet long. It would be impossible to load such a weight on to a modern truck without using elaborate technical equipment.'

As Lissner also observes (op. cit., German original, p. 65), 'It is a most interesting fact that the creators of these gigantic works were evidently acquainted with navigation. The neolithic civilization of Malta must have maintained contact with every part of the ancient world. This is shown by the discovery on the island of objects made of obsidian, jadeite and nephrite, none of which stones are native there. The ivory used by the builders was probably imported too, as elephants had long been extinct on the island.'

Were these builders giants or the descendants of giants? The lower part of a female statue of great height, discovered at Hal Tarxien, tends to confirm that they were, yet the stone implements that have been discovered are not of unusual size. Perhaps they belong to a later era, when the race of 'giant engineers' had been wiped out or relapsed into barbarism. The scale of the Maltese buildings is hard to reconcile with the complete absence of metal tools on the island. Several buildings contain rectangular stone blocks almost twelve feet square, surrounded by walls on three sides and bordered by a stone step. Each block had five holes in it, and in the right-hand corner of the step was a sixth. The holes may have had something to do with the numerous round stones of different sizes which were found near by. Some think that these may have been thrown at the, holes for purposes of divination, while others, mindful of the legends of space-travel, suggest that they were used to symbolize the replenishment of an engine with nuclear fuel.

In general there is more and more support for the idea that 'magic' ceremonies are a childlike imitation of operations and processes that struck the imagination of primitive peoples. For example, a group of Mexican Indians who once witnessed the 'bombardment' of clouds with chemicals to produce rain took to throwing wooden models of aeroplanes at the sky in order to achieve the same result.

On the other hand, the stone marbles may have been unconnected with the holes. They may be akin to the large round stones that are nearly always found amongst Maltese ruins, and we may note that in the jungles of Guatemala and

GIANTS AND THE LOST LANDS OF THE GODS

Costa Rica stones of widely different sizes are found in patterns representing constellations and stellar systems.

Another curious fact is the prevalence in Malta of the spiral design which, in many parts of the globe, signifies the Universe. It is a matter for speculation how the peoples of the ancient world came to adopt this sign, corresponding as it does to the actual configuration of most of the 'islands' of cosmic space.

The Nuraghians

The existence of gigantic monuments in both Malta and Sardinia has led many to suppose that the two islands are closely linked; but this is baseless, as Sardinia was uninhabited for thousands of years after the construction of Malta's mysterious underground passages. If the 'wandering masters', preserving what was left of their heritage after centuries of migration, hardship and contacts with barbarous peoples, did eventually land upon the Sardinian shore, this must have happened in fairly recent times.

At all events, Sardinia's first human inhabitants came there from the East in the Fifth millennium B.C.; they remained close to the seashore, living in straw huts or caves, or else moved on to the European mainland. Another influx from Asia arrived 2,000 years later; this people merged with the Shardena, also from Asia, from about 1400 B.C. onwards. It is to the second race of immigrants that we owe the nuraghi or nuraghs—stone towers with inward-sloping walls, like a cone with its top cut off. There must originally have been over 8,000 of these; 6,500 survive in a ruined state, some of them small, others up to 66 feet high, with walls varying in thickness from 6 to 16 feet. As Lissner tells us (op. cit., p. 92): "They were neither sanctuaries nor burial places, but seem rather to have been defensive positions used by people who were exposed to continual attack. Sardinia was never politically united in its entirety, and its regional groups or tribes were ruled by chieftains who used these towers as houses and strongholds. In the course of time the towers were extended to form larger fortified systems where several hundred people could take refuge in an emergency. The island was repeatedly attacked by Ligurians, Phoenicians, Carthaginians and, eventually, Romans, so the Sardinians were obliged to 'fight and fight again, even though it was always a losing battle.

'Even if an enemy succeeded in penetrating a tower, he was still in mortal danger. The buildings were provided with doors opening on pitch-black cul-de-sacs and all manner of pitfalls and blind alleys from which the lurking Nuraghians could pounce with spear and sword to cut down the unwary intruder.

'A flat roof installed at the summit of the tower for pur- poses of observation and defense and surrounded by a parapet, probably of wood, together with projecting attachments for the launching of stones and missiles, made any assault a

GIANTS AND THE LOST LANDS OF THE GODS

perilous undertaking. The Sardinians' defensive bays were the first military installations of their type in the Mediterranean.'

The Nuraghians had no form of writing, but their origins are revealed by place-names which have remained unaltered through the ages and point back to the Altai, Mesopotamia, Azerbaijan, the Caucasus, Nuristan (the home of the Kahrs in Afghanistan), Kazakhstan, and even Sinkiang and Tibet. In external shape the nuraghi recall Zimbabwe and ancient Peru, while their internal design reminds us of Tiryns and Mycene.

As is frequent in antiquity, the holy places of the Nuraghian civilization were generally close to springs or on high ground; all ancient peoples were impressed by the starry vault, the elemental powers of nature expressed in weather changes, and the connection between water and fertility. To quote Lissner again (op. cit., p. 95): 'The "cosmic mountain" is an age-old Mesopotamia idea. The Altaic peoples believed for many thousands of years that certain trees and poles led upwards to the supreme being, that they represented the centre of the earth and that the Pole Star stood above them. The Greeks rediscovered the cosmic mountain in Olympus, the men of the Old Testament in their Mount Sinai. Tall mountains whose summits pierced the clouds were held to be the abode of the gods in ancient China, Japan, Finland, Crete, Phoenicia and the entire Mediterranean area. The Tower of Babel and the ziggurats of Mesopotamia were nothing other than symbols of the cosmic mountain.'

The upholders of the 'stellar hypothesis' maintain that all these beliefs are based on real facts. Sacred trees and poles, like obelisks, may be regarded as astronautical symbols; mountain sanctuaries, ziggurats and pyramids represent our ancestors' yearning to reach the sky, the home of flesh-and-blood divinities who, as space travelers, actually visited our earth. As for the sanctity of running water, members of this school associate it less with fertility than with the curative or other properties of radioactive springs. The primitive inhabitants of Central and South America give the name 'mirror of the gods' to pools in which soporific plants have their roots; in Sardinia, as elsewhere in the world, there are springs which have the reputation of curing blindness. Lissner speaks of one such in Mongolia which is also famed for curing paralysis; the surrounding country is said to be littered with thrown-away crutches and spectacles.

If there is any link between Malta and Sardinia, however, it consists in the fact that in both islands building materials have been transported over rugged country, sometimes for incredible distances. But this phenomenon is one which confronts archaeologists in every quarter of the globe.

A Buried Space-Traveler

There are other surprises to be found in Europe itself. Our own continent,

GIANTS AND THE LOST LANDS OF THE GODS

which we may think we know as well as a much-thumbed school book, is in fact a storehouse of inexhaustible mystery. Beneath our seas and riverbeds, our cities and countryside and perhaps our very homes, the soil is full of astounding records in which history and science-notion are mingled.

In 1924, for instance, at Glozel, a sleepy hamlet near Vichy, archaeologists discovered a collection of bricks and inscribed tablets, two paring-knives, two small axes and two rocks bearing inscriptions that have been shown to date from 10,000 or 15,000 years ago. Further digging revealed a store of pre- historic treasures: stone implements, other rocks with inscriptions and carving, curious vessels that look like skulls clad in space-helmets - so that one has been called 'the space-traveler' - and over a hundred tablets in a script which has not been deciphered but which contains letters similar to our C, H, I, I, K, L, O, T, V, W, and X. Another remarkable discovery in France were the 'carvings at Lussac-les-Chateaux in the department of Vienne, which also go back 15,000 years.

Stéphane Lwoff, one of the archaeologists who dug them up in 1937, remarked with astonishment that the men, women and children were shown wearing hats, shoes, trousers and skirts exactly like those of the present day.

We should mention, above all, the paintings and carvings at Lascaux in the Dordogne, were discovered by chance in 1940. As the Italian journalist Loris Mannucci wrote, 'These works of art are 25,000 years old, yet they show such perfection in their design, color-scheme (especially red, yellow and black) and sense of movement as to upset many of our ideas concerning prehistoric man. The paintings were made at different times, and it is problem how these artists managed to construct a scaffolding so as to paint the roofs of caves that were several yards in height.' Nor is this the only problem at Lascaux; there is the familiar one concerning the artists' source of light, and also the question how they protected their work from atmospheric damage. As Mannucci says, 'the carbonic acid exhaled by tourists in only fifteen years has gravely' damaged the marvelous wall decorations and has begun to disintegrate the rock in many places.' Whether the caves were a sanctuary or a dwelling-place, they must have been full of people for a long time; yet the pictures survived until our own day, when two or three decades have sufficed to spoil them notwithstanding all precautions.

'To prevent the destruction of this inestimable treasure, elaborate arrangements were carried out at a cost of tens of millions of francs. The air was purified 'and kept at a uniform temperature, by the same method as in submarines; bronze gates were installed to keep out the external atmosphere; the temperature and humidity were regulated by electronic devices; a special system was used to eliminate carbonic acid gas; and only after all this were the caves opened to the public.'

The Lascaux paintings remind us of a fabulous past, with horses 'reminiscent' of Asiatic work, as Mannucci says, or the figure with a bird's head on a man's body, being crushed by a wounded bison. It would seem that the masters of Lascaux came from Asia or even from the legendary Mu, bringing with them an astounding knowledge of artistic technique and also the memory of giants such as we behold in Saharan carvings. The birdman, moreover, is surely symbolic of a race of beings who could fly through the air and perhaps throughout space, who, as Agrest, Kazantsev and Zhirov suggest, may have come to earth from another planet and eventually lost the battle for supremacy with monsters of earthly origin.

Another mysterious civilization flourished 5,000 or 6,000 years ago, on the site where London now stands; a few bronze plates in the British Museum are all that' commemorates its existence. They were discovered by Professor Reginald Williamson, who, with limited means at his disposal, excavated patiently for many years in search of a pre-Celtic metropolis. Eventually he came across some lance-tips, 'then the foundations of houses, then various objects of considerable artistry: ornaments, battleaxes, curious square blades and swords. We have already mentioned the discovery, in southern England, of a representation of a sword like that of the Achaian warriors; can it have been the work of inhabitants of this prehistoric London? It is quite possible, as Professor Williamson's finds exhibit both Nordic and Mediterranean features, so that a variety of hypotheses are justified.

We have indulged in a good deal of bold speculation, but there is a point beyond which even the basis for this is lacking, and only imagination can carry us further. As Lissner writes (op. cit., p. 176): 'Any settlement has to survive a number of storms, has to thrive and eat its way into the ground if it is not eventually to be blotted out by the passage of time. Myriad traces of human existence have been swallowed up by the past, and where natural catastrophes, floods, tidal waves and earthquakes have taken their toll, the sites of whole cities can easily become lost beyond all hope of rediscovery.'

The Mona Lisa of Tartessus

These words are illustrated only too well by the story of Tartessus in southern Spain. This ancient city has not been swallowed up by the ocean or shattered and engulfed by earthquake; it is within easy reach, did we but know where, and we have quite full descriptions of it, yet its ruins have never been located.'

Near the estuary of the Guadalquivir is an extensive marsh which in ancient times was a lake, the Lacus Ligustinus. The river flowed from it in three channels, and one of the islands in the estuary was apparently the site of Tartessus, a wealthy city which the German authority Adolf Schulten identified with Atlantis as described by Plato. For various reasons we do not think he was right, but it may be that this city-state—the only one in the West prior to Roman times—was once a colony of

GIANTS AND THE LOST LANDS OF THE GODS

Atlantis, perhaps at the extremity of its dominions where they bordered on those of Mu.

The chronicles that have survived enable us to get some idea of the civilization of Tartessus and the surrounding country between 1,100 B.C. and the disappearance of the city in about 500 B.C. Its rule extended over the whole of Andalusia, including the sites of Jerez, Seville, Cordoba, Granada, and also Murcia and Cartagena. The nobles were fond of hunting and travel, arts and sciences; according to Justin, the third-century historian, King Gargoris of Tartessus was held to have invented beekeeping. (We mention this only for curiosity's sake; the same claim was made for many heroes of antiquity.) But there is no trace today of the city itself, except for the great squared stones which the Romans used to build other cities, and which were said to have come from the walls of Tartessus.

On the other hand, many objects have been dug up which testify to the cultural level of the 'Spanish Atlantis' and make its secret all the more fascinating. On 30 September 1958 workmen on a building site on the hill of El Carambolo near Seville came upon a priceless hoard consisting of 21 pieces of pure gold: a necklace, two armbands, two pendants and 16 plates which had once formed a crown or belt. Some of the motifs on these plates and other ornaments resemble those found on Mycenean vases, ivory gaming-boards from Megiddo (an ancient Canaanite city) and mural paintings in the Assyrian and Syrian palaces of Khorsabad, Arslan Tash and Tell Barsib. Other similar designs have been noticed in a tomba in Cyprus, in the statuettes of the Cauca Valley (western Colombia) and a celebrated Inca jewel found at Cuzco, Peru.

A bottle or vase in the form of a cockerel, now in the Cadiz Museum, is similar to one at Chimbote, also in Peru. Greek and Phoenician influence is clearly visible in a bronze amphora discovered in 1953 near Don Benito in southwest Spain: Professor Antonio Blanco, of the University of Seville, who is also a curator at the Prado, has described this as the finest antique work of art to have been excavated in the Iberian peninsula. Many other relics of Tartessus might be mentioned, but we will confine ourselves to two of the most important. One is a shaped marble coffin, found at Punta de la Vaca near Cadiz: it contained the remains of a nobleman of the Fifth century B.C., whose effigy on the coffin showed him as a majestic bearded individual. According to Lissner Cp. 180): 'P. Bosch-Gimpera states that it is of genuine Phoenician workmanship but betrays the stylistic influences of Egypt and ancient Greece. Was the prince brought posthumously from Phoenicia in one of the famous ships of Tarshish? Was he a king of Gadir who wished to be interred in his native soil? We may never know, but we can at least see in this magnificent piece of workmanship the links that once bound the seagirt fortress of Cadiz to the ancient Orient.'

A still more enigmatic survival of Tartessus is the 'lady of Elche', sometimes

GIANTS AND THE LOST LANDS OF THE GODS

known as the Spanish Mona Lisa. This is a limestone bust, 21 inches high, which was discovered in 1897 near Alicante. Professor Blanco suggests that it may represent a local divinity. It is reminiscent of Greek and Punic art, but Americanologists see in it a clear resemblance to certain well-known finds in Colombia and Honduras, and above all to Chalchihuitlicue, the Aztec goddess of rain.

Lissner concludes his excellent account of Tartessus (German original, p. 184) with the following passage: 'The fourth-century historian Avienus writes of the decay and desolation of places that he knew from his own experience, and decline in population and their final downfall. And I realized here in southern Spain how many once flourishing cities may lie buried under these fertile plains. They have all vanished, turned to dust or sunk beneath the waves of the Atlantic. But every now and then the earth, grudgingly and casually as is Nature's wont, reveals to us treasures which tell of the art and craftsmanship, the gold and riches of the ancient inhabitants of Tartessus.'

It is unlikely that the ruins of this fabulous city will ever be located, but if they are, they may provide us with the key to many secrets. For Tartessus stood at a confluence' of many ways, leading from Europe, Africa, Asia and even America—ways that remind us of the legendary cradles of civilization, Mu and Atlantis.

GIANTS AND THE LOST LANDS OF THE GODS

CHAPTER THIRTEEN
The Mystery Of Atlantis

'In front of the mouth which you Greeks call the Pillars of Heracles there lay an island which was larger than Libya [i.e. Africa] and Asia together; and it was possible for the travelers of that time to cross from it to the other islands, and from the islands to the whole of the continent over against them which encompasses that veritable ocean.' (Plato, Timaeus.)

These words, placed in the mouth of an Egyptian priest, are part of Plato's description of the lost continent of Atlantis, contained in his dialogues the Timaeus and the unfinished Critias. The details in Plato, incomplete as they are, have provided material for a flood of speculation that shows no signs of stopping, and already comprises some 25,000 volumes and articles by the hundred thousand.

Occultists and pseudo-scientists of all kinds have put forward innumerable theories and have situated Atlantis in many parts of the earth, including Palestine and India. But the problem has also attracted the attention of genuine scholars, some of whom have erred not from lack of judgement but on account of doubtful evidence: for example, 'the French authority Berlioux and the Germans Frobenius and Hermann, misled by ruins of uncertain age, located the lost continent respectively in the Atlas Mountains, in Tunisia and on the Gold Coast.

We need not accept every detail of Plato's account, but his geography may well be more or less right; the 'other islands' may be the West Indies, and the continent beyond would thus be North America. A less familiar piece of evidence is provided by Theopompus of Chios (fourth century B.C.), a Greek historian whose works have been mostly lost but who is quoted by Claudius Eleanus of Praeneste (170-135 B.C.). The following is E. Georg's summary of an imaginary dialogue, composed by this author, between Midas, the mythical king of Phrygia, and the wise centaur Silenus.

'The centaur described to the king the fabulous wealth of a land named Meropis, "far beyond the Pillars of Hercules, on the further shore of the Ocean" This sunny clime, according to Silenus, had been the home of the First men, the Meropids, whose name derived from that of Merope, daughter of Atlas. The soil was wonderfully fertile, yielding three crops a year. The cities were huge and splendid, and gold and silver were so plentiful that they were not valued more than other metals. The king in amazement asked the sage how these things were known in Greece. Silenus replied that in remote times the Meropids had sailed to the land of the Hyperboreans, the "people beyond the north wind" (perhaps the British Isles, Iceland or the Faeroes), and that through the Hyperboreans the tale had reached Greece and Asia Minor.'

Professor Paul Le Cour appears to come closest to the truth when, having studied the relief of the seabed, he places Atlantis between the two Americas on the west and Europe and Africa on the east; however, the latest theories suggest that it was not a single land mass but consisted of a mainland surrounded by archipelagos. Some theorists of the past have identified the whole Atlantis with outlying portions of its territory: e.g. Father Kirker in Mundus Subterraneus (1678), who believed that the Canaries and the Azores were the last of its peaks to remain unsubmerged. Two geologists from the German Geographical Institute, Drs. O. Yessen and A. Schulten, agree that these islands were part of Atlantis but maintain that they belonged to its periphery.

Atland's Last War

Pastor Jurgen Spanuth, on the other hand, suggested in recent times that Atlantis lay in the North Sea, its only visible trace being the island of Heligoland. He recalls that Plato's account purports to be based on a visit to Egypt by the Athenian lawgiver Solon, which took place about 560 B.C. Solon was shown the inscriptions, then about 600 years old, which Rameses III had had carved on the walls of the temple now known as Medinet Habu. Sonchis, priest of Thebes, translated them into Greek for Solon, who wished to use them in a poetic composition; however, he died a year later and his notes eventually came into Plato's possession.

The inscriptions at Medinet Habu relate that the Atlanteans undertook a major expedition southwards and occupied the whole of Greece except Athens and Attica, which they were unable to capture. They landed in Crete and Cyprus, pushed on into Asia Minor and attacked Egypt by land and sea; they succeeded in forcing the Nile estuary with a large fleet, but were finally defeated.

Greek historians tell us that there was an invasion of this kind by Hyperboreans from the North Sea, who allied themselves with the Italians and Libyans and crossed the Mediterranean. This suggests strongly that the Hyperboreans and Atlanteans were the same people. The Egyptian mural paintings, moreover, depict the invaders with winged or tufted helmets and round shields, while their womenfolk wore long tresses; these characteristics are confirmed by abundant archaeological evidence from Sweden and northern Germany.

GIANTS AND THE LOST LANDS OF THE GODS

The Egyptian chronicles say that the Atlanteans used copper and bronze weapons as well as iron ones. The most ancient iron weapons found in central Europe date from about 1200 B.C., which is just the time of the presumed Hyperborean campaign.

The inscriptions of Rameses III describe how the Atlanteans came 'from the islands and the mainland on the great circle of water', 'from the ends of the earth' or 'from the ninth arc,' this last expression, according to Egyptian geography which was adopted by the Greeks and Romans, meant the region between 52 and 57 degrees north latitude. The old historians state that in this region the day lasts for 17 hours, which is in fact true of the 54th parallel. Pliny the Elder also mentions that the ninth arc passes through 'Hyperbores'et Britanniami.

The Egyptians state further that the royal stronghold of the Atlanteans was on an island which they describe as follows: 'High and as if shorn with a knife, rising direct from the sea, with red, white and black rocks, rich in copper and copper ore.' The only island in the world which answers this description is Heligoland. However, the citadel and the chief temple of Atlantis were not on the island itself but 'on a low hill, 50 stadia away on the opposite mainland'. By means of submarine diving at the point indicated, Pastor Spanuth identified the hill and the ruined buildings, together with a well-paved road.

The Atlanteans who marched across Europe and invaded Egypt came from southern Sweden, Denmark and north Germany. Rameses' inscription names them as the Pheres (Frisians), Saksar (Saxons), and Denen (Danes), with their allies the Tursha (Tyrrhenians), Sekelesa (Siculi, Sikels), Sardana (Sardinians) and Vasasa (probably Corsicans). Why was this great coalition formed, and why did it hurl itself against Egypt and Asia Minor? Not from mere lust of conquest, but because of a famine, following on natural disasters, which afflicted the whole of Europe and other parts of the world in 1225 B.C. These disasters are described on the walls of the temple at Medinet Habu and are confirmed by many geological and archaeological discoveries; according to Professor Stechov, they amounted to 'the most fearful catastrophe in the last 4,000 years of human history'.

Many thriving kingdoms were desolated, and Egypt itself, according to Rameses III, was in a parlous condition when he ascended the throne. But the waters of the Nile soon restored it to prosperity, and it thus become a natural source of booty for the Germanic and Italian tribes.

Pastor Spanuth's studies are the most recent attempt to trace the origins of Atlantis, and are certainly based on more than fancy. The old name of Heligoland, moreover, was Atland, which immediately brings the lost continent to mind.

On the other hand, there are Amerindian legends of an 'Aztland' which was involved in a catastrophe much earlier than that of the Medinet Habu inscriptions; and the proponents of a Nordic Atlantis have difficulty in explaining the refer-

GIANTS AND THE LOST LANDS OF THE GODS

ences by Plato and Theopompus to a land beyond the Pillars of Hercules.

Many other ancient texts speak of a continent submerged beneath the Atlantic Ocean: commentators on Plato refer to three large islands dedicated to Jupiter, Pluto and Neptune (the last called Poseidonis) and seven lesser ones sacred to Proserpine, or else of a single island dedicated to Neptune and a number of smaller ones. These accounts do not lay claim to exactitude, based as they were on oral tradition at a time when Atlantis no longer existed. However, the Indian Puranas also refer to a 'great and powerful land' in the Atlantic—the date of this reference is not known, but it must be of great antiquity since it was apparently written at a time when the land in question still existed. Many other Indian texts could be quoted: the Mahabharata refers in passing to 'seven great islands of the western sea, an empire with the city of the Three Mountains as its capital, which was destroyed by Brahma'.

Other Asian documents state that the 'empire of the western sea' was swallowed up by the waves following some natural calamity, and this is confirmed by American traditions. The name Aztland or Atlan appears in the Nahua word nahoatlan, signifying island ('land amidst the waters'), which many tribes use to denote their ancestral home east of America, a land 'where the sun rises and which is now covered by water'.

Our verdict on Spanuth's theory must therefore be that, while we cannot accept that Heligoland and Atlantis are identical, it is quite possible that the last Atlanteans of northern Europe had their headquarters in the region he describes.

Noah In America

If we are not mistaken, Noah's Ark was 'discovered' for the first time in the 17th century by the Dutch traveler Jan Struys, who published a book embellished by an elegant drawing of the Ark poised on the top of Mount Ararat. Since then, many amateurs and visionaries have followed in his footsteps.

In 1948 a Turkish peasant named Sukru Arsena claimed to have seen the Ark amid the eternal snows; several expeditions set out to verify his story, but when the frustrated explorers got back to base they found he had prudently disappeared.

In the same year a Dutch youth of 16 named Hans Roozen had a dream in which he saw the Ark, with its full complement of animals, resting on Mount Ararat at a height of 13,500 feet (perhaps Noah inspired him with the exact figure), and, as he put it, 'he was at once seized by the idea of making himself famous'. In 1949 an American named Aaron Smith went in search of the Ark but failed to find it; meanwhile Roozen appealed to various scholars and newspapers without success.

In 1955 his dream received partial confirmation from a French merchant, Ferdinand Navarra, who made three journeys to the spot and brought back a piece of oak which he said was part of the Ark's bowsprit, the remainder of the vessel being completely covered by rocks and ice.

Roozen was not specially interested in archaeology as such; his main desire was to 'discover some treasure, such as tools or utensils dating from Noah's time'. He put in time as a song-writer, while continuing to cherish the idea of sending an expedition equipped with a dozen helicopters. Before this took shape, however, a momentous discovery was made accidentally in 1960 by S. Kurtis, a major in the Turkish Air Force. This officer was instructed to photograph the slopes of Mount Ararat, which rises to nearly 17,000 feet, and at a height of 6,500 feet he noticed a curious object of an elongated oval shape, embedded in a mass of volcanic lava.

When his photographs were examined in Ankara the experts, whether on patriotic or scientific grounds, immediately thought of the Ark, and they were encouraged by finding that the length of the unknown object agreed with the Biblical specification of 300 cubits. Its width was about 160 feet and the depth of the hull, as far as could be judged from the shadow, about 20 feet. The photographs were sent to Professor Arthur Brandenburger, an aerial survey expert in the service of the U.S. government, who declared that he would stake his reputation on the fact that the object was a ship. If this is so, and if it could be dislodged from the imprisoning lava, we might learn, amongst other things, the answer to the riddle of Noah and his 'opposite numbers' in every part of the globe.

In the Sumerian legend of Gilgamesh, for instance, the corresponding figure is Utnapishtim, who is warned by Ea, the water god, that the human race is to be destroyed in a flood because of its sins. He is told to build an ark to save himself, his family and a pair of animals of each species.

In Greece it is Deucalion, king of Phthia in Thessaly, who, together with his wife Pyrrha, was saved from the wrath of Zeus by the timely warning of his father Prometheus. After the flood the couple landed on Mount Parnassus and were told by the Delphian oracle to 'cover their heads, take off their garments and throw behind them the bones of the Great Mother'. Realizing that this referred to stones, they obeyed the oracle; from the stones thrown by Deucalion there sprang up men, and from those thrown by Pyrrha, women.

The Mayas have a similar legend, which includes the phrase, 'The Great Mother Seyda was among the records of the destruction of the world'. The identity of the Mayan 'Noah' is not quite clear, but one manuscript represents him as Quetzalcoatl, the god-king known under different names, throughout pre-Columbian America.

The Quiché Mayas of Guatemala do not give a clear account of how the earth was populated after the deluge; their epic, the Popol Vuh, say, 'We do not know how they came from the sea . . . it was as though the sea had never been.' How-

GIANTS AND THE LOST LANDS OF THE GODS

ever, the Macus Indians of Amazonia tell us with confidence that the miracle was performed by Maconen, 'king of the floodtime'.

The Aztecs (who also had a 'Tower of Babel' myth identical to ours) possessed a legend of the Flood which agrees closely with those of the Old Testament and of Gilgamesh; not even the dove is missing. Here is the tale:

'In the Valley of Mexico there lived a pious man named Tapi. One day the Creator of All Things appeared to him and said: "Build a boat to live in, and take your wife with you and a pair of every animal there is. Make haste, for the time is at hand!" Tapi did as he was told, despite the insults and mockery of his neighbors, who thought him mad. Hardly had he finished when it began to rain. It rained without ceasing, the valley was flooded, men and animals fled to the mountains, but they too were submerged. The earth became one great ocean, and the only creatures left alive were those in Tapi's boat.

'When it stopped raining, the waters began to sink and the sun came out again. Tapi sent forth a dove: it did not return, and Tapi rejoiced because he understood that the dove had found a patch of dry ground to rest on.'

Many traditions regard the flood as a divine punishment, which is not surprising when we consider the scale of the disaster and the cosmic events which probably brought it about. Thus, ancient Bolivian legends speak of a great flood 'sent to punish men's pride and insolence'. The Sioux Indians tell us that 'time disappeared under the waters'; a mythical bison holds the flood at bay, but it loses a hair once a year and a leg at the end of each of the four ages. 'When it has lost all its hair and its legs, the great waters will engulf the World.' Some ethnologists suggest that this animal represents an ancient divinity in the form of a bull, and that its gradual destruction is the work of an evil spirit determined to undo humanity.

We may notice as a curiosity that the Hawaiian Noah is called Nu-u and the Chinese one Nu Wah, while in the Sierra Parima between Brazil and Venezuela there is said to be a dead city of Ma-Noa, signifying 'the waters of' Noah'.

It is not surprising that many peoples should have preserved the myth of a man and his wife symbolizing the few survivors of an unexampled catastrophe, or that the rescue of these two should be attributed to divine intervention. But the agreement of names and details is so close that we can only explain it by supposing that men were able to communicate over long distances immediately after the Flood. And this links up with the opinion of those authorities who believe that the last remaining centres of old, vanished civilizations continued to exercise an important influence on cultural development in the Mediterannean basin and in America and Asia, until a new catastrophe supervened.

GIANTS AND THE LOST LANDS OF THE GODS

Submerged Continents

According to Plato, who lived from 427 to 347 B.C., Atlantis was engulfed by the ocean about 9,500 years before his time. This does not agree with the Rameses III inscription but is confirmed by other texts, and scientific research has shown that there must in fact have been two catastrophes.

The general view of the authorities who connect the Flood with the disappearance of huge continents in the Atlantic and Pacific areas is that this event took place 10,000 or 12,000 years ago. The Austrian geologist Otto H. Much claims to have ascertained from astronomical data that the exact moment was 8 P. M. (Eastern American time) on 4 June of the year 8496 B.C. It is a remarkable fact that the ancient Americans began a new time-cycle very close to this date, in 8498 B.C., since, according to their tradition, a cataclysm had occurred shortly before, bringing to an end the 'third age of the world's history'.

Plato, at the end of the Critias, thus describes the degeneration of the people of Atlantis and Zeus's resolve to punish them:

'For many generations, so long as the inherited nature of the God remained strong in them, they were submissive to the laws and kindly disposed to their divine kindred . . . But when the portion of divinity within them was becoming faint and weak through being oft times blended with a large measure of mortality, while the human temper was becoming dominant, they lost their comeliness through being unable to bear the burden of their possessions . . . And Zeus, the God of gods, who reigns by law, desired to indict punishment upon them, to the end that when chastised they might strike a truer note. Wherefore he assembled together all the gods into that abode which they honor most, standing as it does at the centre of all the universe and beholding all things that partake of generation; and when he had assembled them, he spake thus: "... ."

Here the text breaks off, but we learn from the Timaeus that 'at a later time there occurred portentous earthquakes and floods, and one grievous day and night befell them, when the whole body of warriors was swallowed up by the earth, and the island of Atlantis in like manner was swallowed up by the sea and vanished.'

This was the same deluge as the 'great waters' of which the Vedas speak; it was described to Zarathustra by Ahura Mazda, the Persian god of light, and was predicted, as the Mahabharata tells us, by the first fish to its creator Manu, demigod and father of mankind, who in due course escaped the deluge like Noah, in a ship which he had built. The Biblical Flood was not, as some have suggested, confined to the Near East but was a universal event, as the above and many other traditions bear witness.

The hieroglyphs on the Mexican pyramid at Xochicalco, deciphered by A. Le Plongeon, refer to the destruction of a land situated in mid-ocean', whose people were 'killed and turned to dust', while the Troano Codex in the British Museum

GIANTS AND THE LOST LANDS OF THE GODS

speaks of a catastrophe which 'obliterated the continents of Mud and Mu'. This seems to refer to Mu and Atlantis, as is confirmed by other Maya fragments; one of these, translated in 1930 by the Brazilian philologist O. M. Bolio, reads as follows: 'The disaster befell on the eleventh day of Ahau Katun . . . it rained fearfully, ashes fell from the sky and the water of the sea engulfed the land in one great wave . . . the heavens collapsed, the earth subsided, and the Great Mother Seyda was amidst the records of the destruction of the world.' This refers to Atlantis, while the obliteration of Mu is described as follows in a pre-Maya document of about 1500 B.C.: 'In the year 6 of the Kan, terrible earthquakes began on the 11th of the month of Zas and continued till the 13th of Chuen. Mu, the country of clay hills, was destroyed; it was raised twice into the air and then disappeared in one night, with earthquakes never ceasing. At many places near the sea, the land sank beneath the water and rose up again more than once. Finally the whole land split up into many parts and was engulfed with its 64 million inhabitants.'

Thus the description in the Purana of the disappearance of a remote Atlantic continent is matched by ancient American accounts of the destruction of the erstwhile 'queen of the Pacific'.

What The Flood Was Like

Here is Much's imaginary description of the Flood and of the cosmic catastrophe which caused it.

'Northeastern Siberia, at 1253 hours on 5 June of the year 8496 B.C. just minutes before the planetoid crashed into the earth.

'The sun is high in the heavens; close to it, invisible in the blue, are Venus and the new moon. The trees on the edge of the virgin forest throw short shadows. Dark green moss grows in profusion at the foot of huge pines, firs and larches. A murmuring stream, emerging from the forest, flows across a large expanse of meadow with rich grass, ferns and flowers.

'Suddenly a noise of crashing branches is heard from within the forest, and the treetops begin to sway. A herd of mammoths is making its way to the river.

'It is now 1447 hours . . . two of the mammoths suddenly stop, halted in mid-rush by an invisible, terrifying force. The asteroid has already hit the earth, but it has taken an hour and 47 minutes for the ejecta to be felt in this part of Siberia. The ground is shaken, at first by a faint tremor and then violently. A groaning noise is heard from the forest; a huge pine creaks, bends and crashes down among the mammoths. Terrified birds dart to and fro.

'The sun appears to be dislodged from its proper place; it dances about in the heavens, then stops, glides slowly towards the horizon and stops again; the shadows of the great beasts, the trees and undergrowth flicker and lengthen, the river's noise becomes louder. The shadows remain long, and the sunshine loses its heat.

'After the earth tremors cease, the mammoths start moving again. They paw the ground uneasily, rock their massive heads from side to side, dig at the earth with their tusks. Slowly they become calm once more, and resume feeding. It has grown cold. Some hours pass during which nothing happens.

'It is now 7 hours and 53 minutes since the asteroid fell. The mammoths are still in the clearing outside the forest, drinking from the stream and pulling leafy branches off the young trees. The evening sun casts a feeble, yellowish light. Suddenly a dull roar is heard in the distance; it swells and approaches with lightning speed, drowning the sound of the river and the birds, and then explodes in an interminable thunderclap.

'The leader of the mammoth herd raises his proboscis, but the sound of his trumpeting is drowned by the appalling din. He gallops off at full speed, the others following him. The earth reechoes to their trampling, but the noise from the sky is louder. The strongest of the mammals, panic-stricken for the first time in his life, rushes wildly about the forest uprooting trees and trampling down the undergrowth. '

'But the mammoths' flight is short-lived. Their chief collapses as if struck by lightning, and dies before his body hits the earth. Within a few seconds all the rest of the herd are dead too, and so is every other animal species in Northern Siberia—mammoths by the thousand, Woolly Rhinoceroses, tigers, foxes and martens, birds and reptiles . . . What had happened?

'Six thousand miles away from that Siberian glade, at 1300 hours on 5 June 8496 B.C., a heavenly body had crashed into the earth with appalling violence in the southwestern part of the North Atlantic. This planetoid, a mere six miles in diameter, was a midget compared to our globe, but the effect of its fall was catastrophic; it broke through the earth's crust and produced the greatest natural disaster in history!

As it says in the Book of Revelation: 'I saw a new heaven and a new earth: for the first heaven and the first earth were passed away; and there was no more sea.' The huge, threatening moon had disappeared from the heavens, and a moonless age had begun. The words of scripture suggested to Horbiger that Atlantis owed its origin, millions of years ago, to a satellite falling into the earth, and, as we have just seen, Otto Much believes that Atlantis may have been destroyed by a similar catastrophe—an asteroid, attracted by the unusual conjunction of the earth, the moon and Venus, hurtling towards our planet and exploding on its surface with a force equal to that of 15,000 hydrogen bombs.

According to Much, who produces a formidable array of astronomical and geological' evidence, the asteroid appeared from the northwest and shot through the earth's atmosphere at a rate of 10-12 miles per second. At a distance of some

GIANTS AND THE LOST LANDS OF THE GODS

250 miles from the earth it began to turn red; soon it caught fire owing to atmospheric friction, and was so bright as to blind anyone who looked at it. By the time it reached a short distance above the Atlantic, the surface temperature of the asteroid was 20,000 degrees Centigrade. At this point it exploded. Its crust broke into a shower of enormous meteors which fell on North America, while its core split into two fragments, weighing together 500 million tons, which struck the earth at about 30 degrees west and 40 north, near the Azores Plateau in the middle of the Atlantic Ridge. This is a region abounding in submarine volcanoes, where the earth's crust is only 10-12 miles thick as compared with 25-30 miles elsewhere. The ocean bed was split all the way from Puerto Rico to Iceland, and pandemonium ensued.

'With an apocalyptic roar', Much continues, 'a fiery column shot up into the sky, composed of burning magma, poisonous gases and volcanic debris. For thousands of miles around, everything was burnt or became incandescent. The ocean began to boil; great masses of water turned into steam and, mixed with dust and ashes, were borne eastward by the great winds that sweep the Atlantic. After a terrible day and night, the royal island of Atlantis disappeared beneath the waves.'

Many facts go to confirm this theory of a cosmic onslaught on the earth: e.g. the craters formed, 10,000 or 12,000 years ago, by great meteorites in Central and South America as well as Georgia, the Carolinas, Virginia and the ocean bed off Puerto Rico. These bodies hit our planet at the very time when a convulsion of Nature created Niagara Falls and thrust upward the peaks of the Andes so that they became one of the highest mountain chains in the world. This period, too, saw the melting of the ice-cap which had covered Scandinavia, the British Isles and most of continental Europe, while Siberia was plunged into arctic cold. The reason for the change in Europe's climate, according to Much, was that the Gulf Stream from now on began to wash its shores, no longer impeded by the mass of Atlantis in between. '

In 1934 a search made on the ocean bed in the place where Atlantis should have been brought to light fossils of small land animals and pieces of lava cast forth by land volcanoes, not submarine ones.

To quote further from Much's account: 'The wound inflicted on our planet did not take long to cicatrize in a dark, hard crust. But the "grievous day and night" of which Plato speaks had very nearly extinguished all life upon earth. Even before the great clouds of steam swept through, the air, the exploding magma had released poisonous gases, invisible to the eye, which brought rapid and painless death to every creature.

'Northwestern Siberia, about 60 hours after the asteroid's collision with the earth . . . Dead mammoths bestrew the open ground and the forest with its shattered trees. Their thick fur is blown about by the storm-wind; the sun's rays are opaque and milky. There is no sound except the bubbling of the river and the howl of the wind, driving the heavy clouds before it over the dead landscape.

'Finally the sun is completely clouded over. The roar of the storm abates, and for two or three seconds there is silence. Then the flood begins. A torrent of water, mud and ashes pours from the sky, and in a few minutes the animals' carcasses are covered by grey-black slime. It pelts down remorselessly, flooding the open country, silting up the river and uprooting enormous trees. For six days and six nights water, mud and cinders rain down on the corpses of animals and on dying vegetation. One dark torrential shower follows another until the whole region is submerged.

'Along with the rain comes the cold. The force of the asteroid's impact thrust northern Siberia 2,000 miles nearer the pole. The deluge freezes to ice, imprisoning hundreds of thousands of dead mammoths and woolly rhinoceroses.'

While Atlantis was engulfed by the abyss that opened between America and Europe, Mu 'might well have been destroyed by the eruption of all its volcanoes, which are said to have been very numerous; even today there are 336 active volcanoes in the Pacific, out of 430 in the whole world. The seaquake caused by the fall of the asteroid must have made every crater erupt throughout the globe, throwing up a dense cloud of ash which hid the sun and precipitated terrific rains.

In Europe and northern Asia alone, it is reckoned that in six days there must have fallen more than 20,000 million tons of water and 3,000 million tons of cinders; the average depth of the flood would have been 100 feet.

Utnapishtim, the Babylonian Noah, describes how 'the south wind roared, the waters roared against it, the mountaintops were covered and the rail fell on all mankind. Torrents of rain fell for six days and six nights; on the seventh day there was a calm as though after a battle. The sea became smooth and the tempest ceased. All mankind was drowned in mud, and the earth was a wilderness without features.'

Seaports In The Andes

At a height of 11,500 feet, a curious whitish streak runs along the side of the Andes for over 300 miles. It consists of the calcified remains of marine plants, and is irrefragable evidence that the slopes in question were once part of the seashore. Scholars ascertained that the streak must have been exposed to view for thousands of years, but for a long time they resisted the obvious conclusion, although Alexander von Humboldt produced other striking evidence 150 years ago.

Near Bogota there is an imposing plateau called the 'giants' field', full of huge fossilized bones. Here von Humboldt saw the remains of the mastodon, a creature nearly as big as the mammoth but with short, stumpy tusks and a trunk almost as long as its body. Various species of this animal inhabited Europe, Asia

GIANTS AND THE LOST LANDS OF THE GODS

and the Americas. It preferred marshy areas with plenty of vegetation, and it is unthinkable that the mastodon could have climbed up to a bare, rocky plateau situated, as it now is, 6,500 feet above sea level. The creatures must have died in their natural coastal habitat, which was laid waste and pushed up to its present altitude by the cataclysm which destroyed Atlantis. The petrification of the bones, moreover, could only have been due to the action of sea-salt.

Further confirmation was provided when scholars devoted their attention to the dead cities of the Cordilleras. It became clear that some of the buildings had no raison dé tre in their present situations; what was the sense of placing cities on inaccessible peaks, palaces on jutting-out shelves of rock, or fortresses on hillsides which ,afforded no possibility of defense? This was borne in on the explorers of Tiahuanaco, in Bolivia, a majestic assemblage of ruins near Lake Titicaca; here the conquistadores were told the Inca legend of the Creation, which runs as follows:

'After a fearful catastrophe which destroyed the world, Viracocha Pachacayachi, the creator of all things, began by forming giants from the earth and afterwards made man in his own image; this happened in the time of Darkness, of the adoration of the Setting Moon, Ka-Ata-Killa. Thousands of years later there was another cataclysm, from which only a shepherd escaped with his family, and he, as a thank-offering, built Tiahuanaco in the space of a single night.'

Legends apart, some of the first explorers believed that Tiahuanaco was only a thousand years old, while others assigned to it an antiquity of several millennia. While the debate was still unresolved it became clear, to the general surprise, that the city was not a mountain metropolis but a properly equipped harbor town which, with a large surrounding area, had suddenly been elevated to a height of 12,500 feet.

Lake Titicaca, it should be observed, is noted for its high salinity, while many of the lakes round about are completely salt: Uyuni, Coipasa and Chiguana in Bolivia, Atacama, Punta Negra and Pedernales in Chile, and Arizaro, Pipanaco and Hombre Muerto in Argentina. Along the shore of Titicaca runs a whitish-yellow line consisting of saline deposits, which has been exposed for more than 10,000 years.

When originally formed it must have been horizontal, whereas now it runs at an angle to the water level. It is thus clear that the land was not only thrust up to its present altitude, but was tilted in the process.

In addition, archaeologists discovered that the great temple-pyramid above Tiahuanaco was not damaged by an earthquake as had been originally thought, but that its construction was suddenly interrupted. According to German experts, the last stone was placed in position in 9000 or 9500 B.C. — exactly the time of the destruction of Atlantis as recorded by Plato.

GIANTS AND THE LOST LANDS OF THE GODS

CHAPTER FOURTEEN
The Realm Of Forgotten Knowledge

If we question scholars regarding Amerindian societies still older than the Incas and Aztecs, we shall get no clear reply; but the traces that exist, enigmatic on the one hand and highly eloquent on the other, are sufficient to justify an imaginative reconstruction of their history, involving once again the lost continent of Atlantis.

The people of what are called the 'archaic' Central American societies cannot be identified with any race known to us. We possess a vague and tentative knowledge of an era which archaeologists date between 3000 and 1000 B.C., when two cultures existed in Mexico, known from the places where their remains were discovered as the cultures of Zacatenco and Ticoman.

These remains are few but of great interest. The ceramics are primitive, but lively and amazingly 'modern' in style. Figures of bearded men, women with carefully dressed hair, elegant ballerinas, mothers with children in their laps, girls with puppies, youths playing ball-games and strange masked apparitions. Not only the style, but the range of' subjects is noteworthy. A people of cave-dwellers, hunters or peasants living in mud-huts would not have depicted such elaborately dressed women, or men wearing hats that are curiously like those of our own day.

The unknown artists remind us rather of a party of modern castaways on a desert island. Living in primitive dwellings, wearing animal pelts and eking out an existence by hunting, fishing and tilling the soil, they beguile what leisure they have by modeling symbols of the civilized world: an old general, a girl dressed up to kill, a famous dancer or a gentleman in a top hat. And, in 'actual fact, the Zacatenco people may indeed have been castaways, lone survivors of an unimaginable disaster.

We find here a striking agreement with what Plato says in the Critias about the survivors of Atlantis: 'The stock that survived was a remnant of unlettered mountaineers. They and their children for many generations were themselves in

GIANTS AND THE LOST LANDS OF THE GODS

want of the necessaries of life; their attention was given to their own needs and all their talk was about them, and in consequence they paid no regard to the happenings of bygone ages. In this way, then, the names of the ancients have been preserved, but not their works.'

The Zacatenco people, and their few fellow survivors on the American continent, must have made shift to recreate a civilization which could only be a pale shadow of the one they had lost. They found refuge near the lake of Texcoco, but immediately after the disaster they must have suffered grievously from the torrential rains. As Pierre Honoré writes in In Quest of the White God (London, 1963): 'It rained for days, for weeks-one single never-ending cloudburst. The surface of Lake Texcoco rose, the huts on the banks were flooded, the people fled up to the mountains. It kept on raining, the lake's surface rose every day, and every day they had to climb higher up the mountains to save their lives. Anyone who stayed in the valley was lost.

'The rain did not abate. Streams came flowing down the mountains, then they turned into rivers, torrents of water, mud and stones. Frightened to death, the people crept into miserable shelters they had made from leaves. The animals sought refuge with them. They had left their huts, their utensils, everything they possessed, and now it was all lying at the bottom of the lake, which had risen by sixty feet and was now filling the whole Valley of Mexico.' Centuries passed.

'The people who had lied from the Flood had come back. Their descendants were still telling tales about it, as if it had happened in their own lifetime. It took 500 years for the water to subside and the lake to sink to its former level.'

The precious ceramics were in fact discovered in a thick stratum of dried mud by the American archaeologist Zelia Nuttall, who excavated the area in 1900. This was an exact parallel with Sir Leonard Woolley's discovery of the remains of Babylon, where a similar stratum was due to the same cause, namely the universal deluge.

The American survivors of Atlantis set about working and building, and enjoyed some generations of relative calm, disturbed only by earth tremors. Then came another disaster: the eruption of the great volcano of Ajusco. A river of molten lava poured down from Mount Xitla into the Valley, destroying everything in its path. Here, in the home of the Ticoman civilization, men had erected a pyramid. This was too tall to be swallowed up entirely, and today two-thirds of it are still to be seen above the ocean of solidified lava.

What was the significance of this pyramid? Some say it symbolized the mountain on which the race of Ticoman had found salvation; others, that it was a placatory representation of the volcano, and that human sacrifices were performed on it; others again, that it expressed a notion of hierarchy and aspiration towards heaven. Our own view, farfetched though it may seem, is that the pyramid was a character-

GIANTS AND THE LOST LANDS OF THE GODS

istic and universal form of building in the pre-diluvian age, and that the survivors of Atlantis and Mu went on erecting pyramids for reasons of half-understood tradition, with which new superstitions came to be associated. At all events, throughout pre-Columbian America we find the same type of step-pyramid with seven grades as the Egyptians built at Saqqara and Memphis, or the Babylonians and Sumerians between the Tigris and the Euphrates.

The lava from Mount Xitla engulfed an area of 32 square miles, and the remains of a notable culture, of which we know very little, are still buried beneath a layer some 20-25 feet thick. The age of this layer has been disputed; geologists now think it dates back more than 8,000 years. Of greater interest, however, were the statues, figurines and vessels which were manifestly too old to belong to the Indian civilizations previously known and which, as we have seen, showed a high degree of artistic perfection.

The Sages Of Olman

It should be mentioned here that many Amerindian societies trace their origin from the fabulous realm of Olman ('country of rubber')—an earthly paradise rich in rubber-trees, cacao and all kinds of fruit, marvelous birds and much gold and silver, jade and turquoise. Its fortunate inhabitants, we are told, wore fine clothes and exquisite ornaments, with rubber or leather sandals. They worshipped an earth-goddess and a moon-goddess, possessed 'knowledge that has been forgotten' and had a 'mighty sage' for their king.

Nineteenth-century archaeologists were not thinking of Olman when, on the coast of the Gulf of Mexico, they began to find objects related to no known culture: statues, statuettes and enormous heads with curious features, half human and half feline. Later, about 1910, a small jade figure in the same style was found near San Andrés Tuxtla. This had a date inscribed on it in characters like the Mayan glyphs, and could thus be referred to the year 162 B.C. Scholars now advanced the hypothesis that all these finds belonged to the civilization of the Olmecs, the legendary inhabitants of Olman. This culture had certainly existed for centuries when the jade figure was made, though before it there were earlier civilizations still. But the Olmecs left a profound impression on most, if not all, of the Mexican races that succeeded them.

After the jade figurine was found, many expeditions set out to discover the Olmecs' capital, and in 1930 Matthew W. Stirling located it at La Venta, an island in the middle of a swamp. Here he found the remains of walls, with a pyramid in the centre of a large complex of buildings. Then, at a depth of 23 feet, he came upon a mosaic of chips embedded in asphalt, a technique used in Crete and Caldea. He also found niches containing statues, high chairs and altars covered with reliefs in which jaguars' heads predominated. The altars were made of stone blocks weighing 20-50 tons; this stone was brought from the Tuxtlai volcanoes, a distance of 80 miles as the crow flies, across the lake by which La Venta was once surrounded. We do not know how it was transported, but certainly the Olmecs had methods which do not square with our notions about the technical backwardness of ancient peoples.

Evidence of the connection between La Venta and the coastal sites came to light when Stirling discovered a number of stone heads, one of the smallest of which is 6 feet tall and 18 feet in circumference; others reach a height of 8 feet. There were no bodies attached to these heads, and this provides a curious link with the mystery of Easter Island in the remote Pacific. The plinths supporting the heads, on the other hand, are very similar in design to those found at Tiahuanaco, and at Pachacamac in Peru. There are differences of style between the Olmec heads, those of South America and the Easter Island ones, but given their size and the enormous effort of making them, they clearly point to the existence of similar traditions and beliefs.

Another curious fact about the Olmec heads is that the physiognomy—setting aside the deformation due to the admixture of catlike features—is unlike that of American Indians or any other known race except some inhabitants of ancient Egypt.

Were these men from outer space or astronauts from Atlantis? Some have gone so far as to suggest that the curious headgear seen on some statues is intended to be a space-helmet; and they quote one of the Easter Island fragments which speaks of 'flying men in hats'.

The Olmecs were acquainted with the stele and the pyramid, both typical features of Mediterranean culture; they shared with Egypt various symbols such as the ankh (a key-like cross, signifying life after death) and the use of ritual axes with openwork blades carved with figures of men and animals. As Honoré points out, these and other similarities - the use of asphalt and jade, the passion for feline heads, and a type of script which we find also in Crete - strongly suggest a connection between the Olmecs and the Old World. But here again there is a paradox, since when the Olmecs are first heard of in Mexico, many of these features had ceased to exist in the Mediterranean countries; the civilization of Crete, for instance, had been extinct for 1,500 years. We are thus obliged to suppose that the Olmecs took them over from an intermediate civilization, and may not this have been Atlantis?

One of the earliest civilizations that sprang up under Olmec influence is represented by a complex of ruins near Mexico City, known by its Aztec name of Teotihuacan. We have no written documents of this civilization, and the ruins of its capital were covered by humus and vegetation when the first Spaniards arrived. It is one of the most extraordinary sites of ancient America, and many of its fea-

GIANTS AND THE LOST LANDS OF THE GODS

tures are unparalleled elsewhere in the world. There is something mysterious and unearthly about its deserted streets, which inspire a sense of beauty and terror. As we contemplate the imposing ruins from an aircraft, it is difficult not to feel as though we were surveying an unknown planet.

Here too the scene is dominated by pyramids, one dedicated to the sun and another to the moon. The base of the former measures 740 feet by 725 feet, which is the same as the Cheops pyramid; its height, 215 feet, is half that of the Egyptian one. It is hard to believe that these figures are a mere coincidence.

Another curious link between Teotihuacan and the Mediterranean is the religious symbol resembling a butterfly, corresponding to clay objects in the shape of a bow that were found at Knossos in Crete. In many parts of the world the butterfly denotes the human soul, or life after death, and this may be the case with the Cretan relics. As to the belief of the Olmecs, there is a legend that the body of the moon-goddess lay, eternally slumbering, in a casket of glass hidden in a crypt under the pyramid that bears her name.

Teotihuacan, according to story, was not built by ordinary mortals, but by gods, demigods or white giants. We need not believe, however, that giants had anything to do with its construction, which probably took place between A.D. 100 and 300. The city was sacked by the Toltecs in 856, but before disappearing it influenced two other important civilizations, those of the Mayas and the Zapotecs.

Dancing Space Travelers

Cortés's diaries tell of fierce battles between the Spaniards and the Zapotecs, a warlike people armed with gigantic spears, who were not completely subdued by either the Aztecs or the European conquerors. In the first-century A.D. they occupied the valley of Oaxaca in southern Mexico, where the archaeologist Alfonso Caso, after a lengthy search, discovered the ruins of their first capital, the 'city of temples', Monte Alban. Later they abandoned this capital for another named Mitla, with an impressive colonnade which recalls that at Chichén Itza (Yucatan) and also those at Knossos and Tiryns, the latter of which dates from about the fourteenth century B.C. Another remarkable discovery was a statue of a squatting naked man with a turban, whose features, dress and attitude were strongly reminiscent of ancient Egypt.

Among the finds at Monte Alban are the reliefs known collectively as the 'Dancers' Gallery', showing men in the attitudes of some mysterious ballet. They are wearing what look like earphones or space-helmets, together with space-suits, gauntlets and curious footwear with turned-up points; fastenings are visible on the arms and thighs. These figures are in a quite different style from others produced by the Zapotecs. This people still survives in the Oaxaca province, and over 100,000 still speak the language. But they have lost their old splendor, and

GIANTS AND THE LOST LANDS OF THE GODS

the ancient spirit only seems to revive during festivals, when the descendants of great warriors put on the rich cloaks and feather headdresses of their ancestors.

A word should be said about these headdresses, which we rightly regard as typical of the Red Indians but which were also worn by many other ancient peoples. Professor Marcel Homer has pointed out that they were common in ancient Egypt, where the style recalls that still found in Brazil, and Pierre Honoré has made a striking comparison between two frescoes, one representing a prince of Knossos in Crete and the other an Indian nobleman from Palenque in Yucatan. The turban, on the other hand, is hardly ever seen in America today, although it was worn there for many centuries, by the Zapotecs and many other peoples; it also adorns the stone giants of Tiahuanaco. Columbus tells of meeting Indians in colored silk turbans, and Father José de Acosta (1539-1600) also reports them from Peru. The conquistadores were startled to find in America what they regarded as typically Moslem headgear, but the turban was in fact worn, many centuries before Mahomet, by the Hittites, Babylonians, Egyptians and Israelites.

Several other cultures flourished in Mexico at the same time as the Zapotecs. The first with whom the Spaniards came into contact were the Totonacs, whose city Cempoala was destroyed by the conquerors; it was situated on the Bay of Campeche, north of the present Vera Cruz, and was built some time between 1200 and 1520. Previously the Totomacs had a much larger city, one of the biggest in ancient Mexico, named Tajin or Tajén, which means 'lightning'. The tales concerning it were disbelieved by many scholars until, in 1935, it was discovered at the end of an arduous jungle expedition by the intrepid archaeologist Garcia Payon. The ruins consisted of a colonnaded building and a huge and a small pyramid —not, this time, the Egyptian type with smooth sides, but the classic Asian niche-pyramid with little square recesses built into the walls of its steps. As Pierre Honoré says, the larger pyramid clearly shows East Asian influence:

'Both in its structure, and in being a niche pyramid, it is very similar to the pagodas of the ancient Burmese city of Pagan. The ornaments of the Tajén style, especially on clay vessels, are almost indistinguishable from the late Chou style of China in the Fifth or fourth century B.C., and this is also true of the finds at Paracas in Peru, which again show the interlocked dragons with short, sickle-shaped wings. The round mirror of China was also found in the Tajén civilization, but made of pyrites, whereas in China the material was bronze.'

In other respects Totonac art shows affinity with that of Teotihuacan, while it has a unique feature in the stone figures known as palmas, shaped like a triangular prism and adorned with reliefs on the back; these are reminiscent of Greece, Egypt, Mesopotamia and further east. In general the Totonac remains are strangely evocative of many different parts of the world, and we cannot help thinking of Atlantis and the other great continent, submerged under the Pacific, which is said

GIANTS AND THE LOST LANDS OF THE GODS

to have connected America with Asia and Oceania.

The civilization of the Zapotecs and Totonacs was not completely destroyed even when the Nahua hordes invaded Mexico from the north; the newcomers imposed their cruel and bloodthirsty religious rites, but in other ways they were assimilated by their victims, and it was they who collected and preserved the treasures of a past that would otherwise have left no records.

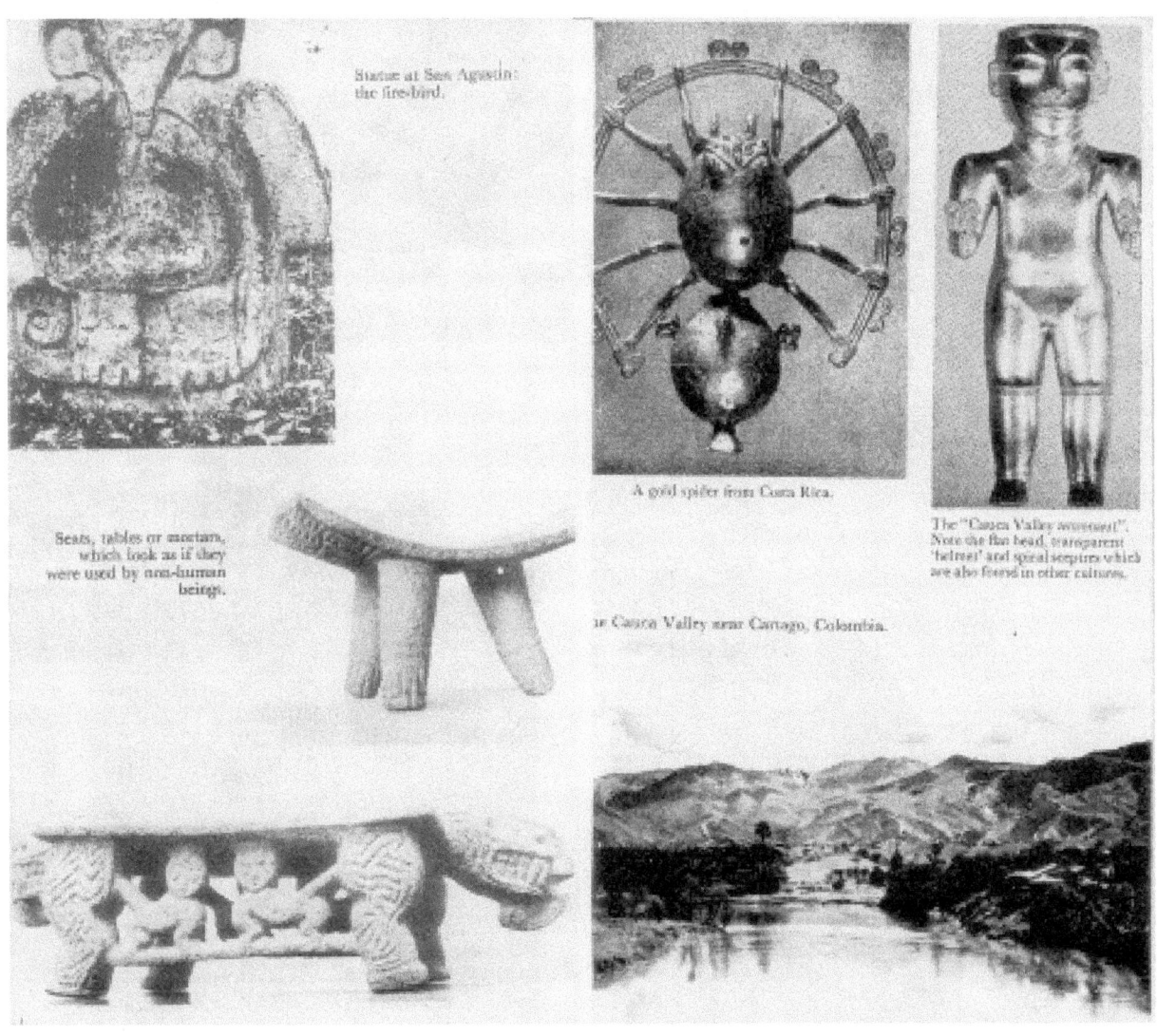

Statue at San Agustin: the fire-bird.

A gold spider from Costa Rica.

The "Cauca Valley monument". Note the flat head, transparent 'helmet' and spiral serpents which are also found in other cultures.

Seats, tables or mortars, which look as if they were used by non-human beings.

Cauca Valley near Cartago, Colombia.

GIANTS AND THE LOST LANDS OF THE GODS

GIANTS AND THE LOST LANDS OF THE GODS

CHAPTER FIFTEEN
The White Gods

The inroads of Nahua peoples from the north took place in the seventh or eighth century A.D., which was a crucial period for Mexico. The first great empire founded by the newcomers was that of the Toltecs, from 856 to 1174; one of their rulers was the famous Quetzalcoatl, said to have been a white-skinned, bearded monarch.

We should remember that it was the Toltecs who built an imposing temple dedicated to the 'god of the morning star' (Venus), which has been discovered on the site of their capital, Tula or Tollan. This city was destroyed in 1168 by a fresh wave of invaders, the Chichimecs, who were in turn supplanted by the Aztecs.

The mysterious planet Venus, and legendary white men— how often we encounter these in pre-Columbian America, and how often they are linked with tales of a lost land where the sun rises, and where there is now nothing but water'. The key legend, according to some, is that of Quetzalcoatl, the fifth Toltec monarch, whose reign began in 977. He is described as son of the sky god Mixcoatl ('cloud-serpent')' and the earth-goddess Chipalman (flying shield'). Quetzalcoatl came from the east and taught men all kinds of knowledge, gave them wise laws and made the crops flourish; during his reign the maize grew higher than ever before and the cotton-plant yielded colored fibers (which we know to be true). He taught mankind to live peaceably, not to kill even animals and to live on vegetable food. But the golden age did not endure; a demon captured the royal sage and made him perform all sorts of ignoble acts. Overcome with shame, Quetzalcoatl left Tula for the seashore and there burnt himself to death; his heart rose to heaven and became the morning star.

In the opinion of many scholars, this legend may be interpreted as follows. Upon Atlantis there descended one day a race of beings so advanced that they seemed like gods (Mixcoatl) in the eyes of the primitive earth-dwellers. They were borne on a slender spaceship (the cloud-serpent) and mingled with the people of earth (Chipalman), whom they raised to a high level of civilization. From Atlantis

GIANTS AND THE LOST LANDS OF THE GODS

the new race spread to America, where they likewise civilized the natives until Atlantis fell into decay and barbarism (the demon). Only by means of sacrifice (Quetzalcoatl's suicide) and by elevating their hearts and minds to Venus, whence the astronauts came, can the men of earth hope once more to achieve better days.

Silver Snakes

'My messengers reported that, having walked for some twelve miles, they came upon a village with about a thousand inhabitants. The natives greeted them joyfully, carried them shoulder-high to their finest houses, kissed their hands and feet and gave them to understand that they knew the white men had come to them from the abode of the gods. About fifty of both sexes begged to be allowed to accompany my men to their heavenly dwelling.'

Episodes of this kind are not unusual in travel memoirs and adventure stores; many a white explorer in the heart of Africa, South America or some other primitive region has been greeted with wild enthusiasm and mistaken for a descendant of the gods. This may simply be due to the natives' surprise and awe at the different color of the white man's skin and hair, or the magical devices with which he is equipped. But on the occasion quoted above, which comes from the memoirs of Columbus himself, the amazement of the natives had a different cause. When the Spanish messengers reached their village on 6 November 1492, they already knew that white men existed and were anxiously awaiting their visit, which for centuries had been linked in their imagination with everything that had made them happy and prosperous.

In this still unchristened continent of America, the Indians worshipped gods who were white and bearded, although they themselves had dark complexions and almost no facial hair. Such a god was Kon Tiki Illac Viracocha of the Incas, whom the Mayas called Kukulkan or Kukumatz; among the Toltecs and Aztecs he was called Quetzalcoatl, and among the Chibchas, Bochica, As we saw, the name Quetzalcoatl was given to the fifth king of the Toltecs, but there is a blend here of history and legend; it was originally the name of the 'white god' and was also a title conferred, from one generation to another, on successive high priests' of the Toltecs.

Kon Tiki means 'son of the sun'; Illac, 'lightning'; Viracocha, 'sea-foam'; Quetzalcoatl, 'flying serpent'; Kukumatz, 'heart of the sea'; and Bochica, 'shining white cloak'.

Do not all these names suggest fantasies of men rising from the foam or descending from the clouds, borne by glittering 'silver snakes'; and may we not imagine them to have been astronauts from distant worlds, who landed first upon Atlantis and afterwards made their way to America and other parts of the world?

Some may dismiss all this as legend; yet may not legend have a basis of truth, and does it not outlast other records by centuries and even millennia? How many people who are not scholars can remember specific facts of Roman history; yet who does not know the stories of Rhea Sylvia, the she-wolf, Romulus and Remus? In just the same way today, everyone in Central and South America is familiar with tales about the 'children of the sun'.

Pedro de Cieza de Leon, a soldier-priest and one of the principal chroniclers of old Peru, tells us that a bearded white man is said to have appeared on the shores of Lake Titicaca long before the foundation of the Inca empire: his name was Tiki Viracocha and, like Quetzalcoatl, he taught men useful arts and commanded them to love one another and abstain from violence. Other Peruvian chroniclers, such as Polo de Ondegardo and Sarmiento de Gamboa, report similar legends and add that the hero and his companions built a huge, majestic city full of marvels. We may remember that Kon Tiki is a Polynesian divinity as well as an American one, and we may imagine a remote age in which the mysterious 'white lords' dominated the world, fostering all its great civilizations.

Many ancient American works of art attest the existence of the fair-skinned strangers. They may be found from La Venta to Monte Alban, from Mexico to Bolivia and Peru. The Maya carvings at Chichén Itza show the last of the white men being vanquished by northern barbarians in a sea-battle, after which they are sacrificed on the victors' altars. Elsewhere, their serene, bearded faces are seen in the masks of Tiahuanaco.

Pierre Honoré tells a curious story of the Spaniards' experience at Cuzco. 'Everywhere in the Inca empire they were greeted and addressed as Viracocha. Hearing the word again and again, they at first took it for a form of salute and had no idea of its meaning. In Cuzco they learned that is was the name of the great White God who had come to the Indians in the dim past and brought them all their knowledge, and had then disappeared, promising to return.

'Then the conquerors heard about the temple which had been erected outside the town to the god who was greater than all other gods. A party of them hurried off there, hoping to find an immense store of gold. They came to the temple of Viracocha, a one-story building about 125 feet by 100 feet. They went in and entered a maze of passages; there were twelve narrow passages going round the building. They made their way from one into the other, and finally penetrated to the sanctuary, a small room paved with black slabs. On the little dais on the far wall there was the figure of a man. When they stood before it even the wildest, roughest and most hardened veterans took their caps into their hands and hastily crossed themselves: they knew that figure from all the churches and chapels in Spain. It was an old man with a beard, standing erect, holding a chain in one hand; the chain was round the neck of a fabulous creature which lay before him on the ground. It was a statue of St. Bartholomew.

GIANTS AND THE LOST LANDS OF THE GODS

'When they had recovered from their surprise they slowly fled out into the passage again. They found no treasure here; the great temple contained nothing but the statue of the White God.'

On various occasions the Spaniards in America came across individuals who seemed to belong to the white race. According to chroniclers the eighth Inca monarch, Viracocha Inca, who reigned in the fourteenth century, was of light complexion, as was his consort.

Pedro Pizarro, a cousin of the famous conquistador, writes of an Inca tradition that 'the sun- god, their ancestor, sent them long ago a son and daughter of his to teach them knowledge; they were perceived to be divine by their speech and fair complexion. The highest class among the Incas are light-skinned; their noblewomen are handsome and are well aware of it. Both men and Women are blond as the standing corn, and some are lighter in complexion than Spaniards. I have seen in this country a white woman with a child of unusual fairness. The natives maintain that such people are descendants of their gods.'

There is evidence, too, of a different kind showing that there must have once been a 'bridge' between Europe and Africa on the one hand and America on the other. For example, throughout South America we find dolmens—megalithic funeral monuments consisting of a large flat stone placed across two or more upright ones—such as are common in Brittany, North Germany, Corsica and Apulia. As Ambrosetti writes, 'the technique of the prehistoric inhabitants of Argentina is exactly like that of the Cypriots and closely resembles that of the Trou aux Anglais at Epone in France'.

We also find in South America menhirs (vertical standing stones, typical of Brittany and central and southern Europe), cromlechs and stone circles of religious origin, best known by the example of Stonehenge. The Brazilian authority Dr. Alfredo Brandao has identified thousands of inscriptions on South American menhirs and dolmens which contain letters from early European and Mediterranean alphabets. Megalithic figures of a type found in France have also come to light in the Amazon basin, and the same is true of weapons, out-of- the-way implements and crockery.

Some dolmens are to be found in the vicinity of the Pedra Pintada ('painted rock'), one of the most striking prehistoric monuments of the Amazon basin, on flat ground near the middle course of the Rio Branco (Parima). This is an imposing block of stone, oval in shape, which, according to Indian belief, covers the remains of a white, fair-haired giant. Near it have been found ancient skulls belonging to an unknown race which shows a strong resemblance to our own.

It may be objected that while the existence of such objects on both sides of the Atlantic points to the fact that there must have been a land-bridge, it does not appear that the inhabitants of the 'bridge' were highly civilized. But if we accept

GIANTS AND THE LOST LANDS OF THE GODS

the theory of submerged continents this objection falls to the ground, since only a handful of people would have survived to pass on their knowledge to other races. We should remember that even today, in the age of nuclear fission and space travel, there are people in all the continents except Europe who are still living in conditions little more advanced than those of cave-dwellers.

The Merciless City

It is undeniable that some great civilization exercised its influence on various peoples of Middle and South America, and that this influence was so strong as to endure for centuries and even affect the barbarian invaders from the north. After the Toltecs and Chichimecs, the next rulers of Mexico were the Aztecs, a small Nahua tribe who came to dominate the whole of Central America. Their chieftains were succeeded by kings of whom the first, Acamapichtli, began to rule in 1376; the dynasty endured till 1521, when it was overthrown by Cortés.

The Aztecs, as we have seen, referred to their original home as 'Aztland', but this was a legend borrowed from some conquered people; they actually came from what is now US territory. After a few decisive battles they established themselves in a large area of present-day Mexico, in a loose agglomeration with its centre at Tenochtitlén near what is now Mexico City. This was a great city with some 60,000 buildings, rich palaces and pyramid temples, surrounded by houses built on piles. It was a city of priests, with more altars and sacrificial stones than anywhere else in America. The central pyramid, dedicated to the war-god Huitzilopochtli, was literally drenched in blood. Almost every day the priests with pierced ears and tongues, their faces and bodies painted black, wrapping about them cloaks that are said to have been made of human skin, would mount the steps of these gruesome edifices to perform the rites of sacrifice. Young men and maidens of noble birth were slaughtered in hundreds by strangulations, by having their throats cut or being buried alive in the pyramid. In the most solemn form of sacrifice, the victim's breast was cut open and the heart plucked out.

When the temple was inaugurated in the fifteenth century, at least 15,000 people were massacred in this way. The Aztecs were not skilled in tillage, but they anticipated modern hydroponic techniques with their chinampas or floating gardens—artificial islands made of a trellis-work of reeds and roots covered with soil. They may have inherited this art from the 'white lords', together with that of growing cotton in various colors ranging from brown to blue; this is attested all the way from Peru to Central America, and is a technique which modern science has been unable to reproduce. Another remarkable fact about cotton in ancient America is that it was a cross between the wild native variety and Mediterranean cotton. The latter could not have reached America via the Bering Strait, as migrations by that route took centuries to reach their final destination, and the plant does not grow in a cold climate. The seeds could not have crossed the Atlantic or been transported by birds, because they could not survive salt water and birds do not feed on them. Once again, the only solution seems to be the land-bridge of Atlantis.

Tenochtitlan was not only a city of human sacrifice and revolting cruelty, however. Pierre Honoré, quoting Cortés and Bernal Diaz, describes how impressed the Spaniards were by the profusion and orderliness of its market. 'Everything the New World produced was to be had... There were special stands for Cholula's jewellers and potters, Azcapotzalca's goldsmiths, Tezcoco's painters, Tenayuca's stone-cutters, Xilotepec's hunters, Cuitlahuac's fishermen, Quauhtitlan's basket and chair weavers, Xochimilco's florists. Every article had its own place in this market, surrounded by great arcades.

There were medicinal herbs and apothecaries' goods and even barbers; the barbers were kept very busy, because the Indians, although they had no beards, used to have their heads shaved.

'There were a great variety of curios you could buy there: golden fishes with little scales of gold, golden birds with golden feathers and movable heads, vessels made from all kinds of wood, varnished or even gilt, bronze axes, warriors' helmets with crests of animals' heads, quilted cotton waist- coats for the warriors, feather armours, Mexican swords with obsidian blades, razors and mirrors from cut stone, hides and leather goods of all sorts, fans made of cotton or agave fibers, tame and wild animals, and also slaves.' Perhaps, too, there were storytellers reciting strange legends like that of Tapi, the local Noah, which made the Spaniards surmise that the natives were acquainted with scripture and that in early Christian times an apostle must have landed on their coast.

Certainly, they found extraordinary parallels in the matter of religion: for instance, the lords of Tenochtitlén baptized new- born children in water; incense was used in the temples, auricular confession was practiced, and the priests distributed small pieces of bread which the faithful consumed with reverence in order to be 'reconciled with the gods'.

Other astonishing coincidences were found among the Mayas, who celebrated 16 May as the 'feast of water': to Catholics this was the feast-day of John of Nepomuk, a martyr who met his death by drowning. On 8 September (the Nativity of the Virgin) the Mayas celebrated the birth of the Mother of the White God; on 2 November they commemorated the dead, and on 25 December the coming of the White God himself.

Some have held that the White God took a hand in destroying the Aztec empire, in order to punish these 'lucky upstarts' (as one archaeologist calls them) for transgressing his commandments and falsifying their own origin. Rather than live by hunting and fishing, they preferred war, trade and rapine: they would exchange goods with stronger peoples and attack and despoil those that were weak and scattered.

At all events, the Aztec priests believed that the White God had left them in the year named Ce-acatl, which recurs every 52 years, and that in that year he would return. Sure enough, on 22 April 1519 Cortés's men landed in Mexico, at the very spot where Quetzalcoatl had disappeared, and the Spanish leader was dressed, like him, in a black cap and cloak.

The emperor Montezuma in due course became Cortés's prisoner, while the latter's men wreaked their will on the Aztecs. In the following year an Aztec rebellion forced Cortés to evacuate Tenochtitlan, and at this time Montezuma was killed. On 13 August 1521 the Spaniards recaptured Tenochtitlan, razed it to the ground and founded Mexico City.

This is not the place to question the verdict of history, but if we survey the course of events in Central and South America we are bound to reflect, with Cieza de Leon, that if the Spaniards had been less cruel and less rapacious we should have more than a few fragments of information from which to form an idea of the mysterious civilizations that flourished there.

The pyramid of Teotihuacán...

...and the Egyptian step-pyramid of Saqqara.

Dancers' gallery at Monte Albán: men of ear-like appearance in outfit resembling a space-suit.

Tomb of the "Pharaoh of Palenque".

GIANTS AND THE LOST LANDS OF THE GODS

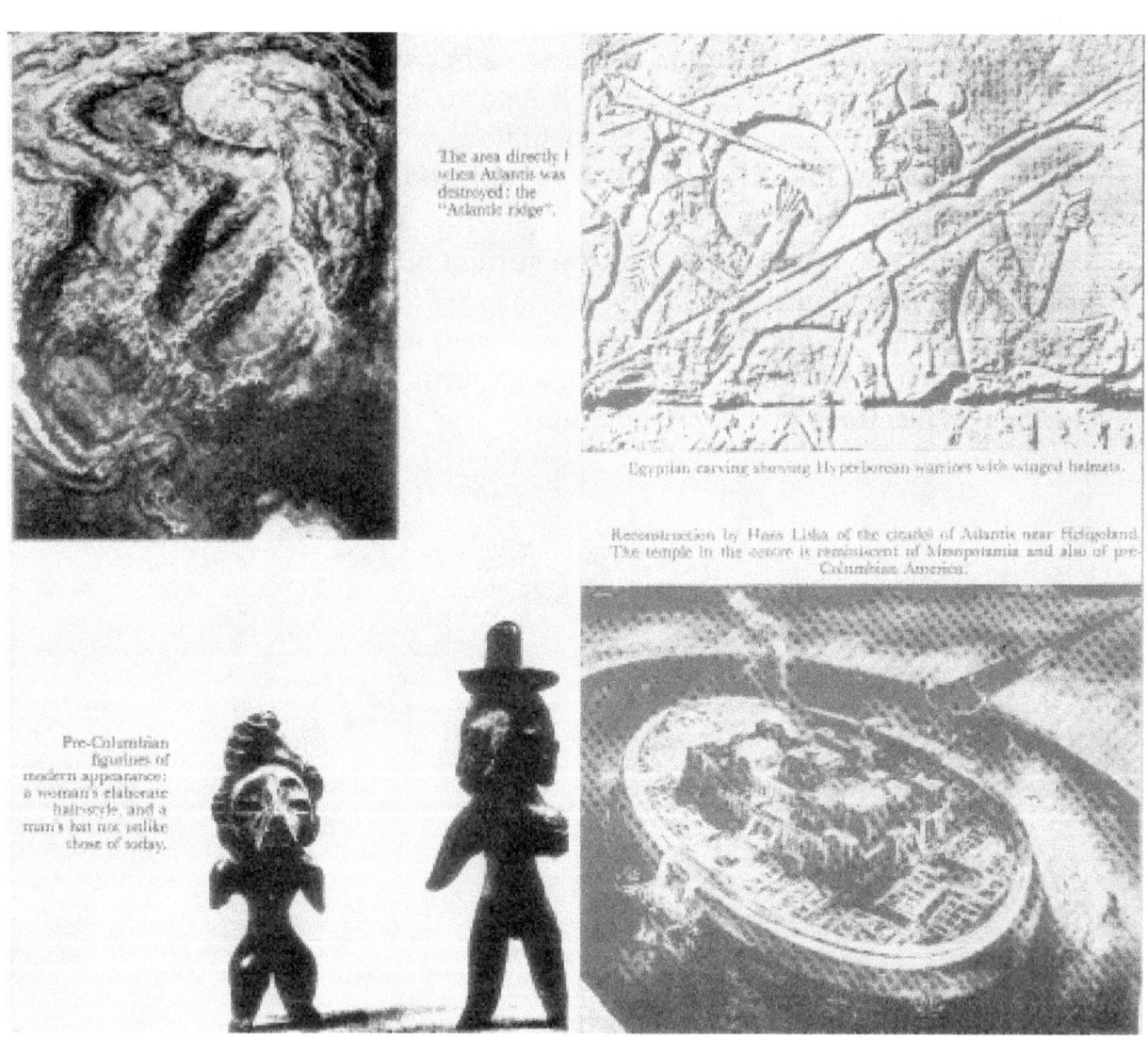

GIANTS AND THE LOST LANDS OF THE GODS

CHAPTER SIXTEEN
Greeks In America

'God took some corncobs and ground up the seeds, soaked the paste in water from Chichén Itza, shaped it in the likeness of a man and baked it in the oven. Then he breathed on it and said "Live!" This is how the Mayas, lords of the earth, were born.'

Such is the Maya creation legend; but where did this race, with their advanced yet enigmatic culture, actually come from? The scholar Luis Chavez Orozco suggests that they reached Mexico from the Mississippi basin, while Sylvanus G. Morley thinks they belonged to the same ethnic group as the Eskimos, the Iroquois and other Red Indian dwellers in the northern part of the continent.

Among the founders of the Maya empire, legend records the names of Balam-Quiché ('tiger with the sweet smile'), head of the Cavek clan; Balam-Ayab ('tiger of the night'), head of the Nitroy; Mawacutah ('illustrious name'), head of the Ahauquicé; and Iqui-Balém ('tiger of the moon'), head of the Tamut and Illorath. All this goes to confirm the evidence of archaeologoy that the Mayas were related to the Incas.

Their civilization probably originated in what is now the Petén province of Guatemala, about the beginning of the Christian era: the oldest remains known to us are dated A.D. 57. From 400 onwards the 'lords of the earth', as they styled themselves, spread towards the north, west and south-west, over Mexico, Honduras and other parts of Central America.

Then, in 909, for unexplained reasons they abandoned their homeland with its flourishing cities and moved to Yucatan, leaving the jungle to engulf all that they had laboriously built up over the centuries. This is the more extraordinary since the country they left was a fertile one, while their new home was arid and inhospitable, infested with wild beasts and poisonous insects. Suggestions have been made that they were driven out by plague, famine or invasion, but there is no hard evidence for any of these.

GIANTS AND THE LOST LANDS OF THE GODS

At all events, the Mayas attempted to rebuild their empire in Yucatan, but they were soon subdued by the Toltecs. Later, when Cortés's men defeated the Aztecs and occupied their capital, the Maya cities were in ruins. At the present day the last descendants of what was once the greatest empire in America are mere jungle savages, without a vestige of their former glory. Yet the Mayas achieved tremendous things in their time. Their oldest city known to us, at Uaxacttin in Guatemala, was an important astronomical centre and contained a feature unique in the world, namely a pyramid built inside another pyramid. Near by was Tikal, the religious and intellectual capital, with majestic temples, hanging gardens and a huge stadium for the national sport resembling basketball. This game was in fact popular throughout pre-Columbian America, and among the Mayas it was fraught with risk for the spectator. The method of scoring a goal was to pass a hard rubber ball through a stone or wooden ring, set vertically at a considerable distance away. When a player succeeded in this he was entitled to pursue the spectators and strip them of anything they possessed, so that the winning of a point was the signal for a general stampede.

Other important centers in Yucatan were Uxmal and especially Chichén Itza, founded in about 534 and still majestic in its ruins, which bear an extraordinary stylistic resemblance to the monuments of Cambodia and other parts of South-East Asia.

Writing of the Atlanteans, Plato tells us that: 'The springs they made use of, one kind being of cold, another of warm water, were of abundant volume, and each kind was wonderfully well adapted for use because of the natural taste and excellence of its waters; and these they surrounded with buildings and plantations of trees and reservoirs round about, some under cover to supply hot baths in the winter.'

Some authorities believe that the main streets of the Maya cities were bordered by fountains giving hot and cold water, and that the former was not derived from hot springs but from some form of heating device. This is quite plausible, since similar installations have been found beneath the ruins of Minos's palace in Crete and on some Asiatic sites.

One of the early explorers of Chichén Itza was Edward H. Thompson, who was the first to suggest a connection with Atlantis. Other scientists were skeptical, but he was given an opportunity to pursue his theory when, about 1885, he was appointed U.S. Consul at Yucatan. For years he spent long periods in the jungle, and in 1896 he discovered at Chichén Itza a small pyramid which, when investigated, provided important confirmation of the Atlantean theory.

A Pharaoh In Mexico

Before E. H. Thompson's explorations it had been thought that the American and Egyptian pyramids differed in that the former were used only as temples

GIANTS AND THE LOST LANDS OF THE GODS

and the latter for burial purposes. However, on excavating a pit inside the small pyramid he found in it the scattered bones of seven human skeletons, and also a cave housing a tomb. Further evidence of the same kind came to light in 1952.

Five miles from the Mexican town of Palenque there is a large field of Maya ruins including an imposing step pyramid. An expedition under Professor Alberto Ruz Lhullier spent a year or two investigating the site, and found a passage inside the pyramid which had been intentionally blocked with rubble. Pursuing his search with great determination, Professor Ruz reached what appeared to be the lowest part of the pyramid and, on removing a heavy stone barrier, found himself in a small chamber measuring 12 feet by 7 feet; its floor consisted of a slab covered by impressive though partly obliterated reliefs depicting the sun, the earth, the moon and Venus.

The weight of the slab, and the narrowness of the space, were such that it could not be shifted without mechanical aid, and it remains a problem how the ancients had put it there.

Ruz was faced by the same difficulty as Howard Carter, twenty-five years earlier, at the tomb of Tutankhamun. Like him, he had recourse to elaborate mechanical devices and was rewarded by the discovery of a large sarcophagus of red stone containing the skeleton of a man measuring 5 feet 8 inches: the tomb contained a treasure-trove of jade, including a mask placed over the skull and reproducing the dead man's features.

He was evidently a Maya lord, of uncertain name and date, but the discovery of his body and the funeral crypt constitutes one more of the innumerable links between the civilizations of the Mediterranean and prehistoric America.

Another such link may be seen in the existence, also at Palenque, of a 'Temple of the Cross'—so called because one of its sides is marked with the sign which, in all manner of forms, was found throughout the world many centuries before the coming of Christ. Elsewhere we see a variation of this symbol in the form of a tree, which tallies almost exactly with the Javanese device of the Tree of Heaven, derived from ancient India.

Buddhist art presents us with figures of gods seated on tigers and other wild beasts, and the same motif recurs at Palenque and other Maya centers. As Honoré says: 'The disc of the sun as a quoit, the mussel shell with a plant, the figures of Vishnu—all these appeared on both sides of the Pacific either in identical form or with so strong a resemblance that they cannot have originated independently of one another.'

The Mayas also used the lotus motif as we find it in India and Cambodia, reptiles with human heads, fire-breathing dragons in Chinese style, and various other emblems that are familiar throughout Asia. As Ivar Lissner points out, 'There are affinities between the art of ancient China and that of the American northwest,

GIANTS AND THE LOST LANDS OF THE GODS

as there are between Shang iconography and certain symbols used by the Mayas and Aztecs. But how are we to explain the time-lag of twenty or thirty centuries between the oldest Chinese bronzes and the Maya and Aztec civilizations, which date respectively from the fourth and fourteenth centuries A. D.'

The explorers who first discovered Tikal were astonished at the height and steepness of its pyramids—one of them rises to 230 feet, like a five-storied house—which were unparalleled elsewhere in America, but closely resembled those of the dead city of Angkor Vat. Again, the stele carved column recording important events, proclamations and so on is a typically Asian device which somehow made its way to the Egyptians, Greeks and Romans; we also find it at Zimbabwe, among the Hsing Nu and the oldest cities of the Near East. Yet who, more than the Mayas, could be called a 'people of the stele'? Confronted by these impressive stone monuments, and especially the famous 'Stele E' at Quirigua in Guatemala, we can hardly refrain, despite the warnings of official science, from letting our minds rove towards 'stellar hypotheses' and the 'gleaming serpents' which were perhaps the spaceships of legendary times.

As Raymond Cartier writes, 'In many fields of knowledge the Mayas outclassed the Greeks and Romans. They were expert astronomers and mathematicians, and thus brought to perfection the science of chronology. They built domed observatories with a more exact orientation than those of seventeenth-century Paris, e.g. the Caracol erected on three terraces at Chichén Itza. They had a precise calendar based on a "sacred year" of 260 days, a solar year of 365 days and a Venusian year of 584 days. The exact length of the solar year has been fixed, after long calculation, at 365.2422 days; the Mayas estimated it at 365-2420 days, i.e. correct to three places of decimals. The Egyptians may also have reached this degree of exactitude, but the evidence for this depends on disputed measurements of the pyramids, whereas in the case of the Mayas it is attested by the calendar.

Further parallels with Egypt can be seen in the highly developed art of the Mayas. In their murals and frescoes and around their vases are depicted men with sharp Semitic profiles engaged in tillage, fishing, building, and political or religious activities, all with a ruthless verisimilitude that we find elsewhere only in Egypt. But Maya pottery also reminds us of the Etruscans, their bas-reliefs are reminiscent of India, and the steep flights of steps leading up to their pyramid-temples recall those of Angkor.

Mathematics In Stone

With most peoples of the world one finds, as one would expect, that the art of writing begins in a rudimentary fashion and that the script evolves in line with the general progress of civilization. But the Mayas are an exception; at the outset of their cultural development, their script had already reached perfection. What is more remarkable still, it provides another link with the Mediterranean world. Many of the Maya names of days resemble the names of letters in the Phoenician and Greek alphabet, and occur in the same order. Maya hieroglyphics show affinity to those of Egypt and to Cretan scripts, to such a degree that, as Honoré observes, the Maya and Cretan scripts must be identical in origin. But the curious fact is that, about 1700 B.C., the Cretans abandoned their ancient script for a less complicated form, and at that date Maya civilization still lay far in the future. The only answer to this riddle lies in postulating the existence of a lost territory—Atlantis—by way of which the old Cretan script could have found its way to America, to some unknown people who afterwards transmitted it to the Mayas along with many other forms of knowledge.

In mathematics the Mayas were acquainted with the zero, a device for which they used the mark of a tiny shell, the decimal system, logarithms and other abstract calculations. As Honoré writes, 'When an ornament was repeated ten times running or more, when a flight consisted of seventy-five steps, when a pyramid reached a certain height, it was no accident but a mathematical statement. The whole of Mayan art was mathematics, literally petrified, turned to stone.'

Astronomy was even more highly developed among the Mayas than in the rest of pre-Columbian America. Their knowledge of the solar system and the constellations is astonishing; a magnificent altar erected at Copan commemorates the last astronomical congress held there on 2 September 503. Their observatories were remarkably similar to ours except for the lack of modern instruments; but without such instruments, how could they have had so exact a knowledge of the heavenly bodies?

Let us try to answer this puzzle by means of an example. We may equate Atlantis with present-day Europe, and the Mayas' predecessors with an African nation that is just embarking on the path of development. The Africans build their first observatory and equip it from Europe, but at that point our continent is wiped out by a cosmic cataclysm. The African nation, too, is devastated; a few scholars survive, but they have no equipment and no hope of receiving aid of any sort. Their knowledge, such as it is, is passed on to succeeding generations; in the process some parts of it are lost, others that appeal to popular fancy are preserved, others again are transmuted into religion, legend or fable.

Centuries elapse; in time civilization is reborn, mankind rediscovers astronomy, and astonished explorers come upon an exact representation of the solar system carved on a stone in the midst of the African jungle.

Bearing this imaginary case in mind, let us consider once more what we know about the Mexican 'lords of the earth'. Their cities were elegant, clean and orderly, with spacious squares and avenues paved with stone or white cement.

GIANTS AND THE LOST LANDS OF THE GODS

The temples were adorned with gorgeous images of strange beings; extensive gardens and fine aqueducts were to be seen, and there was a hygienic drainage system. The roads were not so good as those of the Incas, but should not be underrated: we may mention the 60-mile stretch from Coba to Yaxuna, paved with cement and guarded by parapets, which runs across difficult and marshy territory. Beside this thoroughfare, archaeologists have discovered an ancient 'steamroller', split into two fragments and weighing 5 tons.

The Mayas domesticated various plants and produced a wide range of dyes—blue, purple, indigo and other tints; they also made extensive use of rubber for soling footwear, making balls and waterproof clothing. They even made books out of wild fig-leaves treated with lime and gum. Yet their technical deficiencies were no less extraordinary: they knew nothing of wheels or carts, they forged no tools of metal and had no domestic animals except dogs, turkeys and bees. There was no such thing as a pair of scales, and so these learned mathematicians could not have weighed out an ordinary parcel of goods.

Their religious pantheon was a large one, dominated by Kukulcan, the white god who had come to teach all laws and sciences and was represented in the guise of a feathered serpent; next to him came Itzamné, the sky-god. We may imagine, perhaps, that a man from Atlantis came and told the primitive Americans of a supreme being, governor of the universe, and that the Mayas in due time paid divine honors to both. They were not averse to human sacrifice, which again contrasts with the refinement of their civilization. In time of national distress they would dress up a young girl in her best attire .and throw her over a waterfall. If she did not die it was taken to mean that the gods were appeased, and she was released; but otherwise one girl after another was sacrificed, until the gods relented or a good enough swimmer was found among the victims.

The most curious feature of Mayan art and architecture is that it shows no development with the passage of time, ending up exactly as it began. Only at Uaxactim, where Maya civilization seems to have begun, are there some signs of initial imperfection; but here, too, as already mentioned, the script is perfectly developed from the outset.

We may perhaps compare the Mayas with primitive people who are given paintings to reproduce. After a few false starts they make excellent copies, but they will never improve on these or become original artists by their own efforts. The Mayas, we may suggest, received their culture from some unknown people who disappeared before Uaxacnin was founded. These cannot have been the Atlanteans themselves, nor—as some maintain—voyagers by sea from Europe, North Africa or Asia, since in that case the Mayas could not have been ignorant of such things as cattle-breeding, the use of metals, the balance and the wheel. According to their legend, 'The white gods came from the east, long ago; great ships

GIANTS AND THE LOST LANDS OF THE GODS

with swans' wings and shining sides, like huge snakes gliding through the water. When they reached the shore, men with fair skins and hair and blue eyes disembarked from them. They wore black garments open in front, with round collars and short, wide sleeves. On their brows they wore a diadem in the form of a serpent.' Can these have been visitors from a colony of Atlantis - some island which survived the parent mainland for a time, but not for long enough to enable its inhabitants to rekindle their civilization on American soil?

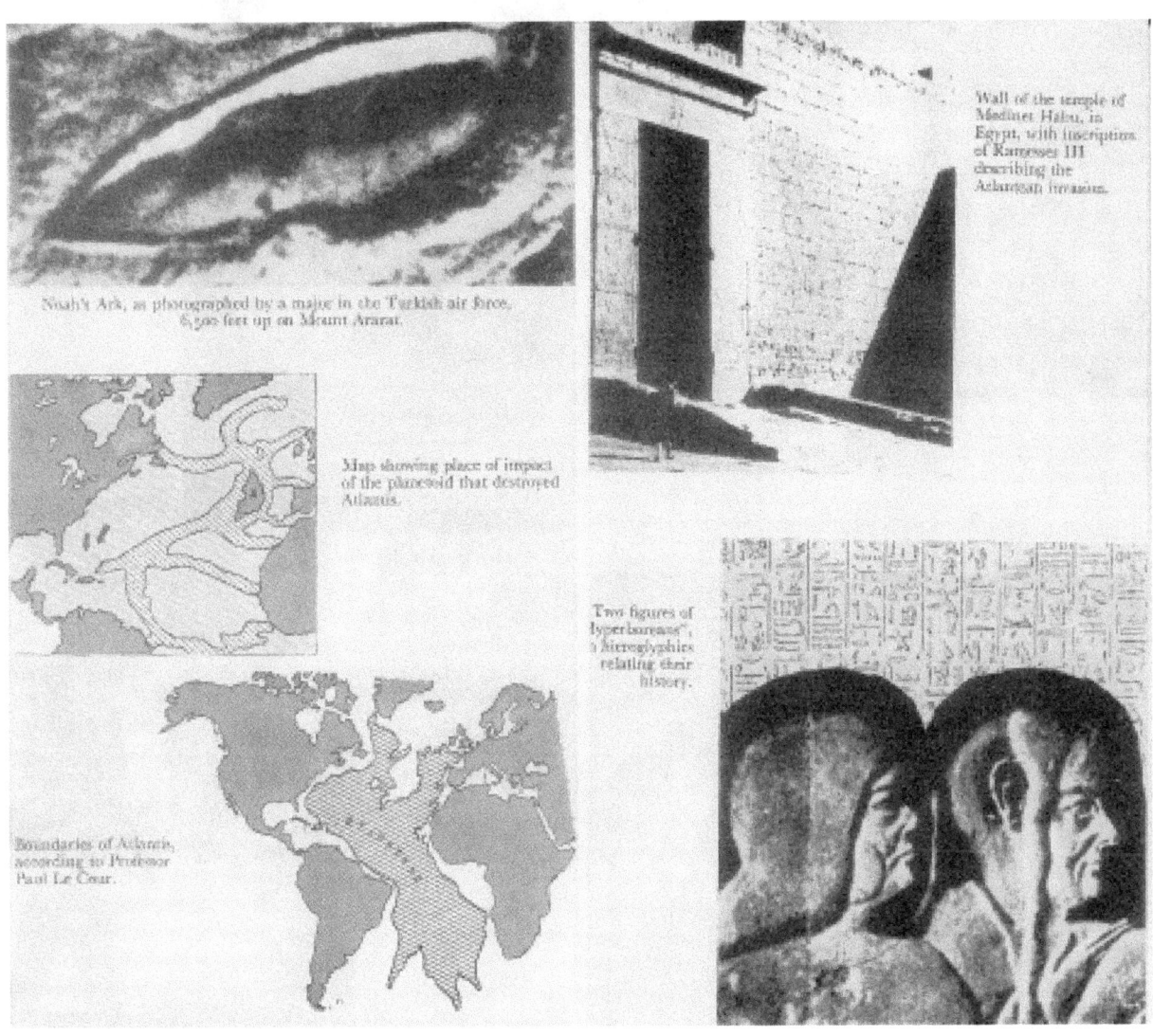

Noah's Ark, as photographed by a major in the Turkish air force, 6,500 feet up on Mount Ararat.

Wall of the temple of Medinet Habu, in Egypt, with inscriptions of Ramesses III describing the Atlantean invasion.

Map showing place of impact of the planetoid that destroyed Atlantis.

Boundaries of Atlantis, according to Professor Paul Le Cour.

Two figures of hyperboreans, & hieroglyphics relating their history.

GIANTS AND THE LOST LANDS OF THE GODS

Left: the Zimbabwe monolith. Right: the Zimbabwe phoenix, resembling the American "thunderbird" totem. Below: the citadel at Zimbabwe.

The Hypogeum, a two-storied underground construction in Malta. Note the spiral design on the ceiling.

Sardinian nuraghi, seen from outside and inside.

GIANTS AND THE LOST LANDS OF THE GODS

CHAPTER SEVENTEEN
Constellations In The Jungle

'The spaceship came roaring down in a cloud of fire, landing almost in the centre of the broad plain. For several yards around the grass and shrubs were burnt up, stones melted and great cracks opened in the parched ground. The ship gave a last, intense vibration and remained still. Nothing more happened for some hours. Then a porthole opened, a gangway was let down and two squat figures in space-suits emerged. They took a few steps on earth, then operated a device on their chests which loosened their helmets, and took them off.

'If anyone had been watching them from the shelter of the forest, he would have been appalled at the sight. For these beings from another planet were not human in feature; they had flat faces, slanting eyes with yellow pupils, a broad, squashed-looking nose and a hideous mouth with four fangs. They looked like cats, or rather catlike creatures from outer space.'

Are we to imagine a scene like this in the earth's remote past? The American civilizations we have so far considered give ground for doing so, and the impression holds good as we move further south.

Beyond the Mexican border we come first to regions in which pyramids and stone buildings are unknown. We may think of them as a 'no man's land' between the great cultures of Central and South America, but this is not so: even the relatively backward tribes of this area were related to the Olmecs, the Toltecs and perhaps the inhabitants of the lost Atlantis.

The Chorotegans, who lived in what is now Nicaragua and northern Costa Rica, are celebrated by Spanish chroniclers for their rich maize fields and cacao plantations and their beautiful women. Here, as with the tribes further north, we find a mixture of advanced civilization and primitive customs. Their chief god was Tamagastad, who is none other than the 'white god' Quetzalcoatl; and their tradition told of a great flood which engulfed the 'middle creation'. We do not know what they meant by this expression; perhaps a lost continent, perhaps a race intermediate between themselves and the men of former time, perhaps even visi-

GIANTS AND THE LOST LANDS OF THE GODS

tors from outer space. Whatever is the key to the riddle, we may be sure that it somehow involves Atlantis.

A similar myth is found among the Chibcha and their modern descendants, the Cueva Indians in the eastern part of Panama. The Chibchas were divided into several more or less civilized groups inhabiting the area between Lake Nicaragua and Ecuador, i.e. Costa Rica, Panama and Colombia. They are said to have possessed skills that are unknown today, and this is borne out by their extraordinary powers of working gold, using vegetable juices for the gilding of copper and applying gold foil to objects made of bone and precious stones. Among the Chibcha finds are gold helmets and exquisite filigree gold chains, either solid or openwork, and amulets of quartz, agate and serpentine. Columbus, on his fourth voyage, was shown precious ornaments representing men with animal heads, women, bats, lizards, frogs, spiders and eagles. These eagles are true 'fire-birds', more like aeroplanes than earthly creatures, and were perhaps intended to imitate spacecraft. As for the spiders, they resemble those found in the Peruvian desert along with huge drawings of other animals; some of these creatures are unknown on earth, and the drawings were apparently made to be seen from a great height.

Fine ceramics have been found in Costa Rica, at Limon and Guanacaste. Some have embossed designs, achieved by the use of wax. The style recalls alternately Mexico, Greece and Africa, while some specimens are so unique that many believe them to come from another planet. Yet the Chibcha masterpieces were produced by people who never built in stone, whose weapons and tools were' made of wood and whose sculpture was extraordinarily primitive.

Unknown Stars

In the forests of Guatemala and Costa Rica, Samuel K. Lothrop and his wife discovered a quantity of round stones varying in diameter from an inch or two to 8 feet. For hundreds of miles around there was no quarry from which they could have come, and it is a mystery how they were shaped with such precision and rolled through the jungle or to the tops of high mountains, a labor which may well have taken decades to complete. As a rule three, four or five of these spheres are arranged in a straight line, serving as a base for triangles and other geometrical figures. The whole arrangement obeys strict mathematical laws, in which the predominant figures are 1, 2, 3, 4, 6 and 8. The only conclusion that suggests itself is that the purpose was to represent constellations or stellar systems. In some cases we can identify these, while others do not appear in our map of the heavens. Perhaps the mystery of their origin was revealed by the 'books of prophecy' of the Chorotegan priests—immense scrolls of deerskin measuring 30 or 40 feet and decorated in black and red— but unfortunately none of these have been preserved even in part.

GIANTS AND THE LOST LANDS OF THE GODS

Legend tells us that these books told the story of the past and future; how all earthly civilizations had been fostered by beings from outer space, and how one day man in his turn would reach the stars. Moreover, the books are said to have spoken of 'men-jaguars' descending from the heavens. May it not be that the grotesque figures depicted throughout ancient America are not pure fantasy but portray beings who came from another planet, bringing war or civilization to the white inhabitants of Atlantis?

We also find in Costa Rica long rows of columns rising as high as 20 feet, the purpose of which is unknown, and strange-looking tablets of volcanic stone inscribed with jaguar motifs. The origin of this motif is attributed to the Olmecs, and according to Honoré it passed from them to the Mayas of Uaxacnin, to Teotihuacan, to the Toltecs and the Aztecs. 'The Olmecs were so dominated by this motif in their art that it has been called a "jaguar mania", and they depicted all types and stages between man and beast.' Honoré adds that 'the ancient Cretans had a similar mania, only with them it was lions: hence the many lion masks found in the Cretan civilization and those which followed it.' However, re- presentations of this kind occur in folklore all over the world, and we shall meet them in other parts of pre-Columbian America. Archaeologists generally take the view that they are related to a jaguar-cult, but it should be noted that they are found in places where no such cult existed, and where native tradition declares that they were intended to portray 'foreign warriors' or 'night warriors'. Moreover, some modern tribes of Olmec origin refer to the men-jaguars as 'gods who came from the moon'.

The Maya civilization is full of mysterious allusions, but in the context of the space theory We may recall the names of three of the first four legendary chieftains: Balam-Quiché, the 'sweetly smiling tiger', Balém-Ayab, the 'tiger of night', and Iqui-Balam, 'tiger of the moon'. Apart from the references to night and the moon, these names have Asiatic overtones; they resemble the titles of various Chinese and Mongol warlords, and this has led Soviet scholars to investigate the possibility of a connection between Asia and the 'men-jaguars'. Many legends relate that monsters of a similar kind once lived in the area of the Gobi desert, so that they may have been connected with the forefathers of the Mongols.

The shamans, when they enter into a trance, are said to be in contact with 'lords of creation, who have the faces of tigers and are borne through the air by birds of fire'. Masks with feline features have been found in several parts of Mongolia, and we may also be reminded of the magic bird Garuda in Hindu mythology, which still figures in religious drama. The Tibetan lamas have a long acquaintance with Mongolia, and as long ago as 1269 one of their number visited the court of the emperor Kublai (Kubla Khan, or Marco Polo's 'Great Khan'). We may thus take seriously the Tibetan tradition that men-tigers lived in Central Asia thousands of years ago, that they and their 'fire-birds' were transformed into deities and that, when the shaman enters into a hypnotic trance, he is not communicating with the world beyond the grave but is recalling memories that have been subconsciously transmitted from one generation to another. Such, at all events, was the version given to Professor Turaniev by the lamas of Tuerin; but they refused to go into further details, and the Moscow-Peking conflict put a stop to further Soviet explorations in Tibet.

With Fangs And Horns

Returning to the Chibchas, we may note that they were not the only masters of the goldsmith's art. Among their chief rivals were the Manabi Indians, coast-dwellers of northern Ecuador who, despite the lack of optical instruments, fashioned ornaments out of little grains of gold half the size of a pin's head, which they sometimes interspersed with even smaller, hollowed-out granules. The perfection of these works of art can only be appreciated by studying them through a strong magnifying glass. The process used was a technique known as 'granulation', rediscovered not many years ago by a German expert, Frau Treskow. It is so intricate and ingenious that scholars are convinced that it could not have been invented by several peoples independently of one another. Yet the same technique was used in Crete for the mane of a lion barely half an inch long, and the feathers and wings of a duck measuring an inch and a quarter; and at Pylos, in Homeric Greece, for the wings of a screech-owl and for the warts on a toad about an inch in length. The Sumerians executed this kind of gold work, as did the Trojans (tiny purses and earrings) and the Etruscans. It is to be supposed, therefore, that the technique of granulation spread all over the world from the place where it was first invented.

Heinrich Schliemann, the famous excavator of Troy, discovered gold death-masks at Mycenae and in the Crimea, very similar to those used for the Pharaohs and also for American chieftains, not only at Palenque. About 400 years ago, as related by Honoré, 'a troop of gold-hunting mercenaries under Pedro de Heredia were marching through Colombia to the valley of the river Cauca. As they penetrated deeper into the country they came upon an old Indian people ruled by a woman. She gave the strangers a friendly welcome, showed them her palace and the great temple, where there were twenty-four large statues of gold, covered entirely in gold foil. In the sacred grove surrounding the temple the Spaniards saw something which took their breath away: every branch of the tall trees in the grove had gold bells hanging from it.

'The queen's guests made a poor return for the hospitality shown them; they took away all the gold bells, and the gold coverings of the statues, and they stole a ton and a quarter of gold from the tombs of former princes. The expedition lasted about nine months, and the booty was appropriately rich. Heredia brought back about two tons of gold in works of art which were quickly melted down.'

GIANTS AND THE LOST LANDS OF THE GODS

Modern explorers have found in the Cauca valley exquisite artifacts made from an alloy of gold and copper; helmets, vases, jars and statuettes of princes, one of which, about 8 inches tall, is in the Museo de America at Madrid. The modeling of the features is such that we can easily imagine the figure wearing a transparent space-helmet with earphones. Other ancient masterpieces have been found in the garden of a villa at Esmeraldas on the coast of Ecuador. The most valuable collection of its kind in the world, it numbers 12,000 pieces including axes, scepters, weapons and implements of all sorts. The majority are of unique design, but there are seals made of precious stones and resembling those executed in China down to recent times, as well as figurines of persons with Oriental-type features, dressed in a manner reminiscent of ancient Egypt. Another noteworthy object is a mirror made from a green jewel two inches wide, which reflects everything down to the smallest detail. The Esmeraldas collection, which must be about 18,000 years old, is remarkable not only for its artistic perfection but for its resemblances to ancient Mediterranean and Asiatic work, though these do not fall into any specific pattern.

The scepters, headdresses and other objects found in the Cauca valley are notable for the frequent use of the spiral as a decorative motif. This symbol occurs throughout the ancient world, from Malta to Samarkand, from America to Asia and from Africa to Europe. Marcel Homer writes as follows (in Sons of the Sun, London, 1963):

'The representation alone of the spiral form plays an important part in the prehistory which links the continents. Montelius and Evans assumed that it derived from the 4th Egyptian dynasty (in the middle of the third millennium B.C.) and only subsequently came to Crete (after 2000 B.C.). Nevertheless we meet with this form on the shores of the Danube as early as 3000 B.C. and at the end of the palaeological age in Moravia. Forms of spirals, engraved or painted on stones, are constantly to be met with in America, where they represent the life of the universe and also the principle of fertility. It was always with the purpose of affecting the faithful that the priests of vanished civilizations put the earthly facts into simple motifs as they were instructed by 'heaven' to do. We must not overlook the fact that not only the Sumerians, Akkadians and Chaldeans but also, and much earlier, the wise men of Tiahuanaco, thanks to procedures of which we know nothing, had grasped that the heavenly path of the stars is an open ellipse. In other words it is a screwlike spiral, and this knowledge they transferred to their stone drawings and engravings.

'Of course, linear and two-dimensional representations can lead the layman astray. So, in searching for a more adequate means of presentation, one must recall the mystery of life, the myth of creation: the serpent and the cosmogonal egg that issues from its mouth. This is a myth widespread in Europe, in the Mediterranean countries, among the Mayas and also the ancient inhabitants of Brazil.

GIANTS AND THE LOST LANDS OF THE GODS

The divinity of the serpent is variously depicted. For the Chaldeans there was the god who held a staff in his hand, which was a double screw-shaped scepter, the symbol of fertility and health. In the graves of the Kurgans in southern Russia, 'one found also screw-shaped tubes and spiral-shaped ear pendants.

'But the cosmogonal egg also represents the spiral movement of the stars. That must be the reason why 'a majority of the gigantic Ibero-Celtic monoliths and those we found in the Amazon region, as for example the Pedra Pintada, have an ellipsoid form and are carefully set in position in relation to the stars.' '

British, American and Soviet scholars have also delved into the mystery of the spiral, and the Russians are inclined to support Homet's view: they consider that it was both an astronomical symbol of the universe and a religious emblem of the Creation, based on the form of a spiral nebula or protogalaxy. The spiral, in fact, is a stylized galaxy, but how could our remote ancestors, who were often wholly ignorant of astronomy, have hit upon this idea or known what a galaxy was? We can only suppose, improbable as it may seem, either that they had actually reached an advanced degree of scientific knowledge by their own efforts or that it was imparted to them by extraterrestrial beings. As Simaniov speculates, 'perhaps the spiral adorned the space-suits of astronauts who landed on our globe in the dawn of human history, and symbolized the mission of these galactic explorers.'

The spiral was a favorite emblem of the Muiscas, a Chibcha tribe living in what are now the Colombian provinces of Boyaca and Cundinamarca, where the rulers, like the Incas and Pharaohs, used to take their sisters as consorts. This people too had a flood legend and worshipped white gods: Bochica, the sun, and his wife Bachue, the moon. Bochica, it is related, came from the east and taught men the arts of weaving and tillage; he gave them laws and showed them how to 'conquer time and disease'. The sun and moon were also Sua and Chie respectively, and the Muisca name for the Spaniards was Usachie—like the natives whom Columbus encountered, they believed the Europeans to be descended from the two white gods.

Other mysterious ruins in Colombia - ancient temples, statues and stelae - remind us of Easter Island, La Venta and other Central and South American sites. We may mention the palace of Moniquira with its fine obelisks and round or oval columns, or the bathing-pool at Lava atas with its sculptured walls and bas-reliefs, including the head of a man wearing horns. This can be paralleled in Egypt, along with the dog-faced god of death and other semi-human monsters. A horned creature, part-man and part-bull (the Minotaur?) and with something of the jaguar, also figures on the 'Raimondi stele' of the Chavin civilization (see anon). But the most impressive relics of an ancient past are at San Agustin near the headwaters of the Rio Magdalena: statues up to 13 feet high, showing warriors striving desperately against demons with flat nightmarish faces. Caryatids are there to remind us of the Mediterranean, and so is the fire-bird. The jaguar motif is represented by a ferocious, catlike face with four fangs, which grins at us derisively as though mocking our attempts to fathom its secret despite the barriers of time and space.

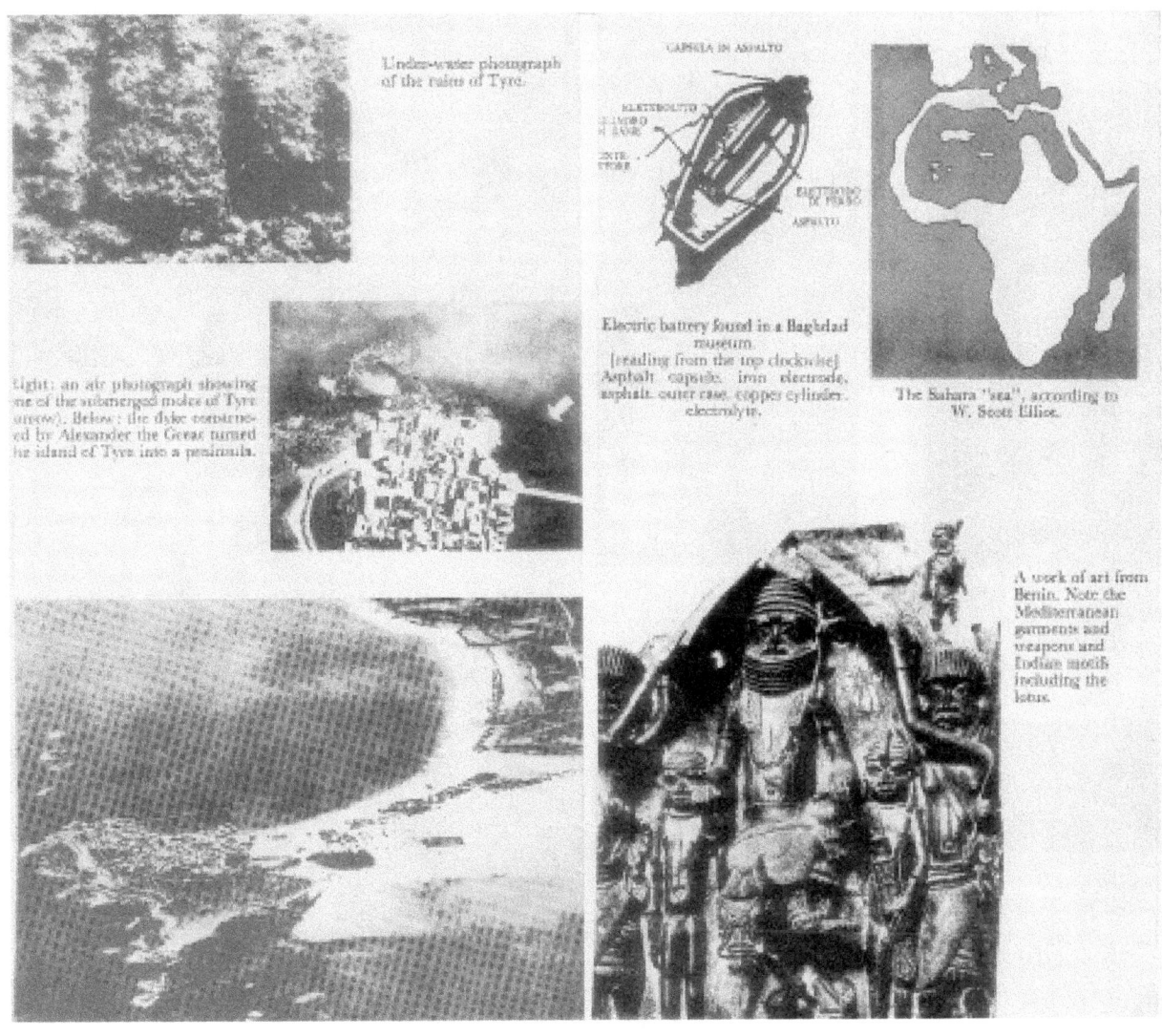

GIANTS AND THE LOST LANDS OF THE GODS

A hook from New Guinea, with a religious design; some think it represents an astronaut.

Two prehistoric astronauts? (Above) African engraving, signed by Gagarin. (Below) Japanese figurine from Honshu.

Part of the massive wall of Mohenjo Daro.

Zimbabwe: a close-up of the wall (left) and one of the curious towers with no door or window.

GIANTS AND THE LOST LANDS OF THE GODS

CHAPTER EIGHTEEN
The Lords Of Fire

On the banks of a tiny stream, the Mozna, which rises in the Cordillera Blanca in western Peru and flows into the Maraion, there is a sleepy village named Chavin de Huantar which has given its name to a great civilization. The culture of which it seems to have been the centre, and whose traces have been discovered for some distance around, was termed the 'Chavin civilization' by Professor Julio Tello, a Peruvian archaeologist of Indian race.

The earliest known strata of this culture date back to 4000 B.C., and some of its buildings were erected in 715 B.C. What- ever the exact dates, it seems to have reached its peak in about 1500 B.C. and to have dominated the area between the Pacific and the headwaters of the Amazon.

The most important animal in Chavin ,mythology is the jaguar; snakes and condors also play a prominent part, as do the part-human monsters that we have already come across in other ancient American cultures. The jaguar or puma plays a similar role, as a symbol of divinity and lordship, to the lion in old-world mythology, while the condor corresponds to the eagle. As for the snake, many scholars have suggested that when stretched out it represents the form of a slender spaceship, while its coils are an image of the galaxy. Another symbolic creature which recalls the notion of a space-chariot is the fire-bird or thunder-bird (the latter name is used by the Indians of the U.S.A., Canada and Alaska), variously represented as an eagle, a hawk, a condor or a winged reptile. This is the animal which we see at the top of a totem pole, and it is identical with the feathered serpent of the Aztecs. It also corresponds to Abmuseurnkab, the winged monster of the Hindus, to the Chinese flying dragon, the 'Zimbabwe falcon' or the phoenix which appeared every 500 years at Heliopolis in Egypt, reborn from the ashes of a special nest which was also its funeral pyre.

It is, to say the least, curious that so many distant peoples should have associated the idea of a bird with that of fire or thunder. As Hans Hansen observes, 'many things in archaeology that seemed obscure only yesterday are clearer today and will be taken for granted tomorrow'. How often have we not read the

GIANTS AND THE LOST LANDS OF THE GODS

description of a space rocket being launched with a thunderous roar and leaving ,behind it a trail of fire, like some splendid yet monstrous bird?

An Egyptian legend tells of a king who 'took refuge in the belly of a white bird which came down from heaven in a trail of ire'. References to 'lords of the flame, riding through the air on the backs of fire birds', are common to ancient America, India and other parts of Asia. As for the phoenix, which builds a nest of spices and is burnt up in it by the sun's rays; would this not be a natural way for primitive people to describe the takeoff of a space rocket? Writing of this and similar myths, Homet takes a similar view to Soviet scholars when he says:

'We are more and more inclined to the conviction that the contents of myths if properly interpreted and understood, are nothing more than the memory of facts far in the past. The point is to extract the core of the myth, saga or legend and to grasp it.

'Thus we should have to deal with the Icarus myth, the tradition of the "flying man", and decide whether this widespread legend is nothing else than a memory, in mythical form, of vanished possibilities. Our modern civilization is only two thousand years old and modern man, with his flight instruments, is already probing into outer space. What if suddenly a geological or cosmic or atomic catastrophe should destroy the mankind of today and all their works, leaving nothing behind but a few elements (called "documents" from our point of view) - would not the descendants of the survivors much later on, thousands of years later, hand them down as something in the nature of an Icarus legend?'

It is easy to imagine such an event as Homet suggests. There is plenty of superstition left in our age of computers, and the survivors of a cosmic disaster might well regard it as a divine chastisement. Taking Gagarin as the type of the new Icarus, 'we may imagine future generations, in a world relapsed into barbarism, fashioning such legends as this:

'There was a man named Yuri who envied the moon for her power and beauty: he aspired to be like her, and flew up to the heavens in a fiery chariot in which he circled round the earth. But the sun, who is the moon's father, took his revenge: he seized a boulder and dashed Yuri down from the sky, destroying all the race of men with him.'

If the catastrophe were a geological one, it might be the goddess of earth punishing her ungrateful sons for deserting her and seeking to flee to the stars. A nuclear war might give rise to a legend of gods fighting for the mastery of heaven, and so on.

As Homer goes on to say, 'Why should it not be that thousands, even tens of thousands of years before us a civilization existed over thousands of years and reached the height of aviational possibilities? Just because such a train of thought is suspiciously easy one must be especially cautious, not only, however, with assertions, but also with a priori rejection.'

Orefona And The Tapir

Are we to suppose that the human race made its way to the stars and thus escaped from a catastrophe that would have plunged it into barbarism, or that space travelers visited the earth and civilized its inhabitants, or that mankind originated on some other planet and colonized the earth from there?

There is room or all these suppositions, and if is not only devotees of science fiction who uphold them. Einstein, for instance, believed in a plurality of inhabited worlds, and is said to have maintained that the navigators of 'flying saucers' are human beings who left earth 20,000 years ago and return to see how their descendants are getting on. The biologist Loren Eiseley suggests that the human race came from the stellar universe, while Soviet scholars such as Agrest and Kazantsev think that our early civilization was due in large part, if not entirely, to visitors from other worlds.

Thomas Gold of Cornell University believes that those planets where conditions are favorable to life have been populated by microorganisms transmitted by space explorers. According to this view, the seeds of life were sown on earth a thousand million years ago and in course of time produced highly intelligent creatures who discovered the art of space travel and thus introduced life on to other planets.

Similar views have been held by the German authority Rensch, the American Howells, and Soviet biologists, anthropologists and zoologists who believe that man possesses counterparts on other planets - being essentially similar to ourselves though they may differ in such details as height and proportion of limbs, skin pigmentation and perhaps internal structure. Most scientists reject this view and believe in a plurality of types of intelligent being; but there is much archaeological evidence, some of it very ancient, that tends to confirm the hypothesis of visits from outer space by human or humanoid creatures.

This evidence offers us a choice of inferences; either there exist in other worlds intelligent beings essentially like ourselves, or the human race came to earth from some other heavenly body, or men in ancient times traveled to other worlds and subsequently paid visits to their former home, the earth, which had relapsed into barbarism. If, like the Russians, we believe in 'parallel evolution' or the possible existence of advanced creatures who differ basically from ourselves, we may conclude that the 'white lords' of Atlantis, the half-feline monsters and other strange figures of myth, tradition or artistic symbolism probably existed simultaneously on our planet and are connected with one another. We may also believe that creatures from another world sojourned among us as friends and enemies, and that the inhabitants of earth reached heights of civilization and re-

GIANTS AND THE LOST LANDS OF THE GODS

lapsed into barbarism as the result, it may be, of some cosmic conflict.

Dr. Cynthia Fain reports Bolivian legends which go back more than 5,000 years and tell of the destruction of civilization in far-off times as the result of a conflict with some nonhuman race 'whose blood was not red like ours'. We may also quote from Beltran Garcia, a Spaniard who 'wishes to revive the sun-worship of the Incas and claims to be a descendant of Garcilaso Inca de la Vega. Garcilaso, who lived from 1539 to 1616, was the son of a conquistador and an Inca princess; he wrote a history of the Incas and is said by his descendant to have left important documents that remain unpublished. One of the most bizarre of Beltran Garcia's stories, allegedly based on these documents, is as follows:

'According to the pictographic writings of Tiahuanaco, in the age of giant tapirs, a race of manlike beings, of high intelligence but with webbed feet and a' different kind of blood to ours, came from another planet and settled on the highest lake on earth. During their passage through space they cast their excrement out of the spaceship and turned the lake into the shape of a man lying on his back, with his navel at the spot where our first mother is said to have reclined, impregnated with the seed of human knowledge.

'This may seem only a quaint legend, but the "frogmen" of modern times have webbed feet like the colonists of Tiahuanaco. Natives of the Andean region live at heights to which no white man can become acclimatized, which shows that they may well have a different type of blood from ours.

'The legend tells us that the visitors from outer space had powerful instruments with which they spied out a suitable place for their future amphibious existence. As for the "excrement" which they jettisoned from the ship to alter the contours of the lake, may it perhaps have been an atomic bomb? It is a curious fact that, in order to rob Lake Titicaca of the symbolic character which the Indians ascribed to it, it was represented on maps up to 1912 as almost circular in shape. Its true name was Titi - lake of mystery and of the sun - but to this was added a suffix which in many languages conveys the notion of "excrement".'

We are entitled to treat the story and the gloss with a good deal of skepticism, and this applies even more to the continuation of Sr. Garcia's account, in which science fiction of an improbable kind is spiced with a touch of pornography.

'In the Tertiary era, some 5 million years ago,' he tells us, 'when there were as yet no human beings on our planet but only primeval monsters, a spaceship, glittering like gold, landed on the Island of the Sun in Lake Titicaca. From this there alighted a female creature resembling a woman from her breasts to her feet but with a conical head, huge ears and webbed hands with four fingers.

This part of the story recalls the Inca nobles' custom of deforming their earlobes by hanging costly ornaments from them in order to draw attention to their

GIANTS AND THE LOST LANDS OF THE GODS

wealth. For this reason the Spaniards called them Orejones ('Big-ears'), and we are not surprised to learn that the mysterious lady was called Orejona. 'She came from Venus' - Sr. Garcia continues - 'where the atmospheric conditions are not unlike those on earth but where water was abundant, as shown by her webbed feet. She walked upright as we do, possessed human intelligence and, for the purpose of populating the earth, had sexual congress with a tapir. The products of this union had the reproductive organs of the animal species and were intermediate in terms of intelligence, but were sufficient to carry on the race.

'One day, having fulfilled her task and perhaps desiring to return to Venus and find a mate in her own image [pleasure after duty, one might say], Oreiona reentered her spaceship and disappeared from earth. Her descendants for the most part lived as animals, but a tribe in the Titicaca region which remained faithful to her memory developed intellectual powers and religious rites and became the home of pre-Inca civilization, as is related on the facade of the Gate of the Sun at Tiahuanaco.'

This farrago is only worth quoting as an illustration of how elements of information which deserve to be judged on their merits are blended with pure fantasy and served in a manner which shows no regard for probability or harm the reader's intelligence. Nobody, as far as we are aware, has ever seen, much less examined, the 'secret manuscripts' of Garcilaso Inca de la Vega. The adventures of Oreiona seem to have been concocted on the basis of several elements:

Kazantsev's theory that the carvings on the Gate of the Sun represent men in space-suits, their vessels and a Venusian calendar; the evidence we possess of prehistoric races, the long ears of the Inca nobles, rock-carvings showing men with conical heads, the 'Kappas' of Japanese legend and the belief that the surface of Venus is largely composed of water. All these elements, of course, date from long after the sixteenth century, at which time Garcilaso is supposed to have penned the story of Orejona.

The writers who base eccentric theories on fables of this kind are usually careful not to refer to them in too much detail but to select the parts that best fit their purpose. This method has the unfortunate effect of discrediting genuine scholars whose minds are open to new ideas, while it strengthens the position of hidebound traditionalists and encourages public opinion to be skeptical of theories which, however fantastic in appearance, may in fact be basically sound. It is not necessary to resort to distortion and extravagant imagery in order to frame hypotheses of much greater interest and verisimilitude than that of Oreiona. It is in fact quite possible to suppose that the blood of voyagers from outer space flows in our own veins, and if we do so we shall be less skeptical of attempts by some Soviet scholars to place the story of Atlantis in its cosmic setting.

GIANTS AND THE LOST LANDS OF THE GODS

Blue Men

Plato tells us that the first Atlanteans were of different race and blood from the other inhabitants of earth, and in 1960 a group of Soviet scholars suggested that-they may have been men of bluish color. This theory was based in part on Herodotus and the Egyptian historian Manetho, who lived in the third century B.C. and wrote a work which we possess in part only, describing his country's past on the basis of the inscriptions on ancient monuments. Other sources are the Palermo Stone and the Turin Papyrus which give lists of the Pharaohs and date respectively from about 2400 and 1250 B.C.

The Egyptians depicted their gods in various colors. Ammon, corresponding to Jupiter, and Shu, god of the air, were blue; Thoth, the moon-god, was shown in a tint between light blue and green, While Osiris, who watched over agriculture, was green in hue. Bearing in mind that Plato's story of Atlantis is ascribed by him to an Egyptian source, and that Atlanteans are said to have visited North Africa in very ancient times, Soviet archaeologists and biologists suggest that the gods of Egypt may be associated with one or other of the races that inhabited the lost continent. The individuals who were, in course of time, divinized as Ammon and Shu may have spent only a short period in Egypt, while the originals of Thoth and Osiris stayed there longer and acquired an olive-green complexion, which would be the natural effect of suntan on a bluish skin.

If, as has been supposed, the Canary Islands are a remnant of Atlantis, confirmation of the Soviet theory is furnished by their inhabitants the Guanches (exterminated by the Spaniards), whose skin was olive in color. Some Andean natives who live at a high altitude are bluish in complexion owing to the deficiency of oxygen in their blood, and there are parts of South America where the term 'blue blood' is used to denote a person of mixed white and Indian origin.

No one has ascertained why this term occurs throughout the world as a synonym for aristocracy; it was used in this way among the Vandals and the peoples of North Britain, central Russia and Mongolia.

The French archaeologist Henry Bac, commenting on the Soviet studies, suggests that the 'blue men from space' were the Atlantean aristocracy, and that it was in their honor that the later rulers of Atlantis wore blue garments, as Plato relates. Such garments are still favored by the 'blue men' of the Atlas Mountains, while the Picts and many other peoples of the European and African lands bordering on the Atlantic Ocean dyed their bodies blue 'to resemble the mighty sons of Atlas'. Bac's followers believe that the lords of the lost continent may have come from Venus, a planet of high peaks, and have preserved their original complexion as the result of living on similarly high ground in Atlantis.

As Robert Charroux reminds us: 'The ancient astronomers recorded strange occurrences on the planet Venus. St. Augustine, quoting Varro, tells us that Castor of Rhodes [first century B.C.] described how the planet, which formerly had many satellites, unexpectedly changed its shape, size, color and direction of movement: this, according to Adrastus, Cyzicenus and Dione, happened in the time of the mythical Attic king Ogyges, son of Neptune and reputed founder of Thebes in Boeotia, whose reign is said to have been marked by a deluge. (The Greek word ogygios means "primal", while in Sanskrit aughaja means "deluge-born".)' The event referred to by Varro may have been connected with an exodus of the inhabitants of Venus, but, as Charroux goes on to speculate, the change of environment was too abrupt and they found it difficult to reproduce themselves on earth. The race began to decline, and the last Venusians, unable to return to their native planet, engraved the message on the Gate of the Sun at Tiahuanaco before their final extinction.

A race such as this may have endowed the human species with all kinds of knowledge. It may be to them that the Popol Vuh, the sacred book of the Quiché Indians of Guatemala, refers when it speaks of 'the first race of men', those 'before the flood, who possessed all knowledge; who studied the four points of the horizon, the four quarters of heaven and the round surface of the earth'. Who were these people with their vast astronomical knowledge? In Guatemala and Mexico, in Colombia, Peru and Bolivia, we find legends of nonhuman races, their wars and their rule over others. They are described variously as blue men or men with round, flat or pointed heads, and it is curious that references to them also occur in places far distant from those in which they are principally remembered.

All-Seeing Eyes

The mention of a flat-headed race recalls the mysterious find of Professor Requefia at Valencia, near the lake of that name (formerly Laguna de Tacarigua) in Venezuela, about 20 miles southwest of Caracas: viz. the skeleton of a man with the skull flattened at the top. This was at first put down to a congenital deformity, but before long, other such skulls were found, including foetal remains with the same characteristic.

Again, huge monuments to 'men with pointed heads' suggest that their makers may have enjoyed modes of perception that are unknown to us.

As Pauwels and Bergier write in Le matin des magiciens: 'A friend of ours, the Peruvian Daniel Ruzo, set out in 1952 to explore the barren plateau of Marcahuasi, west of the Cordillera de los Andes. The plateau can be reached only on muleback, it is 12,500 feet up and has an area of one and a quarter square miles. Here Ruzo found rock-carvings of animals and human faces which, owing to the play of light and shadow, were visible at the summer solstice and at no other time. There were carved figures of animals of the Secondary period, such as the stegosaurus; lions, tortoises and also camels, which are unknown in South

GIANTS AND THE LOST LANDS OF THE GODS

America (this is not quite so, as their fossilized remains have been found).

A hillside was carved to represent an old man's head; when it was photographed, however, the negative showed the image of a radiant youth. Could this phenomenon be connected with some kind of initiation rite? Dating by the radiocarbon method is impossible, as there are no organic remains on Marcahuasi; but geology shows it to be very ancient, and Ruzo believes the plateau to have been the home of the Masma culture, perhaps the oldest in the world?

As regards figures that are visible only in certain lighting conditions, we may note that there are several in Europe and probably many others remain to be discovered. In southern Brittany there is an imposing complex of megalithic monuments which were studied over a period of 40 years by Marthe and Saint-Just Péquart and Zacharie Le Rouzic.

These scholars observed certain marks on one stone of a dolmen known as Kerham; they returned a year later to photograph them, but were startled to find that they had disappeared. However, one of the experts remained for some hours watching the stone, and found that the signs gradually reappeared, becoming more and more visible. In this way it was discovered that some carvings can be seen only at certain hours or on certain days of the year. At Locmariaquer there is a stone in the dolmen called the 'merchants' bench' (table des marchands) which is only visible on the 16th and 17th of certain months.

The number of rock carvings to be seen in every continent suggests the handiwork of migrant artists with titanic powers and titanic chisels. In Italy, Giulio Fronasini gave the names of Virgin of the Rocks and Profile of a Man to two such carvings at Allumiere near Rome. In the second of these the head is pointed at the top (perhaps to represent a helmet) in the same way as the Brazilian 'Giant of Havea' and many similar artifacts.

The mystery carvings which appear and disappear may well be connected with initiation rites, as Pauwels and Bergier suggest, but what is the explanation for the Marcahuasi face which presents one aspect to the naked eye and another to the photographic lens? It is hard to see how an artist could achieve this effect even with the benefits of modern science.

We can hardly imagine that the unknown sculptor was gifted with 'double vision', yet many marvels of the same kind await the explorer of the past.

At Chavin we find a suggestion of parallel evolution in representations of the Gorgon, whose hair, as in ancient Greece, consists of writhing serpents; but this figure was in fact known throughout antiquity, from the Etruscans to the Sicels, in Japan, China, Siam and Java, in Borneo, Hawaii and New Zealand. Cephalopods of similar aspect are carved on several ancient megaliths, including some in France. The Chavin version has the face of a jaguar, but, says Honoré, 'in detail it is so extremely like the Gorgon of Syracuse that one can scarcely help believing

GIANTS AND THE LOST LANDS OF THE GODS

in a connection between the two; hair, mouth and nose are almost exact copies'.

If the unknown artists who carved these figures did so from living models, it does not follow that these must have had human bodies and animal heads, like the Egyptian god of death, or the reverse, like centaurs. They may have looked altogether different, and merely recalled by some feature or other an animal species known to the sculptor. If we suppose, for instance, that there was an intelligent being with many tentacles and a head of more or less feline shape, the artist may well have chosen to represent it as a man-jaguar, and the 'Gorgon of Chavin' might have originated in some such manner. '

Ayers Rock in the southern part of Northern Territory, Australia. An unearthly landscape suggesting a natural monument to Lemuria.

A vanished civilization: scene near the Hsiug Nu capital.

One of the "Kappas" depicted in an old Japanese print.

The "Harappa seal", representing an animal of unknown species.

Negroes and Cushites doing homage to Pharaoh: a wall painting from the tomb of Huni at Thebes. It is impossible to see how such works could have been executed in the dark.

GIANTS AND THE LOST LANDS OF THE GODS

Another view of Stonehenge.

The giant heads of Easter Island.

Another mysterious effigy, this time with a body, from Easter Island.

GIANTS AND THE LOST LANDS OF THE GODS

CHAPTER NINTEEN
The Space-Ships Of Tiahuanaco

The territory known to scholars as ancient Peru is not coterminous with that country as it exists today, but extends to the headwaters of the Amazon, the Andean zones of Ecuador and Bolivia, and parts of northern Chile and northwestern Argentina. Throughout this large area, day-to-day life showed a considerably higher level of civilization than in Central America, and the contrasts between culture and barbarism were less marked.

The Peruvians had an impressive system of cultivation by terraces, with advanced methods of irrigation and fertilization, and had discovered the art of preserving meat and potatoes. Imposing ruins tell of the Mochica civilization (named after Moche, where the first excavations took place), which flourished along the northern part of the coast from Pacasmayo to Casma. In the Mochica tombs there have been found remains of two different races; skeletons belonging to what we would call a white race, and also Indian ones.

The Mochims built a canal 70 miles long, so efficiently that it is still in use today. They wove cotton and the wool of llamas, producing magnificent tapestries and embroideries and using advanced dyeing techniques. They were expert in working gold, silver, copper and their alloys, by processes that have not yet been rediscovered, and they had excellent methods of soldering. Their ceramics are masterpieces of skill and fantasy. As the German authority Gerdt Kutscher wrote: "Nothing seems to have been too high for their skills or too unimportant to be depicted by them. Animals and fruit, hunters and warriors, musicians and dancers, princes and sick people, not to speak of weird demons and gaunt spirits of the dead—all these are rendered on Mochica pottery with fascinating effect."

The ancient Peruvian scene was dominated by pyramids, of which hundreds are to be found along the coast. Those of Mochica were built with clay bricks. From this civilization we possess also the majestic ruins of the temples of the sun and moon (Huaca del Sol and Huaca de la Luna).

Huge irrigation works were constructed in the Chincha Valley near the coast,

GIANTS AND THE LOST LANDS OF THE GODS

where other ancient ruins include a fortress called La Centinela (the sentinel). This area was the scene of the cultures of Nazca (Nasca), Ica and Paracas. Tombs hollowed out of the rock contain hundreds of mummified corpses in the foetal position. These were probably prepared by a smoking process after the intestines were removed. Magnificent textiles have been found here: veils, brocades and 'gobelins', made by the same methods as the famous French product which dates from the fifteenth century, and fabrics covered with a mosaic of feathers. These masterpieces display no less than 190 different shades of color.

Near Nazca, on a plateau 1,200 feet high which is sheltered from sea-winds but patched by the sun, there is a thick network of 'canals' recalling those on Mars, together with enormous figures of known and unknown animals, including the spider and the legendary fire-bird. These constructions are not roads, since they begin and finish in mid-desert, nor do they seem to be irrigation works, since no reservoirs have been located. As for the designs and animal figures, they were discovered by air observation and seem to have been intended to be seen from above. Professor I. Alden Mason of Pennsylvania University is too orthodox a scientist to admit they could have been executed on instructions from men in flying machines, but he observes that 'doubtless they were made to be seen by celestial deities', and he mentions pre-Incaic beliefs that the stars were inhabited and that our earth was visited by divine beings from the Pleiades.

There are said to be many other sites of this kind in Peru and parts of Chile, but the Indians who know of them cannot explain their purpose, though they relate stories which suggest that the figures were intended to guide the course of navigators from outer space who established bases on earth.

Without venturing to say whether there actually were spaceports on Andean heights, we may quote the following as we received it from La Paz:

'The Indians say that thousands of years ago their ancestors traveled on great golden discs which were' kept airborne by means of sound vibrations at a certain pitch, produced by continual hammer-blows. This is not so absurd as it may seem. Vibrations of a set frequency may have had the effect of increasing the atomic energy of gold, thus reducing the weight of the disc and enabling it to overcome the force of gravity.

An Ageless Metropolis

About 450 miles southeast of Nazca and 15 miles south-east of Lake Titicaca are the ruins of Tiahuanaco, the city which, according to Inca mythology, was built in a single night by the herdsman who survived the Flood. Another legend, perhaps an older one, says that it was built by giants, and we may well believe this as we contemplate its ruins.

Other stories relate that the giants did not build the city of their own free

GIANTS AND THE LOST LANDS OF THE GODS

will but were made to do so by beings 'who came from the sky' (by way of Nazca, perhaps?), and who aided the dwarflike inhabitants of earth to rebel against the Cyclopes.

There is still much debate as to the age of this former seaport, which was thrust up to a height of 12,500 feet by the cosmic disaster of 10,000 years ago. The engineer and anthropologist Arthur Posnansky, after careful research, decided that the last city of Tiahuanaco was built 16,000 years ago. Some scholars put the city's age at a quarter of a million years, and this is possible inasmuch as several successive cities may have been built on the same site.

Signs of the direct influence of Tiahuanaco can be traced on the Peruvian coast. In 1920 Professor Julio Tello discovered vases on which were depicted llamas with five toes instead of the usual two. It might be thought that this was a piece of fantasy, the animals being 'humanized' by way of emphasizing their usefulness to man, but in fact it is known that prehistoric llamas had five toes, as did horses and cattle at the same period. The skeletons of five-toed llamas excavated by Tello proved, contrary to the general view, that mankind already existed and, in some parts of the world, had reached quite a high degree of civilization, at the time when the first mammals made their appearance and giant saurians were not yet extinct.

The inhabitants of Tiahuanaco were familiar with bronze, the use of which was unknown to other American cultures for a thousand years afterwards. They were highly skilled in metallurgy and used techniques that are still in part unknown to us for smelting, casting, silver-plating, hammering, embossed work, filigree, damascening and soldering. They also produced marvels of architecture which would be beyond our technical scope at the present day. To quote Pauwels and Bergier (op. cit., p. 197): 'The U.S. archaeologist Hyatt Verrill spent thirty years investigating the lost civilizations of Central and South America . . . In his fine novel, The Bridge of Light, he described a pre-Incaic city protected by a rocky defile which could only be crossed by a bridge constructed of ionized matter which could be made to appear and disappear at will. Verrill, who died at the age of eighty, insisted to the last that this was much more than a legend, and his wife, who survives him, is of the same opinion.'

Laymen are sometimes inclined to view accounts of lost civilizations with suspicion because of the scarcity of their remains; but archaeologists know the difficulty of research and the way in which time can obliterate records that might be expected to' endure for thousands of years. As late as the second half of the last century, travelers to Tiahuanaco were able to admire and sketch imposing colonnades of which there is now no trace. We may get some idea of its former glory from the old commentators.

Garcilaso de la Vega wrote: 'The most beautiful structure is a hill created

GIANTS AND THE LOST LANDS OF THE GODS

by the hand of man. The Indians aimed to imitate nature by this work. In order to prevent the masses of earth from collapsing, they secured the foundations by well-built stone walls. From another side there are two stone giants to be seen. They are clothed in long gowns and wear caps on their heads. Many large gateways have been built from a single stone.'

Diego de Alcobaza: 'Amid the buildings of Chuquiyutu [i.e. Tiahuanaco], on the shore of the lake, is a paved court 80 feet square, with a covered gallery 45 feet long going down one of its sides. Court and hall are one single block of stone. This masterpiece has been hewn out of the rock. There are still many statues to be seen here today. They represent men and women, and are so perfect one could believe the figures were alive. Some seem in the act of drinking, others look as if they were about to cross a stream; women give children the breast . . . '

Jiménez de la Espada: 'One of the palaces is truly an eighth wonder of the world. Stones 37 feet long by 15 feet wide have been prepared without the aid of lime or mortar, in such a way as to fit together without any joint showing.'

An unknown chronicler: "The great throne room at Tiahuanaco measures 160 feet by 130 feet; the smallest and oldest, 100 feet by 85 feet. The terraced temples are precisely like those which rise beside the Tigris and the Euphrates."

Cieza de Leon: 'In a colossal palace . . . there is a hall measuring 45 feet by 22 feet, with great doorways and many windows, its roof built like that of the Temple of the Sun at Cuzco. The steps leading down from the entrance are washed by the lake. The natives say that it is the temple of Viracocha, creator of the world.'

We may recall that today the distance from Tiahuanaco to Lake Titicaca is some 15 miles, and the water-level is going down year by year. The Indian boats which ply across the lake are identical with Egyptian papyrus boats as regards their shape, the material used and the method of construction.

Cieza de Leon goes on to say that the walls and niches of Viracocha's temple are decorated with statues of gold, copper and bronze, stone and clay masks and precious bracelets, and that the marks of gold nails are still to be seen. Some of these objects are preserved at the museum at La Paz named after Posnansky, who did his utmost to save Tiahuanaco from destruction but with only partial success. Many of its great buildings were, until well into the present century, dynamited for the sake of the materials or by incompetent treasure-hunters. The scale of depredation over the centuries will never be known.

Private collections today contain only a fraction of the city's former treasures, yet they include solid gold figurines weighing four to six pounds and cups, plates, spoons and goblets also of gold. Plates and cutlery in modern style did not appear in Europe, it will be remembered, until the end of the sixteenth century, yet in America they had been in use by the Aztecs, Incas and others for many centuries.

GIANTS AND THE LOST LANDS OF THE GODS

A message From The Infinite

In the Mediterranean world, as we have already seen, pyramids were used as mausolea and also (in the step-pyramid form), as temples: the second category includes the Mesopotamian pyramids and the legendary Tower of Babel.

In ancient America we also meet with both types, and at Tiahuanaco they are found side by side. The terraced pyramid known as the Acapana contains the ruins of what is thought to have been a sovereign's burial chamber, with an underground passage leading to it. Can its occupant have been the first 'white' lord in America? At Puma Puncu, about half a mile to the southwest, there was an even larger pyramid of three or four steps or stories, with a building comprising several chambers on each. On the third plat- form can be seen the remains of a big gateway, the 'Gate of the Moon', and similar gates must once have existed on the other levels. An extraordinary fact is that the gates of Tiahuanaco are exactly like those of Persepolis in ancient Persia.

There are other points of resemblance to the Mediterranean countries. As Honoré points out, the water supply was organized by means of long conduits similar to those of Crete and the hanging gardens of Babylon. To quote Marcel Homet, 'The great stone slabs of the temples of Tiahuanaco are joined together by metal cramps or rivets of a kind that have so far been found in one other place only: Mesopotamia, in the architecture of Assyrian palaces.

Also the pre-Deluge goddesses or fish gods of Tiahuanaco seem to be identical with the gods of Mesopotamia who were revered there from the fifth to the third century B.C. And it is especially in Tiahuanaco that we are reminded of the twelve tribes of Israel when among the Cyclopean buildings we find statues with aquiline noses, classic turbans on their heads from which fall the twelve symbolic braids of hair.'

And again: 'The sacred numeral 12 brings many things to mind. First of all there are the twelve tribes of Israel, in a country where turbans were worn around 1000 B.C. Besides, they dreamed in that country of a "Father of All Things" who was called Mot and was represented by the cosmogonal egg. We know that thousands of years before the existence of the twelve tribes of Israel there was another "Father of All Things" who was revered at Tiahuanaco and symbolized by the egg of the cosmos. He too bore the name of Mut.

'There are just as astonishing experiences to be had in studying the religious structures at Tiahuanaco. The Temple of the Sun, the "Kalat Sassaya" of the ancestors of the "Sons of the Sun," was also a fortress. In the language of the Berbers of North Africa, kalat means fortress. The highest-ranking deity of the people of Tiahuanaco was called Pacha Kama, which in Semitic can be rendered "the supreme, armour-clad ruler." The Supreme Being was called, in the Andes, Bacha Tata; in Swahili, the lingua franca of Central and East Africa, tata is "king", and

GIANTS AND THE LOST LANDS OF THE GODS

bacha in Arabic means "overloard".'

As for the name of the city itself, some derive it from tiawanaka, signifying 'this is from God?; the word tia in Aymara denotes majesty, splendor or the horizon.

This corresponds to teotl, the Aztec word for god, which appears in Nicaragua as teot and in Peru as ticsi. We may further compare the Greek word theos (Latin deus, Sanskrit deva) and the Chinese tien. But what kind of god was worshipped at Tiahuanaco?

One of the gateways in the pyramid of Puma Puncu is 24 inches high and 15 inches wide—too small for a man, but big enough for the puma which gave the temple its name.

The god of the ageless metropolis was kept there and worshipped in animal form, a reminder perhaps of the half- human, half-feline creatures who, as some believe, came down from heaven. In the same way, the Gate of the Sun is dominated by a jaguar-god bearing the symbols of thunder and lightning (cf. the fire-bird or thunder-bird motif), in the center of a frieze representing jaguars, condors, cobras and mysterious winged creatures. This gateway is the biggest carved monolith in the world, consisting of a single block ten feet high and over six feet wide. Posnansky believed that it was 18,000 years old and served astronomical and calendrical purposes. Others have suggested that it was meant to resemble the aileron of a spaceship. Kazantsev does not share their opinion, but he agrees with Posnansky in discerning among the bas-reliefs a calendar of the Venusian year. Other astronomers, not only Soviet ones, are of the same belief. It is in fact known that many pre-Columbian peoples used a calendar based on the time taken respectively by the earth and Venus to revolve round the sun, the ratio between the two periods being 13 to 8 (i.e. Venus completes its orbit 13 times in 8 of our years).

The use of a Venusian calendar is a remarkable fact, since, while Venus may well have impressed primitive people by its brightness, it requires a great deal more astronomical knowledge to observe its revolutions than those of the moon.

Those who believe in travelers from outer space point out that if the latter came from Venus, a Venusian calendar would be perfectly natural to them. We may add that Kazantsev, Zhirov and some French scientists have observed that there are figures on the Gate of the Sun which resemble spaceships and rocket engines exactly like the ion propulsion type which is currently under study in the USA.

GIANTS AND THE LOST LANDS OF THE GODS

Neptune, God Of The Apaches

Not all scholars admit that Tiahuanaco was the center from which civilization originally spread throughout Central and South America, though there is abundant evidence of contact between it and the Olmecs, Toltecs and other pre-Aztec cultures. But there are even more curious links between Tiahuanaco and the North American continent.

The US ethnologist Lucille Taylor Hansen tells the story of her visit to an Apache tribe in Arizona, who entertained her with a ritual dance. She had sought them out on the strength of an ancient legend which, she suspected, might provide confirmation of a daring hypothesis. Sure enough, when she began to show them photographs of Egyptian carvings, the Apaches recognized in one of these the 'god of light and fire' to whom the dance was dedicated, and who in their language was actually known by his Egyptian name of Ammon-Ra. This led to further extraordinary revelations based, like the Venusian calendar, on the 'sacred numbers' 8 and 13. When the ethnologist spoke of Tiahuanaco, the Apaches identified it with a centre of their own legendary empire and described, without ever having seen it, the statue of a 'bearded white man' that had stood there. 'The god,' they declared, 'holds a sword upright in either hand, at right angles to the forearm, to signify "friendship within limits".

"The swords and the head together form the shape of a trident, which is our secret sign of recognition. The place where the statue stands is the ancient home of our tribe."

A bearded giant and a trident . . . The statue represents the white god Viracocha, but it displays the attribute of Neptune or Poseidon, and 'Poseidonis' was the other name of Plato's Atlantis, consecrated to the sea-god.

When the Apaches were shown photographs of the ruins of Machu Picchu in the Andes they discussed them with great intelligence, although' they had never seen the ruins and many believed that they were purely mythical. An old sage described the tradition of his race as follows: 'Long before the Deluge we used to live in the land of red fire, in a city whose entrance was hard to find. Our country was the center of the world then; people came there to seek justice, as they now do to Washington. The city was a huge one; ships could not find the right way into the harbor without help. There was not much land, but the mountains were the highest in the world in those days, and deep down in them was the abode of the fire-god. It was through his rage that our old land was destroyed. The god left his underground cave, rose up through the mountain and poured fire and death on the terrified people. All the inhabitants put to sea and fled Westward; then the ocean changed its bounds and was no longer visible from our country, which in the days of its greatness dominated every sea in the world.'

It may be that some ancestors of the Red Indians belonged to Atlantis or

GIANTS AND THE LOST LANDS OF THE GODS

one of its colonies, or were prompted by some legend to identify themselves with its inhabitants. Homet's view is as follows:

'The ancestors of the present-day natives of Peru and Argentina came from the north. These were men of a white race. Even today there are a few survivors of the pure descendants of these peoples and they are pure white, namely the Uros of Lake Titicaca, who live in the same place where the famous civilization of Tiahuanaco once flourished. The same is true of most of the ancient inhabitants of America who derive from the first settlers. Dr. Vernau, who made a study of the Patagonians along the Rio Negro in Argentina came to the conclusion that "These peoples are whites of the same race as the Indians in central Brazil in the state of Minas Gerais, the famous people of Lagoa Santa".'

Part of Stonehenge.

Unfinished Easter Island statue, and engraved designs including letters of our alphabet (right) and the "fire-bird" (left).

Statue at Bamian, Afghanistan, 180 feet high; thought to represent a giant.

A relic of Lemuria: the level surface of Mount Connor, in the north of Western Australia.

GIANTS AND THE LOST LANDS OF THE GODS

CHAPTER TWENTY
Children Of The Sun

If a certain dictator had been aware of what we are about to described, he would undoubtedly have laid claim to the whole of Central and South America, except that the facts are so extraordinary that perhaps he would have refused to believe them.

The Chimu empire, with Chanchan as its capital, extended along the northern coast of Peru from north of Lima to the present border with Ecuador. The Chimu people must have descended from inhabitants of Mexico who sailed southward about the beginning of the Christian era, founding the cultures of Salinar, Gallinazo and Mochica. As time went on, these settlements united with others along the Moche river and subdued their neighbors, creating an empire which lasted from about A.D. 500 to 1400; it was then conquered by the Incas, who borrowed much from it in the field of art, customs and mythology.

The Chimu mostly used clay bricks for building. We can still admire the ruins of the fortress of Paramonga on the southern border of their kingdom, surrounded by circles of ramparts which have partly withstood the destructive effects of time. They had excellent irrigation arrangements and a time road system; narrow streets were flanked by walls to protect them from wind and sand, wider routes led across the desert, and there were arteries of a breadth of 15, 25 or even 80 feet.

The walls of the monumental highland constructions were severe and unadorned, but in the coastal zone the buildings were richly decorated with stylized animals, flowers and geometrical designs. The reliefs at Chanchan are reminiscent of almost every civilization in the world, from Grecian friezes to those of central Asia, from the art of Egypt to that of Mesopotamia and China.

The imposing ruins of Chanchan cover an area of 6 or 7 square miles. The city was divided into 10 districts by walls up to 40 feet thick. The houses have been largely destroyed by wind and weather, but there are also remains of pyramids, cemeteries and reservoirs. Chan signifies 'snake', and the reptile-god was

GIANTS AND THE LOST LANDS OF THE GODS

adored here in the same way as the goddess of Buto in ancient Egypt. But to revert to the beginning of our chapter, a Spanish pilot named, Pedro Corzo who sailed up and down the Peruvian coast at the time of the conquista tells us that everywhere in the temples he found wooden or stone statues of a god named Guatan or 'whirlwind'. This reminds us irresistibly of the Germanic storm-god Wotan, and in fact we find that Wotan was the original name of the Chimu divinity among the Mayas, who 'exported' him to South America. In Guatemala he was the lord of night and darkness, and the Mayas, Aztecs and Zapotecs all associated him with the art of divination.

In Germanic folklore Wotan (or Odin) was the god of battles and also the creator and disposer of the world, the father of civilization and possessed of a prophetic spirit. Thus the European and American divinities closely coincide, and the attributes of Wotan lend color to the 'space theory.' The whirlwind reminds us of an astronaut's vessel, night and darkness suggest outer space, and as a culture hero he may well be compared to legendary visitors of superhuman intelligence.

It may also be pointed out that the Inca year comprised twelve months beginning (as in many parts of the World) at the winter solstice, and that in northern Europe this was 'Wotans' day', the feast of the sun. Again, may there not be a parallel between Wotan's paradise of Valhalla, where the souls of warriors were guided by the Valkyries and welcomed by Odin's wife Frigga (sometimes confused with Freya, the goddess of young love), and a far-off planet full of marvels?

The Valkyries or Amazons are of course found all over the world, from Greece to Scandinavia, from the Caucasus to West Africa (Dahomey) and America. The first-century historian Diodorus Siculus tells of an Amazon queen who fought the Atlanteans and the Gorgons and afterwards allied herself with the Egyptian god Horus, son of Isis. Homet remarks in this connection: 'When Diodorus repeats a traditional tale according to which the Amazons crossed the ocean to fight the Gorgons among the Atlanteans, we can, if we like, call it an interesting fable; the historical fact remains that when Pizarro arrived he found an island to the northwest of Colombia which bore the name of Gorgone.'

If we recall that the Gorgon's glance was supposed to turn the onlooker to stone (a nuclear contraption of some sort?), and compare Agrest's theory of what happened to Lot's wife, we have the ingredients of a remarkable science-fiction story.

The Spanish chronicler Cavegal tells us that the Amazons found their way to America, where they rode horses and camels and obeyed a queen named Conori. Fossil remains of these animals have indeed been found in Colombia, and the white god Bochica is said to have ridden on camelback.

Many prehistoric graffiti of the Amazon basin represent horses, some saddled and drawing carts or chariots. At Palli Aike, on the Straits of Magellan, Dr.

GIANTS AND THE LOST LANDS OF THE GODS

Julius Bird in 1938 discovered a cave containing the bones of men and horses, and in 1950 these were proved by atomic dating to be 9,000 years old.

Apropos of Wotan and divination, we may recall the following passage from Honoré:

'The counterpart of Delphi in the New World was Rimac, a short day's journey on foot from Pachacamac, which is near today's Lima. The chroniclers recorded that the inhabitants of the Rimac Valley worshipped a god of human shape who when consulted disclosed the future like the oracle of Delphi. White-robed priests, who lived as celibates and never partook of salt or pepper, carried out the ritual. Before starting out on a military expedition, or even a hunt, kings and chieftains would consult the oracle at Rimac, which was known all the way to the Cordilleras.

'Nearly as famous was the oracle of the god Pachacamac, after whom the chieftains of Guismancu named their capital. (Guismancu was a small country on the coast of Peru south of the Chimu empire.) According to the chroniclers this city was bigger than ancient Rome, and in its temple a black devil had spoken to the people. In the temples of Guismancu, which became places of pilgrimage for the population, the priests foretold the future from behind gold masks.

'The oracles of the Peruvian coast were so famous that in order to annex them the Inca Pachacuti once mobilized an army of 40,000 men. He took the god Pachacamac along to Cuzco.'

This brings our story as far as the Incas. We shall use this name for them, as do most archaeologists and historians, but it should be borne in mind that 'Inca' was a title originally confined to the ruler and the aristocracy, while the common folk were Quechua Indians (as they still are today). As with many other pre-Columbian peoples, we know little of the Incas' early history. They seem to have had no system of writing, and we can only piece together their story on the basis of scanty archaeological records and, for the latest period, the accounts of Spanish conquerors and chroniclers, mummies, past and present

According to Inca legend, Manco Capac, the founder of the race and of its ancient dynasty, 'came to earth and dwelt on the Island of the Sun in Lake Titicaca, together with his sister and consort, Mama Ocllo. They wandered northwards until they came to the land designated as their home 'by the Sun-god, and there founded the Quechua empire with its capital at Cuzco, which signifies 'navel' or 'centre of the earth'.'

Cuzco is situated 11,000 feet above sea level in a fertile and sheltered valley near the upper reaches of the Urubamba river. The Inca empire, known as the 'land of the four quarters' (Tahuantinsuyu), extended from the south of what is now Colombia to the north of Argentina, a long, narrow territory bounded on the west by the Pacific Ocean and on the east by the Amazonian basin, an area in-

GIANTS AND THE LOST LANDS OF THE GODS

fested by cannibals who were constantly at war with their neighbors.

Some authorities date the origin of the empire back to A.D. 494 and 565, others to 1130. After a rapid period of expansion in the fifteenth century it was conquered by the Spaniards around 1530, though many strongholds in the Cordillera held out for longer.

There was, however, unquestionably a pre-Incan kingdom as well. A painstaking historian has established that at least 103 sovereigns ruled before Atahualpa, the last king of the Incas, who was murdered by Pizarro's order in 1533, and that the origin of the race dates back to pre-diluvian times.

These investigations, carried out in the light of Spanish chronicles, have thrown doubt on the belief that the Quechuas knew nothing of the art of writing. It appears that in prehistoric times they 'wrote on banana leaves by a method invented in the reign of Huayna Caui Pirhua, third sovereign of the dynasty before the flood', but that this was forbidden by the sixty-third Inca, Topu Caui Pachacuti IV, who, on hearing that the process was being used to disseminate predictions of catastrophes that were to befall his country, 'ordered all banana leaves to be burnt and forbade all manner of writing under pain of death'.

The first ruler who emerges from myth into a shadowy form of history is Sinchi Roca, who reigned about 1150. Our chief concern here, however, is with the eighth of the series (counting from Manco Capac), whose name or title was Viracocha Inca. The original Viracocha, as we have seen, was the white god of the Quechuas, and the Spaniards were given this name by reason of their fair skin. The historical Viracocha Inca was of fair complexion and bearded, as we know from his portrait.

The Inca system of government has been called pre-Communistic, i.e. the land belonged jointly to its cultivators and their rulers: the nobility, priests and peasants each received a third of every crop. The nobles were known as 'long-ears' since, as we have seen, they pierced their ears and hung heavy ornaments from them. They and the priests were responsible for the wonders of architecture of which E. Fergusson wrote: 'Neither the Greeks nor the Romans nor the Middle Ages achieved such perfection,' while H. Velarde speaks of a 'country crystallized into geometrical shapes'.

The Incas were devout sun-worshippers, and their priests enjoyed almost unlimited power. There was also a class of 'Chosen Women' or 'Virgins of the Sun', corresponding to the Vestal Virgins in ancient Rome. These were girls of good family who tended the eternal flame on the god's altar; as in Rome, they had power of life and death over condemned criminals, and their own transgressions were punished by drowning, like that of the unfortunate Rhea Silvia.

The ancient American sovereigns were called 'sons of the Sun', as were those of Egypt, Assyria and Crete and also the Chinese emperors, especially the Chou

GIANTS AND THE LOST LANDS OF THE GODS

dynasty. Among the high-born Incas it was customary for brothers to marry their sisters, mothers their sons and fathers their daughters. This, as Honoré points out, was also the custom of the Pharaohs and of ancient Persia in the reigns of Cyrus, Darius and Xerxes, and subsequently until the conquest by Alexander the Great.

As regards links between the Quechuas and Egyptians, in August 1953 Dr. Bird discovered near Lima the tombs of a prince named Capac who died in the fourth or fifth millennium B.C. and was buried in a sarcophagus of Egyptian type. Another such sarcophagus, together with statues in Mexican style, was excavated in the 'Egyptian valley' in the southern part of the Amazon basin, halfway between the rivers Xingu and Tocantins. On 13 November 1954 the Rioide Janeiro newspaper O Cruzeiro reported the discovery, in the village of Durados on the Pira-Veve river, of an 'Egyptian' cameo representing a queen, with an inscription in hieroglyphics signifying that after her death her soul mounted to heaven and her virtues were rewarded by celestial peace.

In 1531, when Pizarro's Spaniards, eager for gain as usual, burst into the great temple at Cuzco, they found some strange bundles that proved to contain mummified bodies in a foetal position, wrapped in precious cloths, their faces covered by masks of gold, silver, wood or clay. Unlike the Egyptians, who used natron and resin packs and anointing with oil, the Incas relied for mummification on the dry climate and saliferous soil of Peru. However, excavators at Ganchavita in Colombia found a group of mummies each wearing a small gold crown and surrounded by funeral offerings—cloth, gold figures, ornaments and emeralds. As Honoré remarks, 'It was surprising that mummies should have been found here, a country with a climate most unfavorable for conservation by natural processes. But chemical analysis has established that resins and oils were used, so the methods of mummification were almost exactly the same as in ancient Egypt.'

The Quechuas in fact used different techniques, as the discovery of mummified bodies has shown. In 1560 Garcilaso de la Vega witnessed the removal of the mummies of five Inca sovereigns identified as Viracocha Inca of the long white hair, Capac Yupanqui, Huayana Capac, Mama Runto and Mama Ocllo. In a sitting position, with downcast eyes and arms crossed over their breasts, the bodies in royal robes were an impressive sight. According to José de Acosta, 'they were so intact and so well preserved with a certain kind of pitch that they seemed as though alive'. Garcilaso added: 'I believe that the Indians' secret consists in burying the bodies in snow and afterwards using the bitumen of which Father de Acosta speaks. When I saw them thus, I felt like touching one of Huayana Capac's lingers, as though it were that of a living man!

The Spaniards removed these mummies to Lima, where they rapidly decomposed in the heat and damp and had to be buried. We may recall that in March 1963 the mummy of the Egyptian princess Mene, who died in 322 B.C., began to decompose and had to be moved to a cold storage chamber at Oklahoma University, where biologists were astonished to find that the epithelial cells were still intact.

Mummies in a perfect state of preservation have also been found in America in recent times. In 1953 a Chilean muleteer discovered, in an Andean glacier, a small sarcophagus containing the mummified body of an Inca girl who had lived about 730 years ago, surrounded by figurines of solid gold including one with a toad's head. In 1959 chance led to the discovery, in a cave in Sonora province in Mexico, of thirty well preserved mummies dating from about 10,000 years ago and belonging to an unknown civilization.

These facts are remarkable enough in themselves, but Sr. Beltran Garcia embroiders them after his own fashion. 'The mummies of the five Inca sovereigns,' he tells us, 'were removed from the temple and hidden before Garcilaso was born, and their discovery was due to an error. From the scientific point of view they were bodies in a state of hibernation, with all their organs inert but living. The Incas were skilled at producing this condition, and they did so in the expectation that scientists would one day be able to resuscitate the bodies. The technique of embalmment was used at the Vatican too, and the "pitch" used by the Incas was in fact a solid, transparent cream consisting of three ingredients, one of which was quinine.'

We report these singular ideas merely as a curiosity, though some people have been taken in by them. Garcilaso's account makes it clear that he is talking of dead bodies, but his descendant, referring to the Chilean discovery, writes as follows: 'Garcilaso de la Vega states that the method of the "frozen toad" (sapo helado) was an Inca secret. It seems that the child was meant to be the bearer of a message to scientists of the future, but that the body's sudden exhumation deprived it of life. The gold figurines, especially that with the toad's head, contained a secret explanation of the experiment.'

If and when Sr. Garcia and those who share his views are privileged to hold telepathic converse with some half-immortal Inca scientist whose hiding-place is unknown to the rest of us, it is to be hoped that they can give a fuller explanation of the gold figurines. Meanwhile, we are assured, other live mummies are hidden in the craters of volcanoes and in Andean glaciers. Those in craters are in a state of lethargy induced by the curare process, while those in glaciers are in artificial hibernation due to the "toad method".'

All Roads Lead To Cuzco

The Inca empire straggled 'like a torn spider's web' over the northwestern and western part of South America. It comprised areas of very different character, and it could not have been held together without an excellent system of communi-

GIANTS AND THE LOST LANDS OF THE GODS

cations. When the Spaniards marched on Cuzco they were amazed to find that the Inca roads were 'better than those of ancient Rome'. Two parallel arteries extended from north to south, over the Andean plateau and along the coast, and were connected by innumerable transverse roads; many of these are still usable, as are the bridges thrown across dizzy heights. Just as the Romans, when they had conquered a new territory, set about binding it with a network of roads that led to the Eternal City, so the Incas created a system in which all roads led to Cuzco. They also operated a surprisingly fast relay service for the transport of messages and light objects: every day fresh fish from the Pacific arrived at Cuzco, high up in the Andes, for the benefit of priests and nobles.

The soil was cultivated with miraculous skill. Barren slopes were transformed into fertile terraces, and artificial irrigation produced fine crops of maize, sweet potatoes, chili peppers, agave, cotton and the coca plant. We are reminded of what Plato says of Atlantis: 'They cropped the land twice a year, making use of the rains from heaven in the winter, and the waters that issue from the earth in summer, by conducting the streams from the trenches.' As Pauwels and Bergier observe, 'some of the pre-Incaic irrigation works are such as could hardly be carried out with modern turbo-drills; and why were huge paved roads created by a people who made no use of the wheel?'

Not only the wheel but the lathe was unknown to the Quechuas, and yet their pottery is among the finest in the world. They were skilled weavers, too, yet they were not in the habit of wearing rich garments, and they had no furniture. A kind of recess in each house acted as a cupboard, pantry, chest of drawers and lumber-room. Had they chosen, they could have enjoyed many other luxuries, and their craftsmanship was such that it has given rise to curious legends. Beltran Garcia—to quote him once more—says that in the sixteenth- century the goldsmiths of Lima produced ingots which resembled ordinary gold in all respects except that their density was less than half that of the gold known to us.

Some Inca necklaces, melted down at a temperature of 1,100 degrees Centigrade, produced ingots with an equally low density (8-9). The same authority tells us that the Incas knew how to extract water from air; but the only credible fact he adduces concerning Inca science concerns the famous 'candelabrum of the Andes'.

South of Lima, on a red cliff-face overhanging the sea, is a deep carving of a trident or three-branched candlestick, over 800 feet high and visible from more than 12 miles away. It is generally thought to have been meant for measuring tides, but its height makes this improbable. Some threads or cords have been found attached to the rock, and this lends a certain plausibility of Sr. Garcia's theory, which for once is not based an 'secret documents'. According to him, 'a long rope suspended in the central column functioned as a vertical pendulum, and horizon-

GIANTS AND THE LOST LANDS OF THE GODS

tal cords were fixed in the branches on either side. The whole system, comprising counterweights, graduated scales and ropes passing through pulleys, "constituted an enormous and delicate seismograph, capable of recording earth tremors and shocks not only in Peru but throughout the world.'

In the marketplace of Cuzco, Pizarro found everything Cortés had seen at Tenochtitlan and, in addition, scales of the same pattern as those of ancient Rome. The Incas were not so adept in mathematics as the Mayas, but, unlike many ancient peoples, they used the decimal system, which they took over from the Chimu along with other devices that have not survived. They could perform complicated calculations with the quipu, a series of colored strings in which knots are tied, and which sufficed for the organization of the whole economy. Some believe that it was more than a mere calculating device, and J. Alden Mason, in The Ancient Civilizations of Peru, refers to the likelihood that it was used for purposes of historical record. Certain Chinese chronicles tell us that an emperor of former times wished to replace the ideographic script by one based on knots; if this is so, it goes to confirm the existence of links between Asia and pre-Columbian America, and also the theory that each quipu is a book, written in a language we cannot read.

The Swedish expert, Baron Nordenskiiild, observed that 'writing need not be the only way of expressing thought', and he believed that the quipu might represent horoscopes or prophecies as well as mathematical calculations. Pauwels and Bergier remark (op. cit., p. 180), that 'modern mathematicians regard the knot as one of the most mysterious of phenomena.

It can only occur in an odd number of dimensions, and topologists have only succeeded in studying the simplest kinds of knot. It is quite possible, therefore, that the quipu records knowledge that we have yet to discover.'

The most extraordinary city that has survived from Inca times is Machu Picchu, a majestic collection of ruins discovered in 1911 by the intrepid explorer Hiram Bingham, and situated 8,000 feet above sea-level and 2,000 feet above the Urubamba valley. Yet it is probable that the Inca city was 'built on the remains of a still older and more splendid metropolis, and there may even have been more than one of these. Whatever the final verdict of scientists may be, we may note that Machu Picchu, like Tiahuanaco, is known to many generations of North American Indians as an ancient center of their race.

GIANTS AND THE LOST LANDS OF THE GODS

CHAPTER TWENTY-ONE
The Heirs Of Atlantis

'We planted a noble tree in the forest: it grew and grew, bearing exquisite flowers and fruit full of sun, and it spread its seed round about, and other trees pierced the soil. A fiery hand burnt it up, fiery air scorched it, the fiery earth devoured its roots. Fire scattered the gardeners and dried up the soul of the earth . Young trees split asunder, trees that flowered for a season only, others that yielded monstrous blossoms, and their fruits turned to dung . The young trees ran to seed, the rains uprooted them and swept them away, and the jungle devoured them.'

So runs a fragment of verse attributed to the great Sanskrit poet Kalidasa (A.D. 350-420). Some think it apocryphal, but others, connecting it with a famous lyric of his which we shall quote further on, believe that it is certainly by him and describes the downfall of some great prehistoric culture— perhaps that of Mu— and the disintegration of its relics. We are not concerned here with a discussion of literary origins, but the passage gives a vivid picture of what may happen to the heirs of a great civilization that is suddenly cut off by the roots. Such must have been the fate of the colonies of Atlantis; in the light of archaeology, we may consider these to have been located in the wilder parts of South America and wherever the outposts of 'Aztland' bordered on the African dominions of the fabulous motherland of Mu.

Professor Homer, in Sons of the Sun (London, 1963), has given a striking account of his explorations and of the exotic secrets that lurk in the 'green hell' of the Amazon basin. The carvings and inscriptions found there include symbols that belong to distant parts of the world and representations of unexpected subjects. Among these are bulls, which historians tell us were only introduced by the Spaniards; a rhinoceros; and men with winged helmets like those of the Vikings or the god Baal, or the bronze figurine at Abini in Sardinia, or certain bas-reliefs in Egypt, Crete and Mycenae.

In Brazil and the neighboring countries we find drawings of boats of a style that cannot have been known to the Amazonian natives. Four or five millennia

GIANTS AND THE LOST LANDS OF THE GODS

B.C., the inhabitants of the island of Maraio in the Amazon delta made votive models of four-masted ships resembling those of Crete, which could carry some 800 people and were equipped with large tanks for drinking-water. The Cretan ships were called cara-mequera, and this is precisely the name given to these receptacles by Brazilian tribes of the Tupi-Guarani linguistic family.

Red Magic

Near Tarame, on a plateau which extends from the Rio Urari Coera to the Sierra Paracaima in southeastern Venezuela, Homer discovered one of the most mysterious and impressive monuments of prehistoric America, the Pedra Pintada ('painted rock'), a huge egg-shaped stone under which, the Indians believe, are the remains of a blond giant who lived thousands of years ago. We quote here some extracts from Homet's description of the rock and of his discoveries in the vicinity.

'The Pedra Pintada is such as imposing mass of stone, isolated in the midst of an immense plain, that it seems almost within one's reach when it is still several hours' journey away. It is a massive monument over 300 feet long, over 250 feet wide and over 95 feet high. It looks like a gigantic ellipsoid or, perhaps better, like an egg. One's mind naturally recalls at once the "Egg of the Cosmogony" in the ancient tales, or the "Egg of the Creation of the World". This thought is immediately related to another: the "Egg Origin" in the ancient lands bordering on the Mediterranean was always accompanied by a serpent. And what did we find on the frontal side of the Pedra Pintada? The old serpent of the tales set so high that the creator of this work must have used a truly gigantic scaffold to carry out his design.

'I saw . . . a human skull, polished by time. Later we found another in the same spot. A quick study convinced me that this could not belong to a Mongoloid race. Nor was it the skull of one of the "giants" as I had expected, for I had been on the track of these "giants" ever since I had been in America. Even von Humboldt, whose voyages of exploration from 1799 to 1804 are still remembered, recognized their existence though he never found them. After searching through almost 8,000 square miles of previously unknown territory, we at least discovered their traces. But even at the Painted Rock we were not able to get at their graves. It was impossible for us to penetrate the substructure; it was filled in with masses of earth which we could not remove with our modest supply of tools. All I could examine was the passageway which ran under the rock to the right. It must have been over 90 feet long, and at the end it was completely blocked with stones and earth. Did it reach the courtyard of the temple? Everything suggested that it did.

'The completely stylized snake of the centre facade measures over 22 feet and commands thousands of inscriptions and letters. They recall the ancient Egyp-

GIANTS AND THE LOST LANDS OF THE GODS

tian, Semitic, Hebrew, Sumerian, Celtic and Old Irish signs.

'The creators of these drawings must have been substantially different from the Indians inhabiting these regions today. It is a recognized fact that when the European conquerors arrived these Indians had neither wagons nor roads nor horses and could not write at all. Yet, covered with the same patina or age surface as the other images on the rock walls, there are sketches of horses, wagons and wheels, many times repeated. They are always drawn in profile and often executed with a special technique, namely that used in ancient Egypt of the third and fourth millennia B.C.'

Near the Pedra Pintada, Homet found dolmens similar to those of Europe and Algeria, inscribed with Greek letters and other symbols common to the Celtic and Semitic peoples. He also noticed that a passage had been carved in the rock itself, too high for his modestly equipped expedition to explore it. According to an Indian guide, this led to an enormous chamber at the very top, where victims were imprisoned before the sacrifice: they were then suffocated by poisonous gases from the bowels of the earth, which reached the chamber by another passageway. One side of the great rock had been hollowed out so as to form caves; these were full of human bones, and gave a curious echo at certain spots.

Anyone who remained for long in these caves was visited by a curious nightmare or vision of human sacrifice, described by Homet from his own experience as follows:

'A great crowd moved along to the accompaniment of loud blows on a bronze gong. Thousands of people, men, women and children, dressed in white, were slowly and solemnly approaching the Pedra Pintada. They came to a complete stop opposite the principal entrance. A voice from on high rang out and echoed five or six times. It rang down on the mass of the faithful, who prostrated themselves in awe. Then out from the crowd stepped certain tall men of majestic bearing and came close to the great stone monument.

'One of them placed himself before the pentagonal dolmen. Another, accompanied by his assistants, climbed to the second, somewhat higher platform, of which the crowd below could see only the four burial caves. A third priest, even more impressive in appearance than his two companions, was also followed by acolytes as he now entered the broad path between the two rocks and disappeared from the view of the pilgrims kneeling on the plain.

'Next two naked men, without chains or guards and scarcely upheld by the servants of the "Sacred Death", climbed to the two visible platforms. They had the appearance of sleepwalkers. They were made to stretch out on the pointed ends of the dolmen, whose red color had begun to glow in the light of the rising sun. Once again the mysterious tones were heard from on high and reverberated five or six times.

GIANTS AND THE LOST LANDS OF THE GODS

'Then the priests of the first and second degree [evidently a similar hierarchy to that of the Ibero-Celtic priesthood, and reflected in the structure of the Pedra Pintada] raised their ritual knives of sharpened stone before the crowd, thrust them into the chests of their victims, tore out their hearts and cut them open. Thereupon they threw the remains to the four points of the compass and announced to the kneeling spectators the fate of their people for the coming year.'

Could this horrific vision be induced by gases seeping up from the earth, and if so, how could it reproduce so faithfully the scenes which no doubt took place on the Pedra Pintada thousands of years ago? This is a question to which we shall never know the answer.

The Secret Of Eldorado

'Manoa is on an island in a big salt lake. Its walls and its roofs are of gold and are reflected in a gold-paved lake. All the palace cutlery, for the tables and the kitchen, was of pure gold and silver; copper and silver were used even for the most unimportant things. In the middle of the island there was a temple dedicated to the sun. Round this temple were statues of gold, representing giants. On the island there were trees too of gold and silver. The statue of a prince was completely covered in gold-dust.' (Honoré, op. cit., p. 209).

Such is the account given by Cortés's secretary, Francisco Lopez de Gomara, in his Historia general de las Indias, of the city of Manoa ('Noah's water'), reputed to be capital of Eldorado, a fabled land of immense wealth which took its name—'the man covered in gold'—from the statue mentioned above. The description is itself a fabulous one, and seems inspired by its author's delirious thirst for gold. For the last four hundred years adventurers and scientists have sought the mysterious land in vain; their longing for gold or knowledge has generally cost them their lives, whether from treacherous rivers, starvation, poisoned arrows or the deadly bite of snakes or insects.

Is Eldorado then a complete delusion? We do not believe so, since many coherent tales concerning it have been collected from the Indians over the last four centuries, and there are solid arguments for locating it in the Serra Parima, an unexplored mountain range on the border between Brazil and Venezuela. Parima signifies in Guarani 'the mountain with much water', an appropriate name for a lake in mountainous territory. The region is inhabited by a tribe known as the Maku, and Homet records that one of their chiefs spoke to him as follows:

'If you follow the Urari Coera upstream for eleven days you will come to a stream which flows into the Great River. You must follow it for four days more, not because the distance is so great but because there are many rapids and the current is very strong. Then you will see a great rock. It is covered with inscriptions and painted red. Opposite the rock on the right side of the river bank is a sort of village. The houses used to be of stone but they are now all in ruins.

'They are built in long rows with broad, regular streets between. When you leave this ruined place and continue towards the place where the sun sets, you will come in two days to mountain country and to a high wall. You cannot go across it, you must search for a stone gate under a great arch, leading below ground. Then you will come to a great city of stone, built in straight lines, but it too is all in ruins. You can follow the lines, but you must be careful at every step, because where the houses used to be there are now only great slabs of stone: many have been split by the roots of trees which have grown up through them. Very close by you will find a lot of water, and in it there are many yellow stones and the powder which you white men seek so greedily.'

The chief's description evidently relates to a lost city of Eldorado buried in the Amazonian jungle. Homet was convinced of this, for although his informant had never seen a city in his life, his account of its whereabouts agreed with a version that was known to Colonel Percy Fawcett, a British explorer who disappeared in 1925 while searching for relics of Atlantis in the Brazilian jungle. Before his last fatal expedition, Fawcett wrote: 'Whether we succeed in penetrating the jungle and come out alive, or whether we leave our bones there, of this I am certain: the key to the mystery of ancient South America, and perhaps of the whole of prehistory, can be found if we are able to locate these old cities of the solar civilization and open them up to science. Their existence I do not for a moment doubt—how could I? I myself have seen a portion of one, and that is the reason why I observed it was imperative for me to go again. The remains seemed to be those of an output of one of the largest cities, which I am convinced is to be found together with others, if a properly organized search is carried out. Unfortunately I cannot induce scientific men to accept even the supposition that there are traces of an old civilization in Brazil. But I have traveled through regions unknown to other explorers and the wild Indians have told me time and again of the buildings, the characteristics of their old inhabitants and the strange things to be found there.'

As related in the memoir Exploration Fawcett (London, 1953, and quoted by Homet, the British explorer came across an old document at Rio de Janeiro describing the adventures of a native of Minas Gerais, whose real name is not known but whom he called Francisco Raposo, in search of the lost gold mines of Muribeca. After months of fruitless journeying east of the Xingu river, which flows into the Amazon from the south, Raposo and his companions came to the foot of a high mountain chain. One of the men, seeking for firewood in the low scrub, caught site of a deer which disappeared into the rocks. While pursuing it they came to a cleft in the face of the precipice, and found that it was possible to climb up through it to the summit of the mountain. After three strenuous hours they reached the top and were amazed to see a huge city on the plain about four miles away. Two days later, having sent out scouts who found the place deserted, they visited the city,

GIANTS AND THE LOST LANDS OF THE GODS

the entrance to which consisted of a triple arch formed of stone slabs weighing at least 50 tons apiece.

Homet's summary continues thus: 'There were unusual inscriptions on the middle arch. They then walked along the wide paved streets flanked on either side by stone buildings. Everything was overgrown by vegetation. The columns at the entrances to the houses were adorned with figures which Raposo took to be "demons". The men walked on in a state of astonishment and came to a large place where they saw a statue of a man on a black column; his arm pointed to the north. On the gateway of a ruined palace there were paintings, sculptures and especially a portrait of a young man stripped to the waist. Under the statue Raposo saw some writing which he carefully copied; the letters' were later recognized as being identical with archaic Greek. In a large temple near the city the discoverers found a small gold coin with the picture of a young man kneeling, and on the reverse side were designed a bow, a crown and a musical instrument. This description may remind us of some lines by Kalidasa which run as follows:

'Abandoned by the king, the palaces and houses with their goodly apartments fall into ruin. Dogs scavenge and howl in places where, at nightfall, amorous girls with silver bells on their ankles once danced before their lovers. Only wild cattle drink at fountains which once reflected ladies' arms clad in gold bracelets. The tame peacocks have fled to the jungle, no longer hearing the bells that used to lull them as they swayed on the branches of garden trees. On the great stairways of the temples, once thronged with praying crowds, tigers sated with flesh lay their bloodstained paws. Serpents hiss and glide amid broken columns. No longer does the moonlight fall in silver splendor on palace roofs, overgrown now with grey mosses and green grass.'

Raposo and his companions quitted the dead city and followed the river through the jungle in the hope that it would lead them towards home. On the way they came across some Indians who had apparently followed them as far as the city and then made off, and the extraordinary fact was that these Indians had white skins . Professor Homet, too, encountered and photographed several white-skinned savages during his Amazonian exploration. It has been proved, moreover, that the Guanchas of the Canary Islands and the ancient Egyptians were physically very similar to the Araucanians who inhabited the last city of Tiahuanaco, a race which still survives in an area reaching from the West Indies to the mouth of the Mamoré, a Bolivian river which, near the Brazilian border, joins with the Beni to form the river Madeira.

Today, close kinsfolk of the Araucanians are to be found in the Berbers of North Africa and the French and Spanish Basques. According to sixteenth and seventeenth century chronicles, the Basques of that time were able to converse with South American Indians with perfect ease, each side using its own language. The

GIANTS AND THE LOST LANDS OF THE GODS

Comte de Charencey (1832-1916), in his Histoire légendaire de la Nouvelle Espagne, declared that Berber, Tamachek (the language spoken by Tuaregs in the Sahara), Euzkara (i.e. Basque) and some words of the ancient Gaulish language are undoubtedly related to Indian dialects of North and South America.

It should also be recalled that old Iberian and Celtic myths tell of a 'land of the blessed' which bears the name Hy Bresail or O'Brasile. Homet discovered at Corvo in the Azores a document which spoke of a statue of a man on horseback pointing in the direction of this legendary Brazil. The Azores and the Canaries are thought to represent two Atlantean mountain-chains, and many believe that records found there contain clear references to Central and South America. Before closing this chapter we may mention some other curious facts relating to the Canaries, which are only 50 miles from the northeastern coast of Africa, yet differ completely from it in their physical geography.

The Island Devils

'Since I wished to know more about the Satyrs I talked of them with many people. Euphemus of Caria told me that on a journey to Italy he was blown oil course by a storm and driven into the outer sea, where no one ever ventures as a rule. There, he said, are many desert islands and other islands inhabited by savage people. They had not wanted to land because they had been there and encountered the inhabitants on an earlier occasion, but once again they were forced to put ashore. These islands were called the 'Satyrides' by the sailors. The inhabitants are fiery red and have tails on their hindquarters as big as those of horses. They came to the ship when they saw it, uttering not a sound but laying hands on the ship's womenfolk, In their fear, the sailors eventually marooned a barbarian woman, on whom the Satyrs took their pleasure.'

This passage from Pausanias, a Greek historian and geographer who wrote about A.D. 175, is believed by many scholars to refer to the Canaries, even though other ancient writers style these 'the islands of the blest'. The Canary archipelago was inhabited by diverse races who maintained little contact among themselves, as Spanish discoverers reported in the fifteenth century. In place of Satyrs, however, the Spaniards encountered olive-skinned Guanches, those on the westward islands having lighter hair, and also members of a handsome white race, 'very strong, with fair hair and blue eyes'.

The idea that the Guanches were related to 'blue men' of nonhuman origin may be supported by the fact that they used a birdlike 'whistling language' in which they were able to communicate over long distances from one hilltop to another—an art still practiced by modern inhabitants of the Canaries. Some think that the islands are peopled by a whole gamut of Atlantean races, and that Pausanias's 'Satyrs' represent the Amerindians. It would be wrong to suppose that

GIANTS AND THE LOST LANDS OF THE GODS

they were a figment of Euphemus's imagination, as we find primitive North African paintings of human figures, bright red in color, equipped with horses' tails which were doubtless a form of adornment.

The Greek historian Plutarch (c. A.D. 50-120) refers to the people of the Canaries as Atlanteans. Homer may have identified the islands, as later writers certainly did, with Elysium, the mythical winterless home of the happy dead. This may not have been due merely to their position in the far west, beyond the Pillars of Hercules, but to the discovery by ancient navigators of the natives' cult of the dead and their belief in immortality. They used to embalm dead bodies, reducing them by some means to a weight of only 7 or 8 pounds, and, like many American peoples, they believed that the dead gave advice to their descendants. When Peruvian-Indians had to appear in a court of law they brought with them all their living relations and also their mummified ancestors, while among the Guanches a dead ruler was never buried until his successor died, so that the living king was, so to speak, assisted at all times by his predecessor.

Some believe that the Guanches learned the technique of mummification from the Egyptians, but in fact the methods were completely different. The Egyptians may have taught the Guanches their writing system and the custom of brother-sister marriage, but in other respects the Guanche civilization remains a mystery. It is known to us only from ruins that call to mind those of Sardinia, Jericho and Zimbabwe, and from the underground structures on the island of Grand Canary, which have much in common with the relics of other ancient Mediterranean cultures.

GIANTS AND THE LOST LANDS OF THE GODS

CHAPTER TWENTY-TWO
Myths Of Vanished Lands

In addition to the contacts between Atlantis and the Mediterranean outposts of Mu, the two civilizations certainly maintained permanent relations via the Pacific. The similarities between ancient American and Asian culture are too numerous and lasting to have been due merely to chance visits across the ocean. Such visits did take place, as we shall see, but they are a phenomenon of comparatively recent times.

As we have already pointed out, the American pyramids have their counterpart not only in Egypt but in the Far East, in the niche-monuments of Burma, Thailand and Indochina. But there are many more architectural features common to both shores of the Pacific, not only in South America where this might seem more likely, but ,also in Guatemala and Mexico, including Yucatan. As Honoré observes, the style of certain buildings in these areas 'is exactly that of East Asia.

The doors and windows might have been the work of an Indochine architect, so close is the resemblance. The hall-columns used for purposes of support or mural decoration are typical alike of the Mayan Puuc style and of tenth-century Cambodia, and the same is true of the facade decorations.'

Nordenskjiild pointed out the identity of no fewer than twenty-four elements of the ancient American civilization with those of Polynesia, including the flute, the couch, the poncho, feathered headdresses, fishhooks and nets, canoes, hammocks, the calendrial system, the quipu, the brewing of beer and trepanning. Apropos of this last, in 1963 the Peruvian surgeon Francisco Grana successfully carried out a delicate operation on the victim of a car crash, using instruments buried in his country at least 3,000 years ago and consisting of an alloy of gold, copper and silver. The remains of prehistoric patients who underwent the trepanning operation show that they survived it and lived for many years after.

According to the Argentine linguist Imbelloni, there are numerous words in common between, on the one hand, the Polynesian languages of the Maoris, of Tonga, Samoa, the Tuamotu (or Paumotu) Archipelago, Tahiti, the Marshall and Cook Islands, and, on the other, the Aymara idiom of Ecuador, Colombia, Tierra

GIANTS AND THE LOST LANDS OF THE GODS

del Fuego and ancient Peru. (The Aymara are an Andean people to whom is attributed the reconstruction of Tiahuanaco.)

Many of the elements referred to above can also be paralleled in the Mediterranean countries, which fact goes to confirm the existence in remote times of land-bridges which were the home of key civilizations and united all the continents as we know them today.

Devourers Of The Moon

Mythology presents common features all over the globe, and this is not merely because, as has been suggested, 'like hopes and fears produce like superstitions'. How can it be, for instance, that Ammon-Ra, the ancient Egyptian sun-god, is known by the same name and possesses the same attributes among the Apache Indians and also in Mexico, Peru and the Amazon basin?

In many regions where a solar cult was practiced, we find the word tepu or tepe used to denote a high place. In the extreme north of Amazonia there is Wei-Tepu, the sun-mountain, and near Boa Vista the Tepe-Quem, an extinct volcano whose crater, according to fable, is lined with diamonds. In the Maya language tepe meant a large stone, while in Troy and Sumeria it signified a hill.

The Egyptians and Mexicans both gave the same name to their god of joy, and an Egyptian figurine now in the Louvre shows this deity with the same features as an American counterpart at Rio de Janeiro. The same resemblance is shown by two mythical bearded giants who held the world on their shoulders: the ancient Greek Atlas, and Quetzalcoatl among the Toltecs and Aztecs.

Among many ancient peoples the world is said to repose on the back of a 'sacred tortoise', venerated as a symbol of Creation, perhaps because it suggests both the egg and the snake motif. This is found in Europe, Africa and Asia as well as in Yucatan, on the Pedra Pintada and elsewhere in Amazonia.

As we saw, a moon goddess is said to lie asleep under a pyramid at Teotihuacan, and there are many lunar divinities with similar attributes in America, Asia and the Mediterranean countries. At Nineveh this deity was called Sin, and the corresponding name among the Chimu is Sin An.

Columbus, in his account of the West Indians, states that their most treasured possession was a gold crescent. This symbol is frequently met with in all parts of America, especially Amazonia, but it was also sacred in Greece and Egypt, at Troy and Mycenae, in West Africa and among the Celts: cf. the golden sickle which the Druids used to cut branches of mistletoe.

Some archaeologists believe that the lunar deity presided over the game of basketball, which was popular in almost all parts of pre-Columbian America. In Central America, games played with counters on special boards had a religious significance and probably represented movements of the heavenly bodies. Games

GIANTS AND THE LOST LANDS OF THE GODS

of the same sort occur at the present day in other continents too, e.g. in Syria, Burma and the Philippines.

Everyone is familiar with the fun-fair contrivance in which seats are suspended by chains from the top of a high mast and spin round in the air. But how many suspect that this already existed in America at the time of the European conquest, with ropes instead of chains and seats woven of basket-work, as may also be seen in many parts of East Asia?

Originally this device was associated with religious rites, and it is by no means unlikely that it was intended to symbolize the revolution of planets about the sun.

Two mythical creatures are linked with the god Ra: the sacred ram, which occurs among the Amerindians, the Egyptians and the Chinese, who represent it by the catlike masks known as T'ao-t'ieh - and the frog-toad, which is also found in Amazonia. Some believe that these represent monsters from outer space that may once have landed on earth. In the same way the scarab, which was sacred to the Egyptians, the Etruscans and the Indians of Mexico and Brazil, is sometimes interpreted as symbolizing a spaceship.

The rabbit or hare was regarded by the ancient peoples of Central America, the Mediterranean basin, China and south-east Asia as representing the setting moon, devoured by darkness. In Mexican mythology the darkness is symbolized by a feathered serpent, and if this animal really represents a spaceship, we may compare the Bolivian legend which relates that the moon was 'eaten up by men from the sky'.

Serpent deities are found throughout America, and in all other parts of the world as well. Among many examples we may mention Charun, the Etruscan god of death, portrayed as a reptile with a bird's beak, and thus reminiscent of the Aztec feathered serpent and the Chinese winged dragon; and the Cretan goddesses who, like the deities of Chavin, are seen grasping a snake in either hand.

Reptiles with human features are also known throughout the world and common in Amazonia. Here too we find a large serpent with arms and a varying number of heads, which also figures in the mythology of Liberia. Its American name is Kou, and it is tempting to agree with those who suggest that it represents a living being emerging from a spaceship. Its body is rigid and cigar-shaped, covered by what look like oblong metal plates rather than scales, and it has four wings that suggest the fins of an aircraft. It is also curious that the human-looking heads of this fabulous reptile are conical in shape.

Beyond The Styx

Some years ago a young engineer and amateur archaeologist named Kama el Malakh discovered, not far from the Great Pyramid, the funeral barques of the

GIANTS AND THE LOST LANDS OF THE GODS

first Pharaohs. These were some 180 feet long and 10 feet wide, and contained everything the dead monarch might need on a long voyage.

They were not destined to put to sea, however, but to convey the sovereign until such time as he should be reincarnated, following the journey round the earth of the Sun, his father.

This custom may or may not derive from ancient memories of space-travel. Until recent times it was thought to be of purely Egyptian origin, the Greeks having borrowed the myth in a modified form—that of Charon's barque transporting the souls of the dead across the Styx. However, it appears that many peoples of the remote past buried their dead in boat-shaped coffins, and some South American tribes do so to this day. As Homet writes, 'We must remember that the early barques were nothing else than simple tree-trunks, hollowed out with a stone axe or burnt out with fire. We find examples still current in Oceania, in central Africa and in the region of the Amazon. These barques served as transitional vessels from one point to another, and most archaic cultures combine the migration of the soul with the crowning of its rebirth. And always, as we have found in numerous documents in Africa, the soul traveled towards the Sun God. But it always traveled in "something" which could also accommodate the body before it was resurrected, hence a "death barque".

'The facts suggest,' Homet continues, 'that there may have been a place of common origin, an earlier culture which was the primordial home of the death barque and the fountainhead uniting all the ancient cultures: Celtic, ancient Egyptian, northwest European and South American. This we call Atlantis, the mother civilization of all "children of the sun".'

In Greek mythology the entrance to Hades was guarded by the three headed dog Cerberus. Among the Aztecs the abode of the dead was surrounded by a sevenfold river, and the god who presided over the departed spirits was the dog-headed Xolotl (like Anubis, the Egyptian god of the dead). A thin leaf of copper has been found in the mouth of certain mummies, apparently intended to pay for their passage to the shades below, in the same way as the obol which was Charon's fee.

In the roof of the funeral crypt at Tiahuanaco there is a round hole exactly like the one found in Egyptian tombs, where its purpose is to allow the 'bird of death' to escape.

Does this, too, represent the corruption of a stellar myth? If so, we may think of the Bolivian legend that tells of white giants borne by a huge bird (the firebird?) through the night (evidently outer space) to the abode of the gods and of the 'dead who will one day return'.

All mythologies likewise relate how men from heaven mated with earthly women, and this may be the reason why some Indian tribes believe that the breath

GIANTS AND THE LOST LANDS OF THE GODS

of life comes down from heaven and reawakens their dead.

The belief in reincarnation was common to many parts of ancient America, and this is why mummies and skeletons are often found in the foetal position; the bodies were bound in this fashion with ropes, even while their owners were still alive, so that they might be ready for rebirth. A similar custom prevailed in ancient Gaul, Mecklemburg, Britain, Sweden and southern Russia, and also in the Tonga islands.

It is still in force in the Amazon region, and so is the practice of 'double burial' which was also once known in Ireland, Crete and various parts of Europe. The bodies were first buried in damp ground to accelerate decomposition (the Indians of Brazil have a different method: they suspend them in nets in running water, where the piranhas soon pick them dry); then the skeleton is removed, cleaned and painted red - the color of blood or placenta, as Homet remarks, after which it is reinterred.

We have already mentioned symbols of life after death, such as yokes (among the Olmecs and Egyptians), knots and butterflies, which are common to ancient America and the Mediterranean peoples. The lotus, which in India is the symbol of birth, is common in pre-Columbian temples and burial-places, especially in the Mayan capital of Chichén Itza.

Here it is represented complete with flowers, leaves and rootstock, in motifs similar to those of India, Cambodia and Indonesia, and with the same accompaniment of dragons, sea-monsters and fierce animals of the cat tribe. We do not know the age of the lotus as a symbol, but in Europe it is found among the Celts, who brought it from Asia as long ago as 2000 B.C., and whose rulers later transformed it into the fleur-de-lys. It is usually thought to have spread from India to southeast Asia, but Homet believes it to be of much earlier, Atlantean origin. His view finds some support in the enigmatic 'Phaistos disc' a round terracotta tablet, six inches in diameter and about an inch thick, discovered in 1908 in a Cretan palace in a stratum belonging to the sixteenth century B.C. (The disc itself may of course be older than this, as we can see if we imagine a future archaeologist excavating a house of the present day and finding there a Roman coin or an Egyptian figurine.) The disc is inscribed on both sides with ideograms, quite different from Cretan writing, arranged in a left-hand spiral. In the centre of one side is a lotus flower, and of the signs which follow it fifteen are identical to those found in Brazilian inscriptions, while ten resemble them closely.

Also depicted on the disc are heads adorned with feathers, constellations—the Pleiades, Serpens and Pisces—a kind of fire-bird and the Quaz, the Egyptian symbol of physical and spiritual strength. The disc remains undeciphered, but Professor Homet, while not claiming to have solved its mystery, believes that it may relate to the destruction of Atlantis.

GIANTS AND THE LOST LANDS OF THE GODS

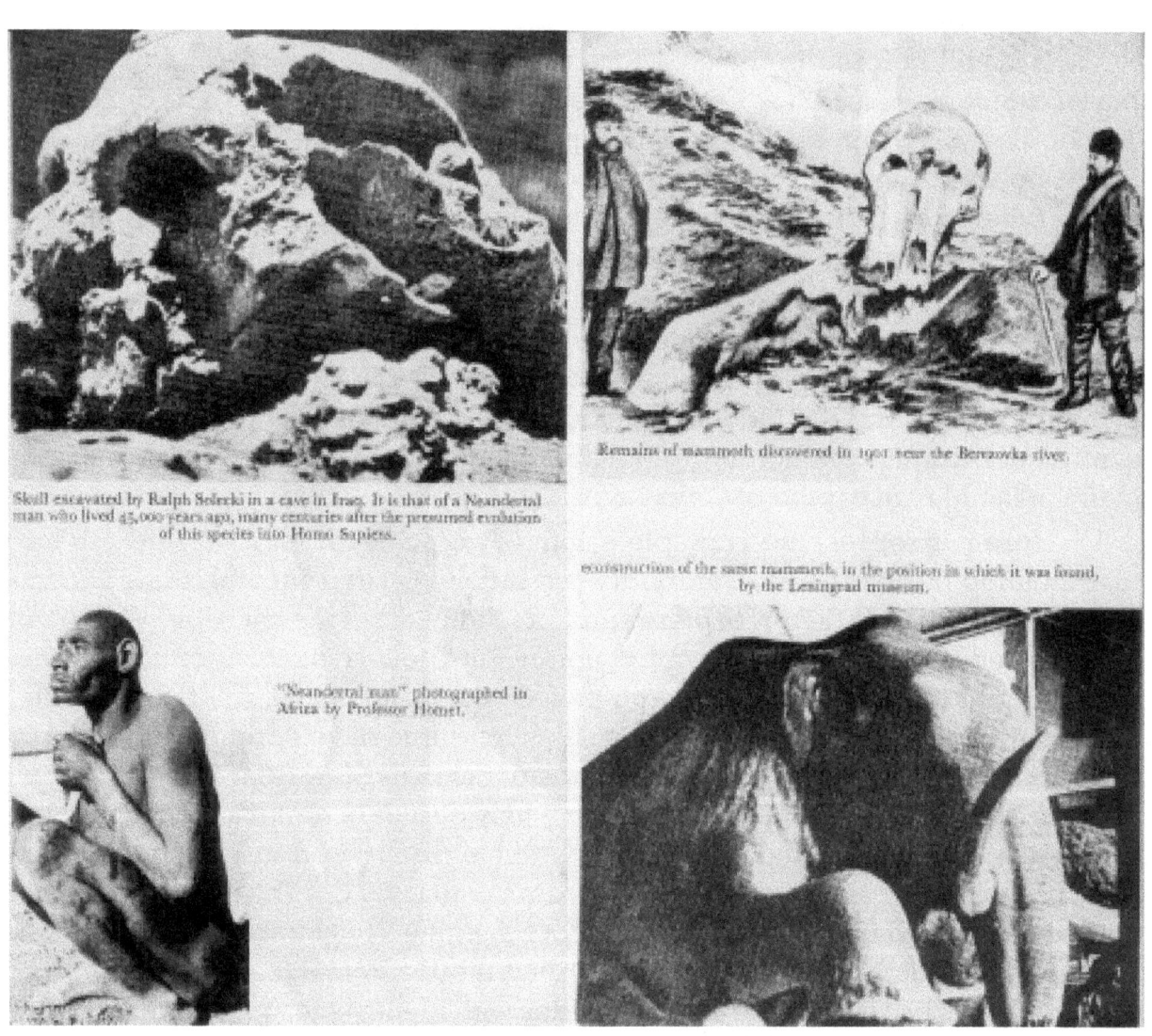

Skull excavated by Ralph Solecki in a cave in Iraq. It is that of a Neandertal man who lived 45,000 years ago, many centuries after the presumed evolution of this species into Homo Sapiens.

Remains of mammoth discovered in 1901 near the Berezovka river.

"Neandertal man" photographed in Africa by Professor Homet.

Reconstruction of the same mammoth, in the position in which it was found, by the Leningrad museum.

GIANTS AND THE LOST LANDS OF THE GODS

CHAPTER TWENTY-THREE
Unthinkable Journeys

In December 1961 a Peking daily published an article by the historian Chen Hua-hsin which, to the amusement or exasperation of some critics, declared that the Chinese had discovered America more than a thousand years before Columbus. 'Naturally,' the Chinese historian wrote, 'we do not deny Columbus's achievement in discovering a new route from Europe to America, but our own claim is based on incontrovertible fact.'

Among the pieces of evidence cited by the Chinese is an account of the travels of one of their compatriots to a 'Buddhist country beyond the seas' which may have been Mexico or perhaps simply India, reached via the South China Sea, the Strait of Malacca and the Bay of Bengal. Professor Chen also mentions archaeological finds in Mexico and Peru, some of which display Chinese and/or Buddhist features; he refers to 'oriental' aspects of Aztec religion and astronomy, and Asian-sounding names inscribed on a tomb near Panama.

Let us examine these arguments more closely. Certainly there are numerous Asian elements in pre-Columbian America, but, as we have seen, many of them go back to distant times before the Chinese empire came into being. They are common to the Aztecs, Incas and Mayas, and to many other peoples, not because they were borrowed from China but because all these peoples inherited them from a great, vanished civilization embracing large parts of Asia and America.

At the same time, there is no reason to doubt that East Asian navigators may have reached the coasts of America. We know that at the beginning of the Christian era the Chinese possessed ships capable of carrying 200 men over long distances. A monk named Fa-hien traveled in one of these, in A.D. 400, to Ceylon and Malaysia and back to northern China. It is quite possible that Chinese sailors made their way via the Asian coast to Alaska and then down the west coast of America, or even that they reached America across the Pacific.

The Vikings, whose ships were cockleshells by comparison, made equally amazing journeys. This was shown in 1898 at Kensington, Minnesota, 1,500 miles from the Atlantic coast, when a Swedish farmer named Olaf Ohman discovered a

GIANTS AND THE LOST LANDS OF THE GODS

stone slab with a Viking inscription among the roots of a felled poplar tree. The discovery aroused some skepticism, particularly in view of the farmer's Swedish origin, but it was proved that the tree must have been at least 70 years old in 1867, when the first Swedish settlers arrived. Ohman himself scarcely knew how to write, but the inscription, in huge runic characters five feet high and eighteen inches wide, was deciphered some ten years later and was recognized as genuine. It reads as follows:

'[We are] eight Goths [Swedes] and twenty-two Norwegians on a journey of exploration from Vinland [Massachusetts] to the westward. We pitched camp between two rocks, some days' journey to the north of this stone. We went fishing for a day, and when we returned ten of our people were dead and covered in blood. A[ve] V[irgo] M[aria], deliver us from evil. There are ten parties of us at sea, eight men to a ship, 14 days out from this island. Anno 1362]'

We shall doubtless never know what these Vikings were seeking in the Middle West and whether their comrades were slain by Indians or bison. We do know, however, from Scandinavian chronicles that in 1354 a great Swedish-Norwegian expedition set out to explore the western seas. All we know of its fate is what the Kensington Stone reveals.

The Redskins And The Proconsul

Whether the Chinese or the Vikings can claim to be the earlier discoverers of America is a somewhat sterile argument, since the New World was certainly discovered at a remoter date by Polynesian navigators in search of a new home, and probably also by chance voyagers from Sumeria, Phoenicia and Egypt, as well as Greeks, Romans and Arabs.

We are prone to underrate the capabilities of antique peoples in this line. Yet, in about 1900, some sponge fishers off the island of Antikythera (or Cerigotto, northwest of Crete) salvaged from the seabed a genuine sextant, thousands of years old. Again, Hyatt Verrill showed that the Sumerians were capable of sailing from southern Iraq as far as Britain or India. A hundred and fifty miles from Cuzco, Verrill's wife discovered an inscription dating from the time of Menes, the traditional first king of Egypt, and describing amazing voyages by the Sumerians. A deciphered fragment runs:

'. . . land of twilight . . . led by Gin-Ti and guided by the fire-god men, from the colony of the Indus valley . . .'

It is of course possible to cross the ocean in extremely frail craft, as intrepid sportsmen have demonstrated in the Atlantic and elsewhere. Chinese junks have been swept by storms from one Pacific shore to the other, and Eskimo or Indian vessels have been salvaged off Ireland, Scotland, France and Germany. Aeneas Silvius Piccolomini (who reigned as Pope Pius II from 1458 to 1464) relates in his

GIANTS AND THE LOST LANDS OF THE GODS

Opera geographica et historica that an Eskimo kayak made a landfall in Germany in 1150. In 1505 a canoe reached Rouen with five dead red-skins aboard and another at the point of death. A kayak was once on view in the church of Burray in the Orkneys, and others are in the museums at Edinburgh and Aberdeen. It is on record, too, that Columbus, before his discovery of America, saw the bodies of two men of unknown race washed up on a beach in the Azores, together with branches of exotic trees.

There is, moreover, a precedent of even greater antiquity. Pliny the Younger and the geographer Pomponius Mela, writing in the First century A.D., speak of a report sent to Rome in 62 B.C. by Quintus Caecilius Metellus Celer, Pompey's brother-in-law, who was then proconsul in Gaul. This describes how the proconsul was visited by emissaries of a German tribe bearing with them rich gifts and also slaves of an unknown race, with dark-red skins. These men declared 'that their homeland lay far off on the shores of the Indian sea; they had set out to visit a neighboring tribe, but a terrible storm had swept them off course and kept them at sea for several days. After much drifting about, perhaps in the vicinity of Greenland, Iceland and the British Isles, they had landed on the northern coast of Europe, where they were captured. As Eugen Georg observes, these could not have been 'Indians' from Asia. The word indicus was in fact used to mean anything exotic or extraordinary in the field of race, geography etc., and we must infer that the men in question were either Eskimos or, more probably, Amerindians.

Moreover, their appearance in the Roman empire was in the nature of a return visit. At the mouth of the Rio de la Plata in Argentine, a dagger and helmet have been found with inscriptions from the time of Alexander the Great, while a Roman sword has also been discovered in Peru. Orthodox science remains indifferent to these finds, which, as Homet observes, 'should have had a sensational effect, and yet they remain unnoticed in the haze of everyday life and the prejudice of fixed opinions. So they wait, forgotten and covered with dust in the corners of museums, as patiently as they waited when they were still buried. They will continue to do so until, one day, they are exhibited as illuminating pieces of evidence.'

Remarkable as these finds may be, they should not surprise us unduly. Both the Greeks and the Romans possessed seagoing vessels over 500 feet long, with a temple of Neptune on board as well as swimming-pools and dining halls of marble and alabaster.

Canaanites In Brazil

It is quite possible that ancient Greek navigators pushed as far as Haiti, which was identified by the astronomer Kepler with the 'island of Cronos' mentioned in Plutarch's De facie in orbe lunae. According to the ancient writer:

GIANTS AND THE LOST LANDS OF THE GODS

'In the midst of the Western Sea [i.e. the Atlantic Ocean] lies Ogygia, the island of Venus and Calypso. But much further still to the west are the three islands of Cronos. Every thirty years, a party of fierce, magnificent warriors resort there from the great mainland that lies beyond, in order to sacrifice to the sea-gods. This continent that forms the Atlantic shore must be at least 5,000 stades [500 miles] distant from Ogygia. The coasts in question were first inhabited by thirteen Greeks descended from the companions of Hercules.

'The barbarians relate, among other fables, that Cronos [Saturn] is held prisoner by Zeus [Jupiter] in one of the islands beyond Ogygia, but it would seem rather that he dwells in the great mainland that lies beyond the islands and the sea named after him. There, for thirty days on end, the sun sets for little more than an hour, and for several months the night is faintly illuminated by the western twilight.' There could hardly be a clearer description of the American continent, the West Indies and the Polar regions.

A similar picture is painted, moreover, by other ancient writers including Seneca, Strabo, Theophrastus, Aristotle and Scylax of Caryanda. Seneca, who died in A.D. 65, speaks in his tragedy Medea of lands between the east coast of Asia and the West coast of Europe ('nec sit terris ultima Thule') and says that 'one day, vast new lands will offer themselves to human view'. Strabo (c. 60 B.C.-A.D. 20) writes of 'other inhabited lands' and says that 'a huge continent will be discovered one day'.

We may surmise from all this that the ancients knew of the existence of America, and remarkable confirmation is afforded by the 'Topkapu maps'. These were discovered in 1927 in the palace of that name at Istanbul. Their author, Piri Reis, was a former pirate who commanded the Ottoman fleet in 1550 but was put to death for treason by Suleyman the Magnificent, having taken a large bribe to raise the siege of Gibraltar. In the mid-nineteenth century two atlases made by him were discovered by one of his descendants, who was also named Piri Reis and was an officer in the Turkish navy.

But the maps found in 1927 created excitement because they showed not only the North and South American coast but also the interior of these continents and of Antarctica, where they gave the correct height of mountain ranges that were unknown to science until 1952. The only major error appeared to be that Greenland was shown in the form of three islands; but during the International Geophysical Year it was proved that this correctly represented the state of affairs over 5,000 years ago.

How could the original Piri Reis, who never sailed beyond the Mediterranean, have drawn up maps of this kind? Some suggest that he may have had access to secret Egyptian libraries. According to glaciologists who have studied the process of coast erosion, the maps represent the earth's surface as it must have

GIANTS AND THE LOST LANDS OF THE GODS

been 10,000 years ago, immediately after the last great convulsion. As regards contours, the U.S. engineer Captain Arlington H. Mallery declares that 'the ancient geographers must have used aerial observation'.

Cartographers of the Hydrographic Department of the US Navy have expressed a similar view, while the historian George Ketrnan writes: 'We are brought up against scientific enigmas which suggest that, thousands of years ago, highly developed civilizations flourished on our earth or were in contact with it from outside.'

If Piri Reis, who spent much time in Egypt, did copy his maps from a secret source there, it is natural to suppose that navigators from the Arab countries may have used them too. We have heard that Arab remains in America are fairly numerous, but have not as yet managed to obtain detailed information. Professor Homet, however, states that he discovered near Manaus (the capital of the Brazilian state of Amazonas, over 600 miles from the Atlantic) a pot buried centuries ago with an Arab inscription 'not written by a European hand— the Europeans always being weaker in this art—but by a skillful calligrapher. The word was sakad-bahar, which in Arabic signifies "river-sea". The Portuguese name for the Amazon is Rio Mar, or River-Sea, exactly the same as the Arabic word I found on the Arawak pottery which is supposed to be 4,000 years old.'

Brazil, however, must have been visited in times past by an even earlier Semitic people, namely the Canaanites. In 1899 the archaeologist Ladislao Netto tried in vain to interest the learned world in some old Phoenician inscriptions he had discovered on the Sugarloaf Mount above Rio de Janeiro.

These were deciphered to read: 'We are sons of the land of Canaan, unfortunate and accursed. We have called to our gods in vain. They have abandoned us, and we shall soon die in despair. It is just ten years since the unhappy day on which we reached these shores. It is terribly hot, the water is stagnant and the air full of noxious insects. Our bodies are covered with sores. Help us, O ye gods! Tyre, Sidon, Baal.'

The Brazilian scholar Bernardo da Silva Ramos found over 2,800 graffiti of similar appearance in different parts of his country. Some are very ancient and only a few of their characters resemble the Phoenician ones, but others are certainly the work of these 'lords of the sea'. They are dismissed as forgeries by orthodox archaeologists, oblivious of the fact that many of the inscriptions have been found in the heart of the jungle or on mountain-tops that no one would scale for the mere pleasure of playing a joke on scientists. Again, in the interior of Brazil Professor Frot discovered cuneiform characters that he identified as pre-Egyptian, while Dr. Narciso R. Colman found inscriptions relating to Egypt in some caves at Teyucare in the Alto Parana in Paraguay. The same scholar discovered at Villarrica (southern Paraguay) carvings that closely resembled Germanic and Scandinavian runes, similar ones have also been found in Siberia, Manchuria, India and Africa.

It is not, after all, so surprising that the Phoenicians should have reached Brazil: they possessed ships of over 1,000 tons and, in the eleventh century B.C., had founded colonies as far afield as the Cape Verde Islands. Equally convincing arguments can be brought forward to justify belief in similar exploits by other ancient peoples. Remembering the Topkapu maps and the innumerable links between early Mediterranean and American civilizations, it is not merely a Utopian fantasy to imagine that bold seafarers may have been spurred to unthinkable voyages in the hope, sustained by vague records and memories, of rediscovering those of their 'Atlantic brethren' who had survived the world catastrophe.

So Near, Yet Lost To Us

One of the last voyagers of this type, perhaps, was Pytheas of Massilia (Marseilles), who in the fourth century B.C. sailed out beyond the Pillars of Hercules and up the west coast of Europe. He set foot on British soil three hundred years before Julius Caesar and, pressing still further north, reached the half-mythical Ultima Thule which, to the Mediterraneans of his time, represented the end of the habitable world. There has been much dispute as to what this territory was. It has been identified with Greenland, Iceland, northern Norway, the Shetlands, Orkneys, Hebrides or Faeroe Islands. Pytheas's own work (Ta peri Okeanou ges periplous) is unfortunately lost, but he is quoted by Strabo among others. The latter says that according to Pytheas there is no true night in Thule at mid-summer and little daylight in winter, and that some believe the winter there lasts six months. Pomponius Mela similarly declares that 'at the summer solstice there is no night there, for the sun can be seen clearly at any hour: not only its beams, but the greater part of its face'.

Strabo, again quoting Pytheas, says that in the region of Thule, 'there was no longer either land properly so called, or sea, or air, but a kind of jelly-like substance in which the earth, the sea and all the elements are held in suspension'.

Tacitus, again, states that 'Thule can be seen at a distance from the extreme north of Britain; the seas around it are said to be very rough and hard to navigate.'

Many scholars have puzzled over Pytheas's description and have suggested that it may refer to thick fog, masses of algae and jellyfish, or the melting of the ice-cap. Others again think he may have been describing a remnant of Atlantis in the form of a huge swamp which remained above sea-level for centuries but was finally engulfed. Ptolemy's map of the World (second century A.D.) shows Thule as an island to the northeast of Britain, but by the late Middle Ages it had disappeared from the ken of geographers. Ultima Thule —our last hope, perhaps, of gazing beyond the point where ferocious savages block the extension of our knowl-

GIANTS AND THE LOST LANDS OF THE GODS

edge and prevent us from journeying back through time, following a trail more fascinating and less obscure than we have been able to indicate in these pages.

But the past is not wholly lost. As Ivar Lissner puts it: 'History is imperishable. Unseen and unrecognized, the past lives on in us in its quiet, imperceptible way. Whether lying dormant in the unfathomable sea of the millennia or buried beneath the ground and swathed in a vast winding sheet of earth and stone, "past" civilizations are still with us even though their tangible remains lie hidden and still undiscovered. All civilizations that have ever been live on in us, and our lives are rooted deep in the remote, mysterious and ancient civilizations of the past. It is our task again and again to rediscover these civilizations, which have a strange way of falling silent as though they no longer lived in us and we in them.

But once a civilization has existed on earth, its effects are permanent. A memory, a new discovery, a visit to an exhibition—any one of these may suddenly alert us to their mute presence. And when this happens we feel a strange desire to weep for something that is near to us, yet which cannot be recalled.'

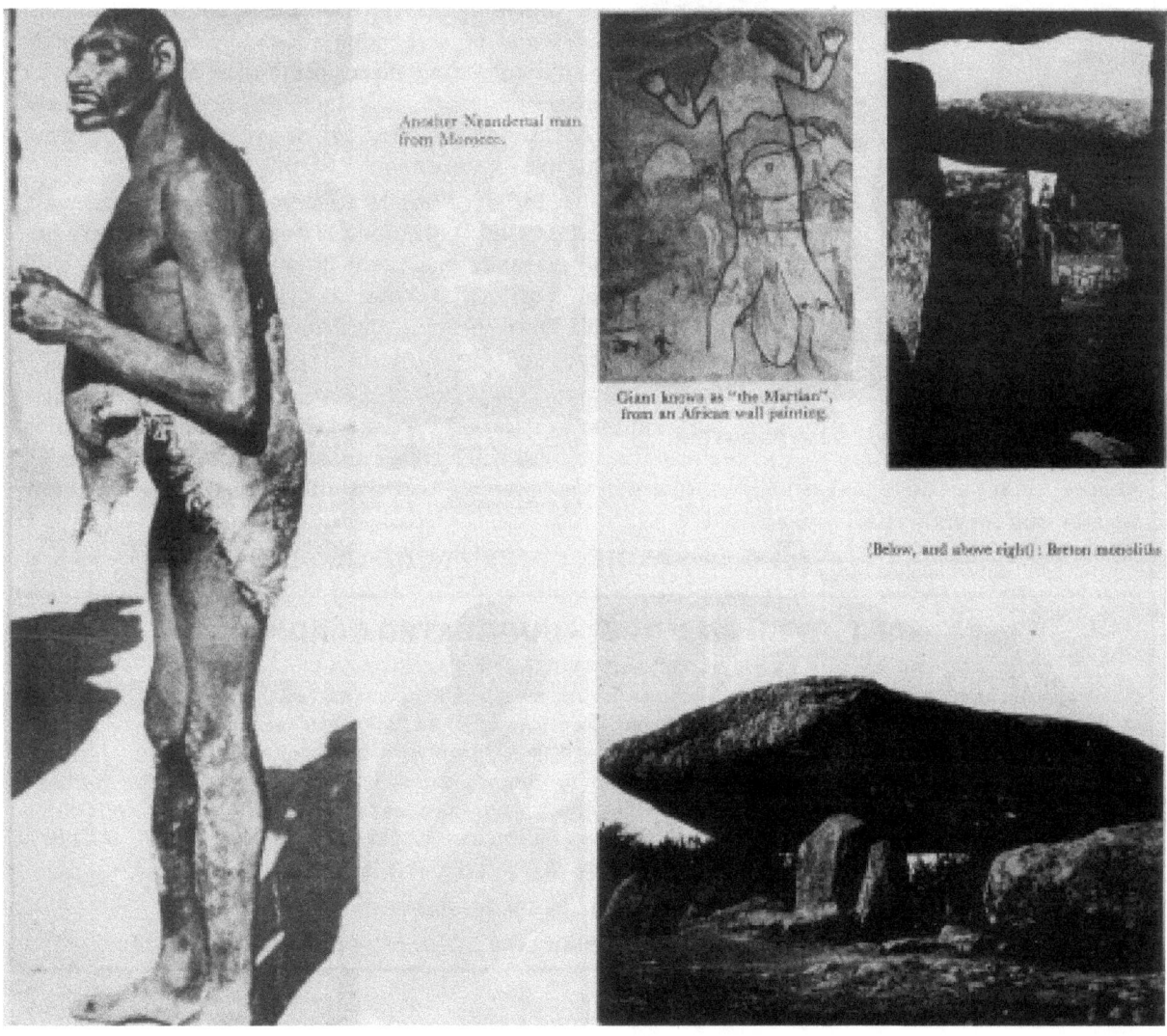

Another Neanderthal man from Morocco.

Giant known as "the Martian", from an African wall painting.

(Below, and above right): Breton monoliths

GIANTS AND THE LOST LANDS OF THE GODS

PROJECT ALIEN MIND CONTROL
The New UFO Terror Tactic — A Threat To Humans Worldwide!

What do you do when the power blackouts keep occurring, and the mysterious disappearances and outright kidnappings continue to mount?

What do you do when you hear an internal buzzing, as your body begins to shake and you go into a deep trance, unable to remember what occurred when you are allowed to return to reality a changed individual?

According to a small group of astute researchers. The Ultra-Terrestrials will not be destroying our world with laser weapons like in Independence Day. Instead, evidence indicates they want to capture our souls as well as our minds in order to accomplish their astronomic "foul deeds." They have no need to blow our fastest military aircraft out of the sky. Their best weapons are not futuristic military ones. Instead, their top-grade artillery against humanity is a numbing form of "high tech alien mind control." Utilizing a series of bizarre techniques, they are able to trick us into accepting their unorthodox and utterly evil belief systems through hallucinatory effects and establishing an emotionless reaction to their far from charitable presence on earth.

Project Alien Mind Control is well under way, and thousands of individuals and entire towns are being mentally enslaved! It is important for the well being of the planet that we all join the alien resistance and learn to elude their mind control efforts at all costs.

This is one of the strangest - most dramatic - dossiers you will likely ever read - the kind that is stamped "Top Secret" by military authorities because of "national security," and because they know it will have a devastatingly negative effect on society. Many believe that as long as we are in the "Matrix," that we will be unable to avoid their sinister, self serving, mind games.

☐ Order PROJECT ALIEN MIND CONTROL - $15.00 + $5 S/H

WANT TO KNOW MORE? - SUGGESTED READING

☐ EVIL EMPIRE OF THE ETS AND THE ULTRA-TERRESTRIALS - 6 leading researchers - including a clinical psychiatrist - provide provocative clues as to the true nature of the aliens and what lies behind their shockingly bold hidden agenda. This is the only work that describes in detail how these "visitors" have affected the personal lives of those caught up in the close encounter and abduction web of treachery and distortion. $22.00

☐ MATRIX OF THE MIND - Are you or someone you know a victim of electronic warfare? Big Brother's covert electronic Mind Control Program operates at the speed of light and can torture, kill and enslave ANYONE — ANYWHERE! Beware of Black Ops, the satellite that goes over twice a day, effecting even your TV set! - $22.00

SPECIAL - 3 TITLES THIS AD - $48.00 + $8.00 S/H
TIMOTHY G BECKLEY, BOX 753, NEW BRUNSWICK, NJ 08903
Send for PayPal invoice - Mrufo8@hotmail.com   Order hot line 732 602-3407

GIANTS AND THE LOST LANDS OF THE GODS

NORDIC LOOKING ALIENS GIVE HITLER PLANS FOR A TIME TRAVEL DEVICE!

THIS IS BY FAR THE MOST SHOCKING AND POTENTIALLY TROUBLING BOOK WE HAVE EVER PUBLISHED.
IT COULD VERY WELL CHANGE THE FUTURE— AND THE TRUTH IS—IT MIGHT HAVE ALREADY!

Here is disturbing evidence that Hitler had a top secret brigade of Nazi engineers working in deep underground laboratories – in conjunction with off world interstellar cosmonauts – to establish space flight and time travel, years before the start of America's rocketry program in which the U.S. sought the help of thousands of Nazi war criminals bought into this country under the auspices of the tight lipped Project Paperclip. Information recently obtained by the authors indicates that the UFO that crashed outside Roswell might have been part of this Nazi space/time travel program cleverly covered up by our military in order to look like the arrival of an out of control interplanetary vehicle. The top brass was ultimately looking to cover their tracks which showed that they were inappropriately working in tandem with war criminals, whom they had excused of all evil misdeeds, eventually giving them citizenship. This "wonder weapon" and time travel device was named Die Glocke or "The Bell," and it is probably being seen and flown to this day; some even manned by Aryan- looking occupants (possibly Ets).

Devices like "The Bell" may have been used to bend both space and time and give the Nazis the unthinkable power to explore the past freely and even to CONTROL THE FUTURE. Are we plummeting headlong toward a world under fascist domination – a nightmare in which sadistic, jackbooted thugs are waiting for us to "catch up" in time with our own predestined subjugation to open worldwide rule by the Nazis, possibly hiding out on the surface of the moon or at "secret cities" at the Poles? Do they lie in wait for us as the clock on our freedom runs down?

The shocking facts can be read in NAZI UFO TIME TRAVELERS / Just $20 + $5 S/H

────── **WANT TO READ MORE?** ──────

☐ **THE OMEGA FILES: SECRET NAZI UFO BASES REVEALED!**

Did Hitler's henchmen escape from Germany and set up secret bases at the South Pole and deep in the Amazon? Are they operating from these top secret quarters to establish a Fourth Reich and take over the world? – **$21.95**

☐ **UFOS NAZI SECRET WEAPONS**

Banned in 22 countries the author was imprisoned for over 20 years because he spoke out on this controversial topic. Did the SS have its own arsenal of super secret weapons which they planned to unleash? Here are pages of drawings showing these devices along with German plans of operation. – **$24.00**

☐ **THE SECRET SPACE PROGRAM**

Do we already have bases on the Moon? Who is responsible? Tesla? Nazis? Secret Societies? NWO? Something pretty damn strange is happening under our very eyes! – **$24.00**

FREE AUDIO CD OF THE MYSTERIOUS INTELLIGENCE OPERATIVE COMMANDER X TALKING ON THE NAZI UFO SPACE PROGRAM WHEN ORDERING TWO OR MORE TITLES FROM THIS AD. Special – All 4 books this advt $79.95 + $8 S/H
TIMOTHY G BECKLEY, BOX 753, NEW BRUNSWICK, NJ 08903

GIANTS AND THE LOST LANDS OF THE GODS

ARE ANCIENT ALIENS THE CUSTODIANS OF EARTH?
HERE ARE NEW LINKS TO THE SPACE GODS

They have been with us since the dawn of civilization, an intricate part of our religious and cultural belief systems. They have guided us, prodded us and perhaps even tried to control us. Some say they are the custodians of the planet, that they are here to show us the path to enlightenment. Others see them as being more nefarious in their intentions. Here at your fingertips are insightful works that reveal the secrets of the ages.

☐ **LEGACY OF THE SKY PEOPLE** Is there an ET origin for Adam and Eve? The Garden of Eden? Noah's Ark? As early as the 1960s, Britain's 8th Earl of Clancarty, Brinsley Le Poer Trench, made an astounding revelation that life on earth had originated on the planet Mars and the first voyagers here had been the Biblical couple. Thus the roots of the various Biblical stories taught to this day. With added material by Nick Redfern, Tim Beckley and Sean Casteel, questions include: Why the CIA and the military show an unprecedented interest in the remains of what many claim to be Noah's Ark that came to rest on Mount Ararat? Is there a new race of humans being formed in these uncertain times? According to the Earl of Clancarty, some of us are rapidly reacquiring the telepathy and psychic abilities we were originally created with. **$20.00 + $5 S/H**

☐ **ALIEN SPACE GODS OF ANCIENT GREECE AND ROME** Was the Mediterranean region of our planet visited by a race of "Super Beings" in ancient times? Was the Oracle of Delphi a conduit for prophetic messages from outer space – perhaps the first telepathic channeler? Researcher W.R. Drake asks: Did giants from space establish a UFO base atop the picturesque Mount Olympus? – Were they the gods and goddesses of "Mythology" idolized and given names such as Apollo, Hades, Athena, Hermes, Zeus, Artemis and Hestia? – Did the powerful deities of Greece help save Athens from being invaded by the mighty armies of Atlantis in 10,000 BC? —Is there reason to believe that the Greeks and Trojans were inspired to fight for the beauteous Helen, surely a space queen? – 318 pages, **$22.00 + $5 S/H**

☐ **THE ARK OF THE COVENANT AND OTHER SECRET WEAPONS OF THE ANCIENTS** Was the Ark of the Covenant a nuclear device capable of killing large segments of the population? Did "God" give it supernatural powers? Was it responsible for the collapse of the Walls of Jericho thus allowing the Israelites to take control of the city? Was Moses able to speak directly to the Lord through the two angels positioned on the Ark's top? David Medina offers proof the ancients possessed "secret technology" that made them exceptional worriers. But how did they develop such devices on their own? Centuries ago "wonder weapons" could be found in many lands, laying waste to man and property. – **$20.00 + $5 S/H**

SUPER SPECIAL – ALL 3 TITLES $52.00 + $8 S/H
ORDER FROM: TIMOTHY G BECKLEY, BOX 753, NEW BRUNSWICK, NJ 08903

GIANTS AND THE LOST LANDS OF THE GODS

SHOCK-O-RAMA

☐ **AMITYVILLE AND BEYOND –**
The Lore Of The Poltergeist And Other Paranormal Phenomena
Authored by Tim Beckley, Sean Casteel, Shawn Robbins, Paul Eno, Brad Steiger, Tim Swartz, William Hall, Butch Witkowski, Michele Lowe, Joshua Warren, Maria D'Andrea, Carol Rodriguez

OUR HIDDEN HISTORY—EXPLORE THE GREATEST MYSTERIES OF ALL TIME!

If you are a reader who has greatly enjoyed – or has been influenced by – the works of John Keel, Dr. Nandor Fodor, or Jacques Vallee you will find this work to be an outstanding breakthrough book. Likewise, if you are just looking for something to titillate your sense of fear, this is guaranteed to be a real page turner.

Six members of the Defeo family were murdered in cold blood in the middle of the night in their home in Amityville, Long Island. Demons were said to be responsible for the hideous slayings inside what was to become known as America's most possessed dwelling. Several best sellers and 20 movies were made.

ALL NEW FINDINGS

Poltergeists come in all shapes and sizes and inspire varying degrees of horror. What might be surprising is that poltergeists are NOT necessarily the spirits of the dead nor the overworked, disordered personalities of the living often thought to have become possessed by demonic forces. That which we call a "poltergeist" could just as easily include a wide range of other unearthly phenomena, such as random denizens of the dark moving through time and space and other dimensions, as well as a manifestation of cryptids, known collectively as shape shifters and "bedroom invaders," and possibly even representatives of numerous alien races.

Here are the most bizarre, the most terrifying, and the most perplexing cases of poltergeist activity that you are likely to encounter, as investigated by the top paranormal researchers of today without bias and without relying on pre-existing conclusions as to what might be causing such unpleasant transgressions. And please note that these bloodsucking parasites can attack not only the most innocent of souls or the average dwelling, but have also been known to follow hysterical individuals across the vastness of the country while maintaining a stranglehold that in some cases is almost impossible to break.

Large 8.5x11 Format. 206 Pages – Profusely Illustrated – Special $20.00

WANT TO LEARN MORE? SUGGESTED READING LIST

☐ **AMERICA'S STRANGE AND SUPERNATURAL HISTORY** – The occult has played a tremendous – but hidden – part in times past. These are TRUE urban legends of the occult plus a bonus section on U.S. Presidents and their battle and opposition to the unknown. **Large Format – 318 Pages – $20.00**

☐ **ANDREW CROSSE: THE REAL DR FRANKENSTEIN** – Did he create the building blocks of life? Or was he delusional? His contemporaries in science were puzzled by the very nature of his work, as they were unable to duplicate his findings or reproduce, under controlled conditions, the striking life forms that were plainly visible and moving around Crosse's workbench. **Large Format – 278 Pages – $20.00**

Special – All 3 Books This Ad Just $50+ $6 S/H
Timothy G. Beckley · Box 753 · New Brunswick, NJ 08903

GIANTS AND THE LOST LANDS OF THE GODS

REVEALED FOR THE FIRST TIME: THE TRUE IDENTITY OF THE MYSTERIOUS WHISTLE BLOWER KNOWN AS. . .
COMMANDER X
WILL THE REAL COMMANDER X PLEASE STAND UP!
NEW! – COMMANDER X FILES UPDATED

For more than a decade the mysterious Commander X has caused dissension among conspiracy theorists, Area 51 aficionados and UFO believers. Some accept his hair-raising accounts of working behind the scenes with the CIA, the NSA and other government and quasi-federal agencies at face value, while others scratch their heads in bewilderment and wonder if his first-hand chronicles cannot be linked to a disinformation program.

For the first time, here is the complete dossier on Commander X's many exploits both with various groups of highly aggressive ultra-terrestrials, as well as his battle with our own earthly authorities hell-bent on keeping these matters TOP SECRET! –

Included among the many shocking – and surprising – revelations in this book:

** The Alien Dinosaur Connection. – ** Who inhabits the Subterranean Regions of Earth? – ** Evidence suggests human victims were still alive, when their blood was drained and body parts removed in underground UFO bases. – ** The many special powers of ETs – including levitation, dematerialization, invisibility, mind control, advanced light beam technology. **A Nazi – Alien collaboration. How the Occult inner circle of the Third Reich contacted grey aliens before World War II using ritual magic. – ** Evidence Hitler shipped equipment and slave laborers to the Antarctic to construct a fleet of flying saucers. – ** Proof that the Nazis transferred into the midst of the American spy and space agencies.

AND MOST IMPORTANT OF ALL – ARE HUMAN CLONES GOING TO BE USED TO REPLACE ASSASSINATED POLITICIANS?

Only Commander X can dare answer these questions.

❏ Order THE COMMANDER X FILES - Large Format. 200+ Pages – $24.00.

❏ NEW! – AMERICA'S TOP SECRET TREATY WITH ALIEN LIFE FORMS – PLUS THE HIDDEN HISTORY OF OUR TIME!

Is The "Treaty" A "False Flag?" – Or Some CIA Sponsored "Smoke Screen?" They arrived without our knowledge or consent and told our military leaders they came in peace for the benefit of humankind, and would gladly start an exchange program with the people of the planet earth which could lead to a "Golden Age." We wholeheartedly believed them and agreed to the "Treaty" almost without any sort of protest. Then they began to abduct our women! Then they returned for our children! Soon after they began to rape the earth's resources! And it became apparent they ultimately wanted to control our minds and capture our souls for their selfish reasons, some too horrific to comprehend.

And because they are too embarrassed to admit they went along with this Treaty, the U.S. government and the military industrial complex refuse to let the public know what has been going on for nearly half a century, keeping a tight lid on this Treaty and its various "exchange programs." But now there might be a ray of hope thanks to the whistle blower known as Commander X. This is your opportunity to find out about the"Treaty," and protect yourself and your loved ones from a possible "enemy attack" that could come out of the sky, as predicted by Nostradamus, as detailed in the Book of Revelations.

Find Out The Truth For Yourself by ordering SECRET TREATY WITH ALIENS.

❏ Large Format – 186 Pages – $20.00.

❏ SPECIAL: BOTH NEW BOOKS BY COMMANDER X - $39.00 + $5 S/H

TIMOTHY G. BECKLEY, BOX 753, NEW BRUNSWICK, NJ 08903

GIANTS AND THE LOST LANDS OF THE GODS

FASTER THAN THE SPEED OF LIGHT!

THE TOP SECRET SCIENCE OF TOMORROW IS HERE TODAY!

Time Travel
Teleportation
Dimension Jumping
Invisibility

THESE TITLES AVAILABLE BASED UPON CONFIDENTIAL INFORMATION DERIVED FROM KGB, CIA AND CHINESE WHISTLEBLOWERS

❏ NAZI TIME TRAVELERS

Whistle blower indicates UFO that crashed outside Roswell might have been part of a secret Nazi space/time travel program covered up by CIA to make it look like an out of control space ship crashed. The top brass were looking to cover their tracks in regard to allowing Nazi engineers and rocket scientists into the US illegally under Project Paperclip. Evidence Nazis had been in contact with Aryan space beings who assisted in developing an advanced "flying disc" technology on advice from members of a German secret society the Vril. —$20.00

❏ TIME TRAVEL FACT NOT FICTION

Einstein had part of the equation correct but did not consider what has become known as the "string theory" of physics which says that everything in the universe exists simultaneously. In this work by Commander X and Tim Swartz a variety of topics are discussed, including: Spontaneous Cases of Time Travel. — Mystery of Time Slips. — Doorways in Time. — People, Buildings and Towns From Beyond Time. — The Restaurant At The Edge Of Time. — Flight Into The Future. — Is Death A Jump in Time? — Are UFOs Time Machines? — Working Time Machines — Nikola Tesla's Time Travel Experiments —$20.00

❏ TELEPORTATION – HOW-TO GUIDE FROM STAR TREK TO TESLA

Commander X says it is possible to master the art of teleportation. The well-known phrase, "Beam me up, Scotty" now has a rational application, the term Teleportation actually having been coined by the world famous researcher of unexplained mysteries, Charles Fort. The author says he worked on a secret teleportation project inside Area 51 in which a "beam ship" did a bit of "dimension jumping" while he was at the controls. Book contains experiences you can participate in.—$16.00

❏ Add $13 for OFFICIAL U.S.MANUAL ON TELEPORTATION released by Air Force Research Laboratories.

❏ TRAVEL TO OTHER DIMENSIONS

Discover how to: ** Become One With The Light — ** Discover The Reality Of Other Dimensions and Planes — ** What You Will Find On The Seven Planes Of Existence — ** Traveling In And Out Of Your Body At Will — ** Entering The Region Of The Disembodied, And The Sacred Resting Place Of The Soul — ** Life And Work On The Astral. -** Find Out The Entities You Are Likely To Encounter. -** What It Is Like To Mingle With Disembodied Souls, and learn to contact the spiritual teachers.—$18.00

❏ LEVITATION AND INVISIBILITY

This book is NOT to be used for unlawful or immoral purposes! Can we learn to fly through the air with the greatest of ease? Is it possible to walk through walls or other solid objects? Now thanks to Tim R. Swartz and retired military intelligence operative Commander X, working in tandem with various sages, shamans and adapts, we are prepared to proclaim the secrets to fulfilling these mystical "dreams" are at hand. Contents Include: ++ The Quest For Instant Invisibility. ++ What Is In The Mysterious Mist? ++ The Realm of Invulnerability. ++ Prayers and Spells For Invisibility. ++ Spiritualists And Mystics Who Have Proven They Possess Incredible Talents.—$21/95

❏ SUPER SPECIAL
Everything listed on this page PLUS A FREE Audio CD just $89.00 + $8 S/H

TIMOTHY G BECKLEY, BOX 753 NEW BRUNSWICK, NJ. 08903

GIANTS AND THE LOST LANDS OF THE GODS

EXPLORE THESE "WAY OUT" WORLDS

Is Disclosure Around The Corner? Are The Ultra Terrestrials Already Amongst Us? Are The "Aliens" Friend Or Foe?

ALL BOOKS LARGE FORMAT – DVD BONUS WITH FOUR-BOOK PURCHASE!

COMING OF THE SPACE GUARDIANS

UFO RESCUE SQUAD, MILLIONS TO BE SAVED—ARE A GROUP OF EXTRATERRESTRIALS KNOWN AS "THE GUARDIANS" HERE TO SAVE HUMANKIND IN THE EVENT OF A GLOBAL DISASTER? — There is no doubt that "THEY" have influenced the human race since our earliest beginnings. Some say they have manipulated our bodies, minds, souls. There is a widespread belief that they are our mortal enemies, while others contend they are here to assist in our SALVATION! — So says Commander X, a former military intelligence operative. Recently, the Russian news media ran a story about a large meteorite that hurtled its way over that nation, but before it could do severe damage – and cause possible loss of life – it was hit by a UFO, causing it to explode and shatter over the Urals. The Siberian Times headline shouted: "WE WERE SAVED BY A UFO!" Are The Guardians warning us that Earth is possibly on a collision course with the mysterious sphere known as Planet X? Or perhaps a massive meteor bombardment? An asteroid strike? Or even a nuclear attack? Any of these events could spell widespread disaster. This book gives you all the FACTS and tells you how to survive these dramatically CHANGING TIMES!

❏ Order COMING OF THE SPACE GUARDIANS - $15.00

THE CASE FOR UFO CRASHES

FROM URBAN LEGEND TO REALITY — WHAT IS HIDDEN IN THE MYSTERIOUS "BLUE ROOM" AT WRIGHT-PATTERSON AIR FORCE BASE? DOES "HANGAR 18" CONTAIN WRECKAGE OF A CRASHED UFO AND PRESERVED BODIES OF ALIENS FROM OUTER SPACE? — For over 50 years the late Senator Barry Goldwater, was denied access. : "I was told in such an emphatic way that it was none of my business — what was in this "room" —that I've never tried to make it my business since." EVERY PRESIDENT SINCE TRUMAN HAS BEEN PART OF THE "GRAND DECEPTION" – NOW IS THE TIME TO EXPOSE THE "COSMIC WATERGATE!" Here are dozens of unpublished Crashed Saucer stories uncovered by the author Tim Beckley during the course of his research, including . . * The night a UFO came crashing down over an Ohio shopping mall. . . * A bizarre tale of an "alien artifact" uncovered by a jogger and displayed in the lobby of a Florida movie theater before it was mysteriously removed and vanished completely. . . * An unbelievable eye witness account of a UFO that fell inside New York City's bustling Central Park after being shot at by the military.

❏ Order THE CASE FOR UFO CRASHES-$22.00. Includes bonus DVD.

THE ASTOUNDING UFO SECRETS OF JIM MOSELEY

INCLUDES FULL TEXT OF UFO CRASH SECRETS AT WRIGHT PATTERSON AIR FORCE BASE — THIS IS NOT JUST ANOTHER BOOK ABOUT UFO SIGHTINGS OR THE CRASH AT ROSWELL! — IT'S AN EXTRAORDINARY REMEMBERANCE OF THE COURT JESTER — THE GRAND TROUBADOUR — THE NUMERO UNO TRICKSTER — OF ALL OF UFOLOGY. In addition to the musings and gossip of those that he remained closest to in life, Jim (with the help of endeared drinking buddy and ghost writer Gray Barker) fans out across the country to personally investigate some of the most peoplexing UFO cases of all time –Cases personally pondered over by Moseley in this book include: ** "I Met Two Men From 'Venus' — And They Had No Fingerprints!" ** What Happened To The "Authentic" UFO Film That Vanished Without A Trace? ** Kidnapped By Aliens? – A Most Strange And Unusual Case. ** The Angels Of Oahspe. ** Adamski, Williamson And The Case For The UFO Contactees. ** Behind The Barbed Wire Fence At Wright-Patterson Air Force Base. ** The OSI And The Lubbock Lights. ** ETs And Alien Wreckage - The Strange Story Of An Air Force Whistleblower. ** The Earth Theory And UFOs From The Antarctica.

❏ Order SECRETS OF JIM MOSELEY -$20.00

UMMO AND THE EXTRATERRESTRIAL PAPERS

THE ALIENS ARE AMONG US! THEY WISH TO COMMUNICATE! AND HAVE EVEN CONSTRUCTED CITIES IN REMOTE PLACES WHILE THEY ARE HERE! The story of UMMO starts with a series of letters and phone calls to various Spanish UFO researchers in 1965 that purportedly came from an extraterrestrial race. While the most commonly reported method of ET contact is clearly by telepathy, the aliens in this case tried a more direct, decidedly earthly method of communication. The letters contained highly detailed discourses on such weighty topics as physics and medicine that could only have been written by experts on the cutting edge in those rarified fields that are light years beyond what a lay hoaxer could have come up with. One of the letters also predicted that a UFO sighting would occur on a certain day at a certain location in Spain, and the ship did indeed appear on schedule and at the appointed place. Photos of their ships and unique symbol have been taken as added verification. A similar account has popped up in Canada and is included. This book is over 250 large size pages and contains never before revealed info on this fascinating episode.

❏ Order UMMO AND THE ET PAPERS - $25.00

SUPER SPECIAL –ORDER ALL ITEMS THIS PAGE - $69.00 + $8 S/H AND WE WILL INCLUDE A BONUS DVD ON AN INTRIGUING ASPECT OF THE UFO MYSTERY

Timothy Beckley, Box 753, New Brunswick, NJ 08903
Secure Hot Line for Credit Card 24/7 646 331-6777

www.ingramcontent.com/pod-product-compliance
Lightning Source LLC
Chambersburg PA
CBHW081916170426

43200CB00014B/2751